Walk On:
Celtic Since McCann

David Potter

Walk On:
Celtic Since McCann

David Potter

Fort Publishing Ltd

First published in 2003 by Fort Publishing Ltd, Old Belmont House,
12 Robsland Avenue, Ayr, KA7 2RW.

© David Potter

Cover photograph: Henrik Larsson scoring his first equalising goal in the 2003
UEFA Cup final in Seville. © Getty Images
All internal photographs © Mirrorpix

Typeset by S. Fairgrieve (0131–658–1763)

Printed by Bell and Bain, Glasgow

ISBN 0-9544461-5-1

Contents

Introduction

T he tears were genuine. It is no new phenomenon for someone who has followed the fortunes of Celtic Football Club to find oneself in tears, be they of rapture or heartbreak, frustration or triumph, but these were different. They were the tears of pride, of love and of affection, not unlike those shed by a doting mother when her lovely boy graduates from university or gets married. But there was also the slight feeling of injustice, of having been ill treated by fate, of not having achieved what was really deserved, of seeing the prize go to someone else who was not necessarily any better.

This was Rugby Park in the early evening of 25 May 2003. Celtic had just beaten Kilmarnock 4–0. In normal circumstances any win at Rugby Park – far from a happy hunting ground for Celtic over the past decade – would be something to be happy about and a 4–0 defeat of the Rugby Parkers would be much bruited and boasted about for the next few games. But this was the last day of the season, and the 4–0 win was not enough to prevent Rangers – who had beaten Dunfermline Athletic 6–1 – from winning the championship.

It had been the second blow in five days. On the previous Wednesday, Celtic had gone down to Porto in the UEFA Cup final once again by the narrowest of margins. The taste was bitter indeed, but everyone connected with Celtic could hold their head up. They had restored Scotland's credibility in European terms, something that the national team was blatantly failing to achieve, and they had beaten two English teams en route, effectively shutting-up those who chortled about Scotland's minor role in world football.

Support is all about love. The Tims left Rugby Park that night in good humour, proud of their men. There was the predictable cursing of those celebrating their undeserved triumph at Ibrox, the execration of Dunfermline Athletic, with their perceived pro-Rangers management team, for 'lying down', the venom poured on UEFA for appointing such a rookie referee on Wednesday night, the time wasting and injury feigning of Porto . . . but there was no bitterness, no lasting hatred. Indeed, humour was much in evidence. 'Where's Kilmarnock's airport?' and 'Dae I still need my passport tae get back to Glasgow' and 'Dunfermline are getting a bed, so they can lie doon proper'. 'East End Park's getting called "the bed" next year.' And so on.

Inevitably, there would be the meeting of Rangers buses on the way home. The usual pleasantries, gestures and greetings were exchanged, but at one service station a brave but decent Rangers fan walked across to a Celtic minibus, shook hands with some Celtic fans and said 'You guys hiv a loat tae be happy aboot.' The Celtic fans were taken aback by this magnanimous behaviour, but it merely reflected the reality that Rangers felt very relieved to have won the league. Perhaps all the insecure gloating and jeering of the other Rangers fans was making the same point.

The *Daily Record* naturally raised its true colours almost immediately, but there were also the more reflective and thoughtful pieces in other newspapers, which pointed out that football was the winner in all of this, and that the Scottish public were once again talking about the game in a way that they had not done for many years. It was an interesting dimension to the old stuff about the Old Firm needing a fresh challenge from other parts of Scotland. Maybe they did, but when it was not forthcoming, they provided their own challenge.

Yet ten years earlier, things had been so different. Ironically, in both 1993 and 2003, Rangers won a treble. But the circumstances were different, totally different. The 1993 treble had been gifted to Rangers because of incompetence, complacency and an unwillingness to face the truth. 2003 was lost through bad luck at key points of the season, over-commitment thanks to a prolonged and exhausting European campaign and one major misjudgement at Inverness. 2003 was by no means a failure.

Summer 1993 had been spent in the deepest melancholy, not only because we had just suffered a bad season. Indeed we had suffered four bad seasons, but even that was not the problem. The root cause of the depression was that there did not seem to be any answer from the existing leadership at the club. There was not even the will to fight. The club was going nowhere, and some of the support were now openly saying that they would either follow a local team or that they would give up football. Celtic were in fact in danger of shrivelling up, if not dying altogether, and Scottish football itself, which has always needed a strong Celtic, would have been in peril, for no other team looked vaguely likely to challenge the hegemony of Rangers, let alone think of making any kind of impact in Europe. To have suggested that tens of thousands of fans would go to Seville ten years later, see the team lose and come back almost as happy as they went away would have been to invite derision, ridicule and a suggestion of a visit to the nearest psychiatrist.

Understanding Celtic cannot be achieved unless you are part of it and share in the labours, sufferings, laughter and tears associated. Outsiders, even those who have strong affections for other clubs, cannot really understand the passions and the feelings involved with *this* club. Deep in the history – perhaps even the pre-history of our club with landlords, famines and repression – there are clues to the intensity of it all. One seldom finds a supporter who is a supporter by choice. He or she is a supporter because it is bred into him or her. In the author's case, it was the force feeding of Patsy Gallacher and Tommy McInally, and no doubt the first words of the younger generation will be 'Simpson, Craig and Gemmell . . .'

Similarly, one cannot stop being a Celtic supporter. At least two well-known Scottish politicians have said publicly that they used to be Celtic supporters but have now ceased to be; both however told me privately that this was not true, but they must say such things lest they alienate the Rangers vote. Celtic is a massive Scottish institution, the bedrock of existence of a large ethnic community and increasingly nowadays many others as well.

The intervening ten years from 1993 to 2003 are arguably the most interesting in the never dull history of this fascinating and riveting club – 'not so much a football club, more a way of life' as someone put it rather well. Changes have come as they have come to all of football, and Celtic have moved with the changes. Indeed it could be argued that in some respects they are ahead of the game.

The main change is now in the attitude and quantity of the supporters. There are a lot more of them now. Every home league game will attract around 58,000 spectators, a large proportion of them being season-ticket holders and a figure that is significantly larger than the support of Rangers. Indeed only Manchester United in the British Isles has a larger support, and very few teams on the continent of Europe can expect to top that mark.

But let us consider this in historical perspective. A look at the attendances of season 1992/93 will show that although the games against Rangers attracted large attendances, Celtic played Airdrie at home on 6 April 1993 in front of 10,671 spectators and Falkirk on 20 April with only 10,151 gracing the slopes of Celtic Park. These statistics in comparison with the attendances of 2003 show the progress made by Celtic, and it is only natural that the huge crowd will understandably entertain great expectations. Celtic's crowd is simply so vast that it will not allow standards to drop to the pathetic level of the Kelly epoch. Celtic are a big, big club, and although there remain traces of the inbuilt, endogenous paranoia, the other psychological disturbance of the past – the inferiority complex – has now long gone. Celtic may well lose on occasion to Rangers, possibly even over a period of years they will lose out to Rangers, but they shall never again be afraid of them or be intimidated by them.

There is another dimension as well. Since the share issue of 1994/95, there is a feeling that the fans now own the club. This is of course not true, but what is indisputable is that no Celtic management of the future will ever dare lose touch with the fans or indeed with reality as the Kellys did. The prompt sacking of John Barnes in 2000 after the disgraceful Scottish Cup tie against Inverness Caley Thistle was a clear indication of that. Had the directors not done so, there would have been major civil unrest in the environs of Celtic Park before every home match. The Kellys on the other hand were able to ignore the undercurrents, because they were simply that – undercurrents – but Brian Quinn and Dermot Desmond will always have to be very aware of what the supporters feel and what they want.

The ground will be the permanent monument to Fergus McCann. It is a marvellous structure, much admired by opposing fans, journalists and casual visitors alike. Watching a game from the upper tier of the north stand, for example, is a truly awesome experience. The eruption of the crowd at the appearance of a late winner for example will remain in the memory for a very long time – and one can recall two such phenomena both scored by Johan Mjallby against Dundee in 2001 and Hibs in 2003. It is often claimed, on the other hand, that there is a lack of atmosphere at some points in the game. There may be some truth in that, but lack of atmosphere is a feature of most modern all-seater stadia.

Celtic's support, apart from being large, is also predominantly well behaved with 'incidents' like the sad happenings on the aeroplane home from Vigo in December 2002 being very rare indeed. Crowd misbehaviour has seldom been a part of Celtic Football Club since Jock Stein's time. Stein successfully launched a crusade against this in the early days of his managerial career in 1965, and from then, trouble involving Celtic fans has been very rare. The trip to Seville was a total triumph in this respect, and Celtic have also managed to a very large extent to eliminate or at least reduce sectarianism from the support.

This is hardly surprising, given the amount of nominal (and sometimes practising) Protestants who now proudly wear the green. For historical reasons, Protestants are in the minority (if this matters) of the support, but they are a significant minority, often well-educated men and women who grew up in the 1960s and 1970s and learned to despise the narrow-minded bigotry that one sometimes hears elsewhere in Glasgow and in Scotland. This author for example is proud to say that he is a member of the Church of Scotland where he finds not a few footballing Tims in his congregation.

Yet this has been done without in any way minimising the history of the club. That Celtic are rooted in Ireland is patently true, and Celtic has made no effort to deny this. Indeed it has fostered this link with the official encouragement of the singing of 'The Fields of Athenry' for example. In this respect, there is perhaps a parallel with the Irish Republic itself. A visitor to Dublin, for example, will find tricolours proudly displayed, the 'Soldiers' Song' played and respectfully listened to at the close of functions, great stress laid on patriotism at Kilmainham Jail and Glasnevin Cemetery, but also a true acceptance of people of other nations and of other cultures. It is a nation that has learned to forgive and to move on without in any way minimising what the past was like. Celtic must try to achieve all this as well . . . and they are succeeding.

The bus park at Celtic Park on match days (a minor criticism of the club but one that is frequently heard is that the bus park could do with a facelift including tarmac rather than the mud and gutters that remind us so much of the bad old unhygienic days of Hampden Park) will show a fair amount of Irish buses from Donegal, Belfast, Derry and elsewhere. This is a comparatively new phenomenon for there were never Irish fans in such large numbers in previous generations, except for big occasions like Scottish Cup finals.

But Scottish Saltires were also clearly visible among the Celtic fans in Seville. A generation ago, this would have been unthinkable. Two generations ago, it would have been impossible, for in the 1930s, at an Old Firm game, the flags on display would have indicated that Celtic equalled Ireland and Rangers equalled Scotland with Rangers fans even hijacking lovely Scottish songs like 'The Wells O'Wearie' and 'Loch Lomond' and claiming them as their own. Now one can look at not a few white-coloured tops at Rangers games, and validly ask the question 'which international team do they support?' All is changed, changed utterly, as W. B. Yeats might have said. Celtic have Swedish flags as well.

Now why would that be, one wonders? It is because Celtic possess in their multi-national and multi-talented team one genuinely and undeniably world class player by the name of Henrik Larsson. Great Celtic teams need to have a personality goalscorer – one thinks of Jimmy Quinn and Jimmy McGrory of long ago, of Kenny Dalglish and Dixie Deans of more recent times. Larsson is fit to be mentioned in any company and although he could not possibly claim that Celtic were 'the only team he ever wanted to play for', he will now be remembered for all time not as Henrik Larsson of Sweden, but as Henrik Larsson of Celtic. He is truly one of the all-time Celtic greats.

Managers have come and gone. Since 1993 there have been Brady, Connor, Macari, Burns, Jansen, Venglos, Barnes, Dalglish and O'Neill. Connor and Dalglish were stop gaps. Burns and Jansen achieved some success, and O'Neill a great deal. He is certainly a good manager, but the jury is still out on the question of whether he will be a great manager in the sense of Maley and Stein. Time will tell, and it is to be hoped that O'Neill will stick around Celtic Park long enough to give us a chance to make a judgement on this point. He is certainly a fine man and judging by his behaviour on the touchline and elsewhere, a true Celt sharing the same sort of extremes of emotions that we all do.

The questions are perennially and boringly asked: 'Whither Celtic?' and 'Whither Scottish football?' It is true that the rise and rise of Celtic and Rangers has meant that the rest of the teams in Scotland are in a pretty bad state. It is now a forgone conclusion that the winners of the Scottish Premier League will be one of the Old Firm sides. Other teams may win the Scottish Cup or the Scottish League Cup but the league will stay in Glasgow. Even in the two cup competitions we find this happening. In 2003, for example, a good team like Dundee reached the Scottish Cup final and played well enough for a spell against Rangers, but then appeared to accept that, 'We are not allowed to win. We must obey nature's law and lose' as of course they did.

Clearly the Old Firm clubs see their future outside of Scotland. Celtic and Rangers have tried to join the Premiership in England and also to form an Atlantic League with the leading clubs from countries such as Holland, Belgium and Portugal. The option of moving to England is clearly the most attractive in commercial and sporting terms and the issue was raised yet again in the run up to the UEFA Cup final, most notably by Dermot Desmond, Celtic's biggest shareholder. It is clear that the scale of Celtic's support in Seville – the city experienced an influx of between 50,000 and 80,000 Celtic fans – brought home to many the undeniable fact that Celtic are one of the biggest clubs in the world. The desirability of Celtic moving south was subsequently argued by a number of leading English journalists, not least Paul Hayward of the *Daily Telegraph*, who had recently been named Sports Writer of the Year by his peers. In an article written two days after the final, Hayward even suggested that the initial moves were already under way: 'Behind the scenes powerful alliances are forming in Glasgow, Liverpool and Manchester. The most dramatic scenario would be a second Premier League breakaway in which the lesser top-flight clubs were dumped and the top English division became an elite Anglo-Scottish coalition.'

Yet there are apparently insurmountable obstacles in the way of a move that would be welcomed with open arms by the vast majority of Celtic fans. The Scottish and English football associations, UEFA and the lesser clubs in the Premiership have all tried to pour cold water on the idea. And at an official level the Premiership itself kicked the idea firmly into touch when its member clubs recently voted 20–0 against the idea.

But my belief is that it should, and will, happen. It would undoubtedly be good for Celtic and Rangers. But it would also benefit the English game. The Old Firm are probably the only clubs in Britain with the potential to rival Manchester United in terms of support and, ultimately, finance. This could only enhance the level of competition in a league that is now too often won by the Old Trafford club. There would also be commercial benefits. While the Premiership is enjoying an unprecedented level of support from supporters and television companies, and may not need the Old Firm at the present time, the boom will not go on forever and there is sure to come a time when action will be needed to maximise the sale of media rights. Quite simply, the excitement generated by Scotland–England clashes would be irresistible, both to the diehard fan in the stadium and to the armchair viewer. As Dermot Desmond perceptively remarked in the aftermath of Seville, 'When you own a theatre you want to put on the best plays.'

The other Scottish teams are in a cleft stick about this. From time to time, they throw tantrums about not getting a bigger share of the media cake, even in 2002 resigning (all ten of them) from the Scottish Premier League in one of the most bizarre moves in Scottish football history. But they know that without the big two, the Scottish game would very quickly become like the Irish League or the League of Ireland. Scottish football needs Celtic and Rangers. It is a pity that at least one other team cannot keep some sort of pace with them in the way that Dundee United and Aberdeen did in the 1980s and Hearts did as recently as 1998.

It is of course television: BBC, Sky, Five and occasionally STV or Setanta, which calls the shots. Celtic played sixty competitive games in 2002/03. No less than thirty-five of them were shown live on television, and indeed most of the big games were on BBC, certainly in Scotland. Let us praise this. It has meant that Celtic fans who live in places like the Orkneys, Benbecula or Inverness have been able to see Celtic on a regular basis, and can support their team, talking knowledgeably about whether Petrov had a good game or whether Hartson really was offside.

It has magnified and solidified the Celtic family, and it is a total contrast to the position adopted by Sir Bob Kelly in the 1960s when he would have done anything to prevent supporters from seeing Celtic on television. His argument always was that it would prevent fans going to the game and we used to hear clichés like 'life's blood' and so on. In fact, whether the game is on the box or not, Celtic will attract 58,000 or 59,000 to a home game – an attendance twice or even three times what Sir Bob Kelly could have expected in the 1950s or 1960s.

It is now time to examine in some detail this mighty decade in Celtic history. These tumultuous, momentous, ten years have meant a great deal to everyone connected with the club. In 1994, it might have gone out of existence (although the author is one of those who thinks that this would never or could never have happened); by 2003, Celtic were once again a major European power with eye-brows raised in countries such as England and Germany, which had been patronising the Scottish game for decades.

The historian, Tacitus, who wrote about the Roman Empire in the first century AD, pledges himself to write '*sine ira et studio*' – 'without passion and bias'. It is an ambitious claim which the good Roman does not achieve, for he does emphasise the bad points of the Imperial system. To write good history one must have some passion and indeed a little bias. This author will not even make such a claim, as Tacitus does, for the concept of Celtic simply does not lend itself to the dispassionate and the neutral. Celtic will always arouse strong feelings. The author would not be honest if he were to try to disguise his.

1

1993/94: The Kelly Legacy

T he Scottish Cup final of 1993 had come to its end. Father and son had watched it, as they had done so many Scottish Cup finals in the past, in father's case since Joe Cassidy scored the only goal in 1923 against Hibs. Son recalled with amusement 1954 when he was chided by tense father for sliding along the linoleum floor to show how Johnnie Bonnar was keeping Paddy Buckley of Aberdeen at bay and to add a visual dimension to the radio commentary. Minutes later, the tension now over, a silver teapot was produced so that son could pretend to be Jock Stein, Celtic's captain, and receive the Scottish Cup at the end of the game, as Peter Thomson's dulcet tones over the radio informed the nation that 'Celtic have won the Scottish Cup for the seventeenth time.'

The Scottish Cup was of course the competition that Celtic loved. It was the only domestic competition that they had won oftener than Rangers, and it is the competition which lends itself to what might be termed the Celtic ethos in which there is all the romance and sorrow associated with the club. Celtic had first won the trophy in 1892, and had, generally speaking, kept their noses in front of Rangers in terms of how often they had lifted it. One of the constant features of Celtic's history is that whenever the team is badly organised and managed, Rangers begin to catch up in terms of winning the Scottish Cup, even for a brief spell in the 1960s overtaking Celtic.

Both father and son had shed tears of relief in that massive green-and-white tide at the dawning of the glorious Stein management era in 1965 when Billy McNeill propelled Celtic to that same Scottish Cup, rising majestically above the Dunfermline defence to head the winner and to launch the club to further glories, as yet undreamed of. Bobby Davidson's refereeing (described by the charitable as bizarre and by the unforgiving as cheating) had been dissected and venomously spurned in 1970 when Celtic went down by three goals to one against Aberdeen. Agonies and ecstacies had been shared over the phone as cup finals had been played out on television in living rooms, particularly the two great comebacks from the dead against Dundee United in the mid 1980s. Valentine and Strachan had been bitterly cursed in 1984 when Roy Aitken was sent off for a foul that had been made much of. Cowardice had been in evidence, as garden sheds had been used for hiding in lest Rangers equalise in 1971, 1977, 1980 and 1989.

But this was 1993 and there was no Celtic in the Scottish Cup final. Ironically it was played at Celtic Park, as Hampden was being redeveloped, but the contestants were Rangers and Aberdeen. For this purpose father and son had forged an alliance with an earnest young male nurse who supported the Dons. The other patients were left in their own wee world, and hardly noticed, for this was the dementia ward of the hospital. The young Dons supporter would be disappointed at the end, but professional that he was, smiled and joked with the old man as he escorted him to his bed. The sage told the other patients that it wasn't always like this and that 'Jimmy McGrory would have shown them' and 'Look, you never saw Patsy Gallacher'.

The son, now a respected professional teacher and who really should have behaved better and with more decorum, bade farewell to his beloved father and headed morosely to his car. By this time, the car radio was saying that the cup was being presented with its blue ribbons. Son shouted in a loud voice (fortunately nobody else heard) 'Bastards! Bastards! Bastards! Don't these Kellys realise what they've done to us?' A few months later when he dutifully laid the green-and-white scarf over the coffin, he thanked God that dad had been spared some things.

The damage done by the Kelly dynasty to Celtic Football Club was considerable and, some felt, permanent. The House of Kelly had been a mixed blessing for Celtic. The original member of the family, James Kelly, signed (some might say poached) from the Dumbartonshire team Renton in 1888, was an outstanding player and earned eight Scotland caps. Although technically an amateur – as all Scotland was in 1888 – he was nevertheless made an offer he could not refuse by one of Celtic's founding fathers, John Glass. Kelly played soundly for the club until 1897 and then went on to serve with distinction in an administrative and directorial capacity before becoming chairman until 1914, and continuing as director until his death in 1932.

James Kelly was the first legendary Celt, a great centre half and captain. His arrival at Celtic Park was an instant indication that the new club meant business. He was a genuine superstar in his era, and his landlady would tell the newspapers what he had for his tea. He became closely associated with Willie Maley and the tremendous Edwardian team that won six league titles in a row from 1905 until 1910. It was Kelly and Maley between them who represented the progressive, forward-looking parts of the Irish community and who realised that one way to satisfy the demands of the underprivileged was to give them a great football team.

The contribution of James's son Robert was ambivalent and more difficult to assess. A withered arm and other health problems had meant that a career in professional football was out of the question, but he had served the club as director and chairman. Certainly he believed that the name 'Celtic' was important and that good football and good sportsmanship were equally beneficial to the maintenance of that good name. Laudably, in the early 1950s he stood up to George Graham's dictatorial attempts to remove the Eire tricolour from Celtic Park which, as the saying went, resembled a constipated hen. No power on earth could bring it down.

Less laudably, he insisted on an ill thought out youth policy which led the club to disaster in the early 1960s. There were two ways of looking at this policy. Yes, it certainly was a good idea to bring on youngsters like McNeill, Murdoch, Crerand and Clark. Matt Busby had done the same at Manchester United, as indeed to a lesser extent would Alex Ferguson at the same club thirty years later. But good youth teams have to be blended with experience. Occasionally a good player must be brought in from another club. The problem was that they cost money, something that Mr Kelly was reluctant to disburse in spite of the obvious abundance of it at Celtic Park.

In addition it was Kelly who chose the team, often hiding behind the much loved Jimmy McGrory, the nominal manager. Kelly whimsically picked favourites and dropped (and transferred) those he did not like. Four Scottish Cup finals were reached in 1955, 1956, 1961 and 1963. In each of the four cases, the wrong team was chosen and Celtic lost. Yet Kelly did have the courage to admit he had been wrong when he brought back Jock Stein in 1965. It would have been no easy matter for Kelly to invite a Protestant – albeit one who had played for and captained the club and who was as imbued with the Celtic philosophy as anyone – to become manager of the club. The European Cup was won when Kelly was chairman and therefore he deserves some praise, although his insinuations that Jock Stein was leased out, as it were, from his reserve and youth team responsibilities at Celtic Park to Dunfermline and then Hibs in order to be brought back to win the European Cup are simply not true. Nevertheless, those who believe in such things were pleased to see that Mr Kelly got a knighthood in January 1969.

But by the early 1990s the Kelly dynasty was now represented by Sir Robert's two nephews, Kevin and Michael. Michael had once been Lord Provost of Glasgow, and Kevin had been with Celtic for many years. Frankly they had led the club to tragedy and woe on a scale which could hardly have been contemplated ten years previously. The 1980s had seen one or two fine moments – several very good Scottish Cup finals and a great centenary season in 1988 for example, but no impact whatsoever had been made on Europe. Worse, there had been the total inability to live with the new Rangers from 1989 onwards.

Rangers were now in the hands of money magnates of a blatant and unrepentant kind. Graeme Souness had been appointed in 1986 as player-manager and the ante had been upped. Ruthless, occasionally even savage, Rangers had been efficient, spending money on English and foreign mercenaries on a lavish and apparently irresponsible scale and showing the world that Rangers meant business. If anything good could be said about this, it was that it at least temporarily reversed the flow of talent from Scotland to England. The depressing departures of Scottish players to England where they sometimes made it, and sometimes didn't, had come to an end. Now established England internationalists like Terry Butcher, for example, played for Rangers.

This approach had wiped out the cottage-industry-economy

teams like Aberdeen and Dundee United, whose contribution to Scottish football had hitherto been very creditable, but had also imposed severe pressure on the only team that could live with Rangers, namely Celtic. Celtic's response had been nothing short of disgraceful. Heads had been buried in sand, the counsel of despair had been heard over and over again and the phrase 're-arranging the deck chairs on the *Titanic*' would sum up the efficacy of the club's approach. The phrase 'the biscuit-tin economy' was frequently used to describe Celtic's response to the vicious, yet brutally successful, capitalism of their opponents.

There was even the perception that Celtic were the poor team of Glasgow, and certainly the ground, 'dear old Paradise', often gave that impression. Leaks reached the fanzines that the state of the dressing rooms had been the subject of an official complaint from some of the players, one of whom said, only half jokingly, 'It's a great honour to use the same dressing room as Jimmy McGrory and Charlie Tully, but to hell with the same towels and the same soap!' To justify the non-appearance of an all-seater stadium, there had been ludicrous statements from the board that 'our spectators prefer to stand' and even one or two bogus opinion polls conducted in the *Celtic View* (dubbed *Pravda* by the cynics, after the propaganda organ of the Soviet Union). Yet more progressive teams like Rangers, Aberdeen and even Clydebank had had all-seater stadia for years!

Poverty, in terms of Celtic, was of course a nonsense. The support was massive, possibly the biggest in Great Britain, and all that was required was clear leadership. That did however tend to involve spending money or inviting someone on to the board who had the cash to do the needful. This, the Kelly family and their associates refused to do, apparently oblivious or indifferent to the damage that they were doing to a great Scottish institution, its heritage and those who loved it. And they apparently continued to draw a salary, £40,000 each per annum, it was rumoured! It was a supreme irony that the family which had had so much to do with making the club great a hundred years ago to establish Celtic in the twentieth century now had no conception of what was required as we approached the twenty-first. Still less did they appear to have any conscience or even awareness of what they were doing to the supporters.

In August 1988, Celtic had been thrashed 5–1 by Rangers at Ibrox. In retrospect this was a watershed and the beginning of the end for the Kelly regime. The humiliating reverse could have been counteracted and possibly even overcome given the right attitude, but the club, management, directorate, players and eventually even fans were psyched-out into believing that Rangers were unbeatable. There was the occasional good Celtic moment, but sadly, such moments became in the context of history little more than aberrations from the norm that Rangers must win. This attitude, which always flourishes in the absence of a firm sense of direction at Celtic Park, had of course prevailed in the early 1960s as well in the heyday of 'Uncle Bob' Kelly – and it is a sad truism of life that such beliefs are self-fulfilling.

An excellent example of how the club allowed itself to be made a fool of by Rangers occurred in summer 1989. The day before the Old Firm Scottish Cup final (which Celtic won 1–0; the last honour, as it turned out, to be won by the Kelly dynasty) Celtic signed Maurice Johnston – apparently. Some argued that he should never have been allowed to go in 1987. Others were less than happy to see him back, given his reputed involvement in murky dealings. But like him or not, he was back from Nantes with his beautiful girl friend and his Celtic scarf, flaunting his crucifix and saying that it was good to be home and, infamously, that Celtic were the only team he ever wanted to play for. Celtic having won the propaganda war, for the moment, also won the Scottish Cup the next day.

The last point needs to be stressed. The propaganda war is every bit as vital as tactics on the field. The late Jock Stein always knew how to handle the media and to knock Rangers off the back pages of the newspapers. For the moment in 1989 when the Scottish Cup returned to Celtic Park, there was the feeling that the fightback was on. The game had been won well, even though the score was only 1–0 and with Maurice Johnston back at Celtic Park for the following season, there was no reason at all to believe that the future was not going to be rosy. Sadly, some problem arose (or was allowed to arise) about Johnston's income tax, the deal died the following week and about six weeks later, Johnston signed for Souness's Rangers.

Naturally all Celtic fans hated Maurice Johnston – and not without cause. But antipathy towards the treacherous Mo could not disguise the fact that this was an appallingly incompetent piece of business by the Celtic board, which had now been comprehensively taken to the cleaners by both Johnston and Rangers. Celtic had been shown to be gullible, simple, naïve, penny-pinching and downright stupid. Not only that, but the moral high ground had been surrendered to Rangers. Johnston was a Roman Catholic, nominally at least, and he certainly was prepared to make a show of his religion, although whether his attendance at mass and confession were what they should have been is a different matter. Rangers had now publicly signed a Roman Catholic, jettisoning, it would appear, a policy of bigotry which had obtained since soon after the First World War. Scottish opinion – even the quality papers like *The Scotsman* and *The Herald*, which had frequently been intellectually dishonest enough to pretend that the policy did not exist – had to give them credit for that.

Celtic were always thereafter a very poor second (sometimes not even a second) to Rangers in the league. Even when they did get their nose ahead of Rangers, in the Scottish Cup for example, they never capitalised. In both 1990 and 1991, they beat Rangers but failed to win the competition, losing in a heartbreaking penalty shoot out to Aberdeen in the final of 1990 and to Motherwell thanks to an inept performance in the semi final (and its replay) of 1991. Europe invariably meant an early exit – on one occasion, in September 1989, Jackie Dziekanowski scored four goals at Celtic Park against Partisan Belgrade, but careless defending meant that they went out on away goals! A sympathetic Rangers supporter remarked that there should be a law against what Celtic did to their supporters.

Indeed Celtic did not always qualify for Europe, and managers came and went. Billy McNeill ('too much of a supporter to be a manager' as one fanzine put it) was shown the door in 1991. Liam Brady followed him. He was a surprise choice given that he had never managed any team previously, and his only qualifications seemed to be that he was an Irishman, that he supported Celtic as a boy and was a member of the Juventus team which put Celtic out of the European Cup in 1981! His naivety was exposed when he tried to explain away a League Cup defeat by Airdrie on the grounds that it was no big deal to lose to Airdrie. Airdrie, after all, had also beaten Aberdeen! 'This guy does not understand Celtic, or Scotland', reckoned the punters, and they were right. Liam lasted only two years and a bit, hampered by lack of resources to buy quality players. His team played, nevertheless, some brilliant football in the second half of the 1991/92 season, the pivotal night being a very unlucky

Scottish Cup semi final in April where Celtic did everything but score against Rangers in the Hampden rain. Crucially, Brady failed to win anything tangible and by autumn 1993 Lou Macari was *in situ* – an appointment which, given Macari's desertion of the club in 1973, raised more than a few eyebrows about the judgement of the Celtic directors.

1993 was a dreadful year, but the board seemed to be convinced that everything would be all right as soon as the club moved to a new stadium at Cambuslang. Certainly an all-seater stadium needed to be built and Celtic Park was outdated, but the actual site in Kerrydale Street was big enough and there was no need to throw the baby out with the bath water, supporters felt. Besides there were at least two objections to the site at Cambuslang: one was that toxic gases were apparently given off by nearby industry and the other, more basic, objection was that nobody seemed to have the slightest clue how the money would be raised.

Yet plans were drawn up, artists impressions were printed in the *Celtic View* (including an infamous one where the players all seemed to have one leg and the goalposts had bits missing) and either one of the directors or chief executive Terry Cassidy repeatedly appeared in the press or on television assuring everyone that everything would be hunky-dory, that Rangers would be defeated and the European Cup would soon return to Celtic Park, or at least to Cambuslang. Similarly, Hitler's bunker in Berlin in 1945 had a few astrologers who predicted the arrival of supernatural armies to defeat the Russians. Pigs were also reputed to be seen flying up the Gallowgate and along London Road!

The luckless Terry Cassidy, chief executive from 1991 to 1993, was relentlessly pilloried by the fans. He started off with the advantage of his name, an undeniably Celtic one particularly in the minds of those who recalled Joe Cassidy of the First World War years and immediately thereafter, but that was about all that was impressive about him. His role seemed to be that of a human shield behind which the directors hid. His appearances on Friday night television were frequently embarrassing, as he answered the presenter's question with 'What do you think?' and 'Who knows?' before assuring everyone that everything was going to be all right.

Celtic's fans are themselves gullible on occasion. They are also far too loyal. A stand against this nonsense should have been made as early as 1989 when it was becoming clear that Rangers were buying players on a hitherto unprecedented scale. As it turned out, mediocre teams and trophyless seasons had to be tholed in 1990, 1991, 1992 and 1993 before the worms eventually turned.

To be fair, supporters did find themselves in a dilemma. It was easy to criticise what was going on in the name of Celtic, yet no one wanted to appear disloyal and to be seen to belittle the honest efforts of the players. They were giving of their best, although it was clear that in some cases their best was more than a little short of good enough for Celtic. Supporters did not wish in any way to detract from their efforts or to undermine their confidence. Yet, they were doing themselves less than justice if they kept quiet about it and stayed complacent in the belief that 'something might turn up' as Mr Micawber in David Copperfield would have said.

Season 1993/94 with all its horrors oddly enough saw a few good things happen to Celtic. For one thing, they actually lasted longer in Europe than Rangers did. The Ibrox men went out to a Bulgarian team called Levski Sofia whose name lent itself to an 'Ave Maria' chant, something that quietened Rangers fans at work for at least one day. Celtic however had little to boast about, for they were destined to go out to Bobby Robson's Sporting Lisbon long before Christmas. The team had many, or at least some good players, notably Paul McStay and John Collins, wholehearted men like Peter Grant, a few golden oldies like McAvennie and Nicholas who had returned after deserting the club in the past, the best goal-keeper around (arguably) in Pat Bonner still fondly remembered all over the world for his starring role for Ireland in the 1990 World Cup. And there was also Tom Boyd, who had arrived from Chelsea in February 1992 in a straight swap with striker Tony Cascarino; Boyd became not only a defensive stalwart but also club captain and only left the club at the end of season 2002/03 after playing a total of 361 games. The support still seemed prepared to be 'faithful through and through' as their song went. But were they? Attendances were dipping and were now considerably below those of Rangers, whose ground was filled mostly by season-ticket holders who paid their money in advance during the close season.

Tragically, Rangers beat Celtic by the only goal in the League Cup semi final of 1993/94 when the hard working Mike Galloway made a mistake. League form was mediocre, to put it mildly. The team had registered only two wins by early October. Wednesday 6 October saw a defeat at McDiarmid Park, Perth, fisticuffs (allegedly) in the dressing room and the fall from power of Liam Brady, who thought about offering his resignation on the bus home that night, but waited till the following morning. Indeed he had been considering it since the summer.

The directors then clumsily allowed Joe Jordan – who had been a good, if short-lived assistant manager and a wholehearted Celt – to depart and would have done well to have given the brusque, but sincere, Frank Connor, the caretaker manager, a longer run. Frank had had a chequered and interesting career, starting off as a fairly unsuccessful goalkeeper with Celtic in the early 1960s. This was actually his third stint as a backroom bhoy at Celtic Park. He had worked under Jock Stein and Billy McNeill from 1977–1980 before becoming manager of Berwick Rangers. He was then brought back to Celtic Park in 1983, the year of McNeill's departure to Manchester City, was sacked as assistant manager by Davie Hay in 1986, but had then gone on to resurrect Raith Rovers from the Second Division. Now he found himself in charge at Celtic Park.

Peter Grant stated that the dressing room to a man were behind Connor. The likeable Frank, an earnest and down-to-earth character, has the distinction of being the only Celtic manager never to lose a game, and his 'reign' included the first leg of the UEFA Cup tie against Sporting Lisbon! His other two games were against Dundee and Hibs. In both of these games, he had seen Celtic come from behind, something that betokened a certain enthusiasm on the part of the players, and a definite desire to work for him.

But Frank was made to yield in favour of Lou Macari, who was appointed manager on 30 October 1993. Lou had been a fine player in the early 1970s but had then left Celtic for Manchester United. His playing days and subsequent managerial career had not been without a few allegations of scandals at Swindon Town and Stoke City, and like Nicholas and McAvennie, he was now being granted a Celtic resurrection that was less than totally merited. He was summoned from Stoke City to save the club, and it is fair to say that it was a move that had the supporters not a little perplexed and baffled. He made sure that he was photographed under the portrait of Jock Stein – indeed there were a few superficial similarities in that Macari didn't drink but gambled extensively, but even before he abandoned Stein for Manchester United in 1973, no one could say that the relationship between Macari and Stein was a good one. But Macari showed a certain amount of street wisdom at the outset. He made the perceptive comment that: 'The punters don't care who runs the club. They want results. I want results, preferably good results.' Perhaps Lou was here showing a sense of humour and poking a little fun at the clichéd rhetorical claptrap of managers, players and journalists who talk about 'getting a result' without specifying what kind of a result!

Be that as it may, he started well with a win over Rangers at Ibrox on 30 October. Granted it was an ill-deserved, late winner and the team had been chosen by the interim manager Frank Connor (who was going to be kept on in some capacity, it appeared) rather than Macari himself, but any win at Ibrox is a good one for a manager. From then on, Celtic's domestic form gradually improved with only one defeat (to Dundee United at Tannadice) before the turn of the year. Macari could not keep Celtic in Europe however and raised an eyebrow or two by trading Andy Payton, a passable forward, for Wayne Biggins, a total unknown and 33 years old. This was in a deal with Barnsley and cost Celtic an additional £100,000. He also bought a goalkeeper, Carl Muggleton, from Leicester City for £150,000 and Manchester United's reserve full back Lee Martin for £350,000.

These players were all cheap. The style of play also caused more than a few rumbles. Macari put the emphasis on defence, and seemed unaware of the Celtic tradition of attractive, attacking football. Bertie Auld would relate how Jimmy McGrory in the late 1950s would often say one word to his team as they went out: 'Entertain!' In Jock Stein's day, there was also a clear emphasis on good football with loads of goals, and even in more recent times, Celtic had perhaps gone down, but they had done so gloriously, none more obviously than in the Cup Winners' Cup of September 1989 when Dziekanowski had scored four goals in the home leg . . . but Celtic had lost. Macari seemed determined to change all that, even if it meant alienating the fans still further.

Rangers had had a few bad games as well in late 1993. Indeed they were no great shakes, but didn't need to be to win in Scotland! Celtic approached the New Year's Day game at Celtic Park by no means out of the title race, at least in theory. But the supporters were not to be fooled any longer. Several home gates had dropped to well below the 20,000 mark, and the protest movements like the Affiliation of Registered Celtic Supporters' Clubs under Peter Rafferty and Celts For Change under David Cunningham were beginning to make their voices heard. Indeed in November 1993 an audacious takeover bid had been launched. It was fronted by David Low, but had the support of one Fergus McCann, a Canadian millionaire who had spent his boyhood following Celtic from the Croy Supporters' Bus, and also former director Brian Dempsey. The board had stuck together and had been able to resist it. A counter bid from the multi-millionaire Gerald Weisfeld, and fronted by Willie Haughey, was also in the pipeline. These bids had the interest and support of the fans . . . but the board, although temporarily successful in thwarting the rebels, failed to read the danger signals.

It was the Fergus McCann bid that earned most public attention. McCann had qualified as a chartered accountant before leaving Scotland in the mid 1960s, and had learned a great deal about the world of finance before embarking on schemes that would make him a millionaire. The golfing holiday was the main product provided by his company and as this meant that he dealt with the very rich, money flowed readily into his coffers. He had made one or two unofficial offers to help the club but the directors, suspicious that he was trying to oust them – as indeed he was in the long term – refused his help. Yet the board could have saved themselves, at least temporarily, if they had allowed McCann to join them and provide not only capital but also his considerable business acumen.

It was an excellent example of how real power is often maintained by yielding occasionally to pressure rather than by an obdurate refusal to countenance any opposition. Suggestions and offers of help to the beleagured establishment were treated with paranoia, as the net began to tighten. In the meantime everybody connected with Celtic began to suffer. At least one player at the time has refused to talk about this period of Celtic history because 'it is just too painful'.

The New Year's Day fixture with Rangers at Celtic Park would have been a crucial match at the best of times. In the circumstances of season 1993/94, it was even more significant. The very future of the club was at stake. It was a bizarre atmosphere. For once the 'guests' from Ibrox did not feel the full brunt of the visceral hatred.

The vitriol was reserved for the Celtic board. Yet, such is football that a good result for Celtic might just have saved them.

This last point is worth reiterating. Celtic supporters do not, as a general rule, worry too much about what goes on behind the scenes, as Macari himself had spotted on joining the club. The arcane worlds of business and finance, with their jargon and technical terms, present a deliberately forbidding front to the media, let alone the general public. What fans, and Celtic fans in particular, do understand is football. Fans will be able to ignore or condone a little pocket-lining, or even vast fortunes being made at their expense, provided that the team on the park are worthy of the club and doing a good job.

At the end of 1993, however, Celtic fans now clearly understood that their team was letting them down, that no trophies were being won and that they were the subject of unremitting sneers and ridicule from Rangers supporters and their fellow travellers – people who piously claim to support Motherwell or Hearts, for example, but nevertheless muscle in on the side of Rangers when Celtic are doing badly and true colours can therefore be shown.

The start of that fateful Old Firm game could hardly have been worse for Celtic. After only a minute Rangers took the lead with a goal from Mark Hateley, and the Celtic central defensive pairing of Gillespie and Wdowczyk were nowhere to be seen. Three minutes later, Hateley was again involved as Mikhailichenko applied the finishing touch and the amateurish home side were 2–0 down.

The atmosphere, already tense inside the ground, now became murderous. The impression was even spread around (and found ready belief) that the Celtic players had deliberately let these goals in to bring matters to a head. This was of course arrant nonsense, but revealed the mood of the Celtic fans. In the main stand, objects were thrown at the directors' box, some missiles apparently hitting the Rangers directors but only as *The Herald* points out 'because of their close proximity to Celtic's directors.'

Things became worse after Rangers scored again on the half-hour mark. A Celtic fan, apparently receiving first aid, suddenly broke from those attending to him to rush at Rangers goalkeeper Ally Maxwell before police removed him. At half time there was the chilling sight of a Celtic fan clambering on top of the dugout to dangle his Celtic scarf in the shape of a hangman's noose at the directors' box.

Bravely, the directors returned from the comfort of their plush lounge and bar for the second half. One had to admire their courage (some would have said arrogance) in facing the public, and they were immediately rewarded with a goal. John Collins scored it and it heralded a Celtic fightback of sorts. Rangers would eventually win 4–2 but at least the spirited Celtic performance helped to prevent the trouble getting any worse, although mounted police were in evidence at full time to prevent further outbreaks of violence.

As it was, things were bad enough. Fifty-four people were arrested, numerous people were slightly injured including, ironically, a Catholic priest! Father Peter McBride of Renton, Dumbartonshire, who was also a chaplain in the Royal Navy, was later able to preach a fine sermon on the evils of bigotry and the need for tolerance, using a vivid visual aid, namely a gash on his forehead caused by a coin after Rangers scored their third goal. He happened to be in the way of it. And the irony was that it was not thrown by some Orange bigot. It was thrown by one of his 'own' people! In fact the good Father's sermon missed the point somewhat. The problem was not religious intolerance, rather it was a vivid example of what happens when justified protest at incompetence crosses the line and leads to violence.

The aftermath of the game found the Celtic community in a state of uncertainty and confusion. Bewilderment filled the air as supporters speculated about what would happen next. What would 1994 bring? Celtic's game at Motherwell on 3 January was postponed because of bad weather. This was possibly just as well, for it helped to take the heat out of a very dangerous situation. Meanwhile Lou Macari used the opportunity to go scouting in England, but such was the financial situation (an overdraft of many millions was now being mentioned) that he was forced to confine himself to the lower reaches of the English leagues. That Lou himself was far from happy with this situation was made apparent by this quote that he gave to journalists, 'Look at them [Rangers] – one or two dodgy results and they go and sign Gordon Durie for £1.2 million. Our supporters feel if they can do it, why can't we?'

'Why can't we indeed?' asked the forlorn Celtic supporters, whose New Year had been far from pleasant. Although some of them seemed fatalistically to accept that this was the way that it was and the way that it had to be, an increasingly angry number refused to believe that what Rangers could do, Celtic couldn't also do. They had fan bases, after all, that were approximately the same size. Celtic's might be currently diminished, but the potential was vast.

The board meantime sat tight. There was a historical precedent where supporters' unrest had seemed irresistible, but had gradually fizzled out, and the board had emerged triumphant. This occurred in August 1963 when supporters protested at Bob Kelly's intransigence and incompetence after an appalling game against Queen of the South, which had come a week after a 3–0 defeat by Rangers and a few months after another 3–0 defeat by their Old Firm opponents in a Scottish Cup final replay. Only the presence of Glasgow's mounted police in full riot gear had prevented serious disorder that day. 'Uncle Bob' had ridden that one out. His nephews might do the same now.

It was clear however throughout the month of January, in which the team lost to Partick Thistle and Motherwell and drew with Aberdeen and Dundee United, that the old regime had to go. The media talked of little else and barely a day passed without a new story on the travails of Celtic. These were invariably quirky or irrelevant or even erroneous pieces of imaginative journalism, it has to be said, but they further undermined the name of Celtic. The Saturday football programme on BBC Radio Scotland in particular gave the saga saturation coverage from the time that it went on the air at lunch time. The impression was often given that when the games did start at 3-00 p.m., they were merely a filler until the commentators could get back to the real business of discussing, with some relish, what was wrong with Celtic. Indeed, season 1993/94 was a dull one in terms of football, as everyone had known for some time who was going to win the Premier League.

Wise Rangers fans took no real pleasure in all this. Only the most ignorant bigot could believe that this was in any way good for the future of the game in Scotland. It is often said in world economic terms that if the USA sneezes everyone else catches a cold. Celtic had sunk far below the 'sneezing' stage, and all of Scottish football would soon become desperately ill. Celtic fans found themselves in the unusual position of being sympathised with and even comforted quite sincerely by the more enlightened Rangers fans. They quite clearly saw that Celtic, in the position they were, were neither threat nor challenge to the current Rangers hegemony in Scottish football. It could even be that the Rangers fans actually

missed the competition, and realised that a poor Celtic team did nothing to help them prepare for the rigours of European competition.

There remained a last-chance saloon for the embattled Celtic
board. It was the 1994 Scottish Cup. Historically, many tepid Celtic
seasons had been rescued by a good run in the Cup, and the board
may have felt that this could once again rally the faithful to their
fast-sinking ship. The draw did not oblige them. A game against
East Stirlingshire or Forfar at Celtic Park might have earned more
breathing space, but cruelly, Celtic were drawn away to a strong
Motherwell side at the end of January.

Celtic fans were in a quandary about this one. It would of course
be better for the long term interests of the club for Celtic to lose
heavily. The board would certainly not survive that, it was argued.
On the other hand, those of us with Celtic engraved on our hearts
find it difficult to see the green-and-white jerseys defeated, whatever the circumstances. Celtic did go down that day to a narrow
defeat, with the only goal of the game scored by ex-Celt Tommy
Coyne. Ironically the team fought well and were unlucky on one or
two occasions, but the fact remained that they were out and that
Celtic were in for another barren, trophyless and unhappy season.

Incredibly, the self-satisfied, arrogant board stayed in place. In an
atmosphere more akin to South American politics than to Scottish
football, supporters now organized street demonstrations, tried to
persuade the Bank of Scotland to withdraw support, pointed to the
massive debt and 'Sack The Board' became a chant heard more reg-
ularly and with more volume at Celtic games. The first game after
the Cup defeat was at Stark's Park, Kirkcaldy. Celtic had tried to
improve the side by going for another player – Willie Falconer – a
decent, hard working, honest journeyman, who had played for
Aberdeen and was now with Sheffield United. The asking price was
£350,000. Willie would indeed play well for Celtic (winning a
Scottish Cup medal in 1995) and later for a number of other clubs.
But at £350,000, he was hardly likely to have the ability to turn things
around – and in any case, Macari failed to deliver the signing before
the Kirkcaldy match.

'Sack The Board' drowned out any other chants that day, and as one
newspaper put it, Celtic looked 'unenthusiastic and unimaginative'
in that 0–0 draw. Indeed, there were even some suggestions of a
players' revolt and it was clear that the real Celtic supporters

among the staff – Peter Grant, Pat Bonner, Paul McStay and Charlie Nicholas (although Nicholas's claims were rendered less credible by the way he had deserted Celtic for Arsenal in 1983) – had had enough. They would never of course deliberately lose games, and indeed the week after the game at Raith Rovers, Celtic delighted their few supporters at Tynecastle with a good 2–0 win over Hearts. This delighted the rebels as well, for their slogan was now 'Back the Team, Sack the Board' – something which seemed to encompass their belief in, and love for, the club, yet expressed contempt for those who were currently running the organisation.

Yet the slogan was, in essence, a contradiction for in the long term the eleven men on the field are the paid representatives of the board. Looking at it from a different angle, one could argue that the eleven men on the field were the best that the board could do. Celtic is not about a stadium or a takeover. It is about a football team. This football team and its employers were clearly failing to live up to what the supporters wanted of it, or to the rich and august traditions of Celtic Football Club.

A boycott was organized for the next home game against Kilmarnock on Saturday 26 February but, before that happened, the board played its last desperate card. On Friday 25 February 1994 two directors, Kevin Kelly and David Smith, appeared in public to unveil the plans for the proposed move to Cambuslang in 1996. It would be a state-of-the-art stadium with seats for 40,000, and to raise the £20 million required to build it there would be a share issue and additional finance from a company called Gefinor.

It would have been very impressive in another context and at another time, but in the circumstances it did not even look vaguely credible. Almost as soon as it appeared, it was torpedoed. Over the weekend stories began to appear to the effect that Gefinor's name was being used in vain, and that the whole business was little more than wishful thinking. It reminded one, once again, of the last desperate days of Hitler in the bunker when he was deluded enough to believe that phantom armies would miraculously appear to drive the Russians back, or that he could forge an alliance with the British and Americans to do that job for him.

In any case, the stadium issue was not what interested the fans. It was the need to get a good football team on the park, whether at Celtic Park or at Cambuslang. Even with the stadium in its current unsatisfactory state, supporters remained more concerned about the quality of fare being offered by those who wore the green-and-white jerseys, and the need for some kind of a challenge to be put up to Rangers. This board did not look vaguely like capable of delivering on that one.

The board had one piece of luck though, when weather conditions compelled the postponement of the 'boycott' game on Saturday 26 February until Tuesday 1 March. The idea was for supporters to go to the environs of Celtic Park but not go in, or if they did go in, to leave en masse on the sixtieth minute. Such a move would attract huge media attention and would surely have been the leading item on the national news that night, to say nothing of the sports' programmes. Although the Saturday game was postponed, it was only a temporary reprieve for the board. Scotland's Sunday papers, devoting many pages of newsprint to this issue, all said (some had been saying it for some considerable time) that it was now time for the board to do the decent thing and go. The Sack the Board campaign had broken out from the football pages and now extended even into the leader columns of newspapers, which were showing a genuine concern for the apparently terminal decline of a great Scottish institution.

There is a certain dispute about what the crowd that Tuesday night for the Kilmarnock game actually was. Through the antiquated turnstiles there passed 10,882 according to the board, 9,887 according to *Rothman's Yearbook*, but only 8,225 according to the rebels. For many years, it had been suspected that Celtic falsified attendance figures when it suited them but, ironically, quite a few Premier League clubs would have been delighted with that attendance. The lowest recorded gate at Celtic Park was in any case 4,986 for an end of season game against Dundee in 1984, after the league and everything else had been lost.

Paul McStay was absent with a virus. This may or not have been true, but no one in the crowd had any doubt. They thought that McStay was staging his own boycott or was simply embarrassed and upset by the whole business – as he had every right to be. During the first half, a fox, of all things, appeared, ran up the touchline and disappeared. Where it came from, nobody knew, nor does anyone seem to know what happened to the beast afterwards. Naturally it was called 'Kelly'. The supporters did desert (not all of them, it must be admitted) from the sixtieth minute onwards as a dreadful game of football petered out. In an atmosphere akin to that of a reserve fixture, John Collins scored the winner in the last minute, a goal that was greeted with what must be the smallest-ever cheer for a Celtic goal.

However the real drama was enacted on the night of Thursday 3 March 1994. The precise sequence of events is not all that clear except that by Friday 4 March Fergus McCann emerged victorious. The Bank of Scotland, under pressure it seemed from all of Scottish society, including leading politicians, was about to put the club into administration because of unpaid debts. Stories that Celtic were a few seconds or minutes away from extinction are only partly true, for if that had happened, a new Celtic would have sprung up immediately. It seems that McCann satisfied the creditors that he could pay the debts. Chris White and David Smith were asked to resign, did so, and were joined at the exit door by Michael Kelly (although Kevin Kelly remained).

Nemesis had thus visited the old regime in a big way, but it was no more than they deserved, for they had brought the grand old club to the verge of ruin. It was difficult to feel sorry or sympathetic for them. It was hardly possible to even consider them with equanimity or say that they tried their best in difficult circumstances. This, they had manifestly not done. They had brought misery and dev-astation to those who loved the green, while making a very good living for themselves out of the ruins of the club. Michael Kelly continued to pen self-justifying articles in newspapers but was per-manently discredited, whereas the other two slunk off into deserved oblivion.

McCann had said that the old board would get 'not one thin dime'. In fact, they had to be bought out and given considerable amounts of money, reputed to be about £2 million between them. This must have hurt McCann and certainly angered more than a few support-ers when they heard, but it was nevertheless money well spent. The power of the Kelly family was broken. Never again would they be allowed to ruin this club and spoil the cultural heritage of tens of thousands of supporters while bleating on about tradition.

The supporters on the other hand were upbeat and cheerful. It was hardly like celebrating a triumph on the field in a cup final, for example, but it meant that everyone could now get behind the club. The new directors promised instant action – and seemed to mean it. We, the boycotters and the deserters, could now get back to the business of supporting Celtic. We could be Celtic supporters once again.

It was Brian Dempsey who appeared at the door at Celtic Park to tell the public and the television cameras that 'The rebels have won', and one would have thought that he would have taken a seat on the new board (he had been ejected by the old board in bizarre circumstances a few days before the League Cup final of 1990/91), but for some reason, he never did so. Credit must also go to to financier David Low who did so much behind the scenes to undermine the stability and credibility of the previous regime.

So who was this mystery men who had saved the club? McDiarmid Park, Perth saw Fergus McCann there in his new capacity as full-time chief executive. Seldom can such an insignificant looking man have had such an impact on so many people. When interviewed by the media he did not know too much about Celtic's current playing record, and he did not seem to have had much recent experience of watching Scottish football. It was in all probability his first visit to McDiarmid Park. Small, bespectacled and wearing a bunnet he looked for all the world like a punter, and would not normally have been noticed in a crowd. But he certainly was taken notice of that day as the world's media gathered to get a glimpse of the man. His father had once been headmaster of St Modan's High School in Stirling and McCann himself had a magisterial bearing, once one got a good look at him. One does not make a fortune by being a fool, and Fergus was clearly nobody's fool.

As if sensing a new mood, Celtic scored in eighty seconds through Paul Byrne, a young Irish player who would not be destined to survive the McCann revolution for long. But if we thought that Byrne's goal was to be a spectacular rebirth of Celtic on the playing field, we were to be sadly disillusioned, for St Johnstone rallied and almost equalised on several occasions. Celtic however held out to gain a victory in a singularly unmemorable game of football which would never have been mentioned in any history of the club if it had not been for the circumstances surrounding it.

The rest of the season was insignificant in playing terms, other than for a 1–1 draw at Ibrox in a game where no away supporters were present, banned by a vindictive Rangers chairman to appease his own supporters after a comparatively minor piece of vandalism on a previous Celtic visit to Ibrox. Yet, although green-and-white scarves were conspicuous by their absence from the Broomloan Road stand, a helicopter flew overhead trailing a green banner that read: 'Hail! Hail! The Celts Are Here!'

A crowd of 36,199 attended McCann's first home game in charge on 26 March at Celtic Park. This was approximately double the attendance at the last two home games (if we ignore the boycott game against Kilmarnock on 1 March) against Dundee United and Aberdeen in late January. Sadly the increased crowd saw no improvement in performance as a dismal Celtic team went down 1–0 to Motherwell. That however was not the significant factor. The important thing was that Celtic fans were back . . . and in large numbers. They had not fallen out with Celtic, only with the irresponsible and foolish stewardship of the previous regime.

Very aware of this, the media organised a 'sop to Cerberus' campaign to keep Celtic supporters sweet and give them some compensation for the season that, in playing terms, had been so disastrous. They too realised that a weak Celtic team is bad news for them, for fewer newspapers are sold, fewer radio programmes are listened to and fewer television programmes are watched. The 'cheer them up' campaign centred around Simon Donnelly, a talented enough youngster but whose fair hair and good looks made him resemble Leonardo di Caprio from the hit movie *Titanic*. All this was enough for wholly spurious comparisons to Kenny Dalglish. In truth, Donnelly did end the season well, but he would struggle to live up to his media billing as the next Dalglish.

Perhaps there was a certain optimism among the support at the end of the season. Certainly, there was a clear sign that Rangers were rattled when they lost the Scottish Cup final to Dundee United, thus giving the people at Tannadice something to cheer about at last. It was, incidentally, an interesting exercise in perspective to consider the fate of other teams. It would be difficult for example not to hand that particular title of 'longest suffering' to the loyal fans of Tannadice, for their team, no matter how talented or successful in Europe, did have the tendency to lose Scottish Cup finals in Glasgow! This was the seventh such occasion for them since 1974 but, in 1994, Craig Brewster's bizarre goal was enough to do the trick.

And if Dundee United had suffered, what about Hearts? Their last trophy had been in 1962 at the time of the Cuban Missile Crisis! In the meantime, they had suffered bankruptcy, relegation and innumerable changes of board and managers. Across the border there was Newcastle United, which had in 1992 been a whisker away from the Third Division. Celtic did not have a monopoly on misery. To the fans however, it seemed that they did, for there was the glorious past and the current, all-pervasive and oppressive presence of Rangers.

At Celtic, with the old board gone, a decision was quickly taken to redevelop Celtic Park, instead of moving to Cambuslang, an idea that was not so much thrown out the window as allowed to die a natural death. It had indeed been ill thought out, unnecessary and absurd. The redevelopment work would involve playing home games at Hampden during the following season as Celtic Park, where the club had played since 1892, was to be flattened, apart from the main stand. The impressive thing about all this was its swiftness. There would be no shilly-shallying. Work was to begin almost at once. The McCann man was already making an impact. In any case there was little room for complacency because the Taylor Report had to be implemented. Following the disaster at Hillsborough in 1989, which had seen the deaths of so many Liverpool fans, safety at football grounds had become a major political issue. All-seater stadia were now a legal requirement for leading clubs in England and Scotland, and Celtic's current ground was woefully inadequate. The authorities who were implementing the Taylor Report were not likely to be impressed by claims that 'our supporters prefer to stand'.

There was to be a share issue so that the fans could literally 'share' in the club's fortunes and 'own' the new ground as it was being built. Given the arrogance shown by the previous regime towards the involvement of supporters, this was indeed a decision of great historical significance. It would not be launched immediately though, as supporters needed time to digest all that had happened. In fact it took place in the middle of the following season. It was an instant and phenomenal success, with £14 million being generated from ordinary supporters in spite of scepticism in the newspapers. The £8 million debt would soon be wiped out, and money would be available to the manager to buy players. The

7,000 season-ticket holders would soon be added to as well, once the new stadium was up and running.

Another important decision would clearly have to be taken about the manager. Macari had been appointed by the old board and therefore his job was particularly on the line. It had been clear for a while that some of the players had little respect for him, and criticism centred on his continued residence in England and frequent absences from Celtic Park in midweek. Early on in his tenure, McCann wote an official letter to Macari on these issues, but the manager refused to budge as his children were at school in the Stoke area.

Tactics also were rarely discussed, and Lou gave the impression of not being particularly interested in the current bunch of Celtic players. He was clearly hoping that the new board would finance the buying of a new set of players, although in all fairness, it has to be pointed out that the ones he had already brought from England did not in any way inspire confidence in his judgement of a player. Lee Martin, Carl Muggleton and Wayne Biggins were no one's idea of Celtic greats.

Whether Lou knew it or not, the axe was about to fall. In retrospect he would say that Fergus McCann was out to get him anyway, and indeed Macari would take the club to court on the matter. He brought an action in autumn 1997 before the Court of Session in Edinburgh, demanding £400,000 for alleged breach of contract. The judge, Lady Cosgrove, having listened to eight weeks of tedious evidence, rejected his case, ruling that Macari's refusal to move house to the Glasgow area, and breaches of other contractual conditions, had given Celtic grounds to dismiss him.

It has to be said however that very few supporters sympathised with Macari, even though the actual manner of the sacking was tactless and even brutal. In mid-June 1994, after Macari had been in post for about eight months and just as he was about to take his family to the United States to see the World Cup, a phone call gave him the baleful tidings. His departure had been predicted in certain sections of the press and had been a hotly debated topic among Celtic fans whenever they met. It was not a surprise. More interest centred on who was to replace him, and indeed speculation on this issue had been rife since the arrival of McCann.

2

1994/95: Disaster and Triumph

The speculation about who the new manager would be did not last long. It would be Tommy Burns. Tommy was born in Glasgow's Soho Street in the Celtic heartlands, in December 1956, and as early as 1970 signed on for the club on a schoolboy form. He made his debut in 1975 and then went on to play over 500 times for the club scoring 81 goals, until his transfer to Kilmarnock in December 1989. He was fated to play for Celtic in turbulent times, and knew at first hand the highs and the lows of football from the cup triumphs of the 1980s to the dreadful days of the early 1990s. The highs had included a brilliant goal which won the league at Tannadice in 1981 and an inspirational performance against Sporting Lisbon in 1983. He was Celtic through and through, and one incident above all revealed his wholehearted commitment to the club.

It was the day after the infamous 5–1 thrashing at Ibrox in late August 1988, a game that Burns played in. Tommy accepted Scottish Television's invitation to appear on their programme the following day, and it was then that we saw a sensitive, hurting, dignified but determined man, making no attempt to minimise the catastrophe, refusing to point the finger at one or two people that the fans were blaming and showing a quiet resilience in the face of a dreadful result. A sincere and devout man, it would be difficult to imagine anyone with more love for the club or with more knowledge of what Celtic meant and should mean to the community that it represented.

As a manager, Burns had done well at Kilmarnock. He was

clearly a popular choice to succeed Lou Macari. The problem was that Kilmarnock also rated him highly and so, on 9 July 1994, refused permission for Celtic to approach their management team of Burns and Billy Stark. This was understandable, for they had consolidated Kille's place in the Premier League, and seemed to be developing some fine players. But in a clear and early indication that the new Celtic meant business, Celtic went for them anyway and engaged them on 12 July (of all days).

This resulted in a complaint from an embittered and spiteful Kilmarnock and two fines for Celtic for poaching. The Scottish League fined Celtic £100,000 and after a protracted dispute the Scottish Football Association fined them another £200,000. McCann fought the case and complained about unfair treatment, but eventually coughed up. He had got the man he wanted, and it was proof that he was not going to let anything stand in his way. In any case, the fines, though by no means negligible, paled in comparison to some of the money that was being thrown around the football industry at that time and even by McCann himself.

Burns, being a man of impeccable Celtic credentials, was immediately accepted by the support. He may have had a conscience about leaving Kilmarnock, but invitations to join Celtic do not come along very often. Billy McNeill had had a similar experience in 1978 when, after a successful year at Aberdeen, the call to take over from Jock Stein proved irresistible. In Burns's case, not only was there the clear emotional tie, but it was also a great opportunity to do well under what seemed to be a progressive chairman and an equally progressive board of directors.

Billy Stark was also much loved by the Parkhead faithful. The only problem had been that he was 31 before he joined the club in 1987, almost as an afterthought, it appeared, in Billy McNeill's ingathering of talent for the centenary season. He had already played for St Mirren and Aberdeen, often impressing against Celtic, but no player did better for Celtic in that glorious 1987/88 season than Billy Stark. He was also a man who seemed to have the two necessary qualifications for the job – namely a deep knowledge of the game and a clear recognition of what Celtic meant. This was despite a background that was not necessarily Celtic, as the reference book, *An Alphabet of the Celts*, records that he once played for the Rangers youth team.

It was clear however that Rome would not be built in a day even by such energetic and knowledgeable men as Burns and Stark. Hard work would be necessary over a few seasons, and the question now being asked of the support was, 'Would they be able and willing to wait that length of time?' Tommy Burns's start was not a bad one. After an edgy draw at Brockville, Falkirk, on the opening day of the season, three straight wins were registered. The best one was the 2–0 win at Ibrox over Rangers, goals coming from the ever reliable John Collins and Paul McStay. On 9 September, following weeks of speculation, Burns stepped into the transfer market, paying a club record of £1.75 million for Motherwell's attacking midfielder Phil O'Donnell. O'Donnell immediately rewarded his new employers by scoring twice in his debut the following day against Partick Thistle.

At this point, things were looking good for Celtic. Rangers were clearly struggling, already out of Europe and the League Cup (where they had surprisingly lost to Falkirk), and it did seem that Celtic were playing with a spring in their step, relishing the change of direction of the past six months and even enjoying the experience of playing all their home games at Hampden. The SFA and Queen's Park would find this experience a tidy little earner for them, and exorbitant charges were imposed, knowing that Celtic had no choice but to pay them. Supporters noticed with horror the appalling rise in ticket prices, although a few gimmicks were used to sweeten the pill. Now and again, for example, entertainers were employed; for example, a Rod Stewart lookalike entertained everyone at half time in a game against Kilmarnock!

It was also the time when the song 'The Fields of Athenry' took hold of the Celtic faithful. It had a lovely melody and lyrics which, although involving 'stealing Trevelyan's corn' and 'rebelling' against the 'Famine and The Crown' enjoyed the apparent endorsement of the club. There was a feeling too that board and fans were at long last marching together – and in step!

One change that was certainly coming (in tandem with 'The Fields of Athenry' policy and some thought in contradiction to it) was the employment of people who were not Roman Catholics in executive positions. It had certainly been true that, unlike Rangers, Celtic had from the earliest days been non-sectarian as far as players were concerned. There was the famous story of a goalkeeper called Tommy Duff who played several times for the club in season 1891/92. He came from an Orange background and his Parkhead career came to an abrupt end after New Year's Day 1892 when in a friendly against Dumbarton, the team went down 8–0. His poor perfomance that day was never attributed to his sectarian background – it was caused, apparently, by a more basic dysfunction which frequently affects many Scotsmen, Protestants and Catholics alike, on New Year's Day!

Since then, men like James Young, (before and during the First World War) John Thomson and Willie Lyon (1930s) had worn the green with distinction, having no problems with religion. From the 1950s onwards a whole host of non-Catholics played for the team and, in 1965, the famous barrier broke with the appointment of Jock Stein, a non-Catholic, as the manager.

But the board of directors had remained obstinately all Catholic. Indeed they had been concentrated in a few families. Now that the lowest point had been reached, it was rather like an alcoholic hitting the gutter. The only way to look was upwards, and looking upwards involved employing men of calibre in key posts, irrespective of their background. Those in the past had certainly been 'Celtic minded' in that appalling and over-used phrase; they had however failed to produce the goods.

The initial success on the field in season 1994/95 was transitory, apparent rather than real. There still remained obvious shortcomings in the team. In goal Gordon Marshall was competent enough, but Burns also reinstated Pat Bonner to whom Lou Macari had ludicrously given a free transfer. In defence Mark McNally was a hard worker but lacked pace, although this problem was partly compensated for by the speedy Tom Boyd. Tony Mowbray was far too often caught out of position and in any case picked up a bad injury at the end of September. The likeable Mowbray ('Moggy' to the fans) had in any case his own domestic problems with the serious illness and subsequent death of his wife, something that the support was genuinely upset about. The forward line contained men like Andy Walker (who had returned from Bolton Wanderers in the summer) and Charlie Nicholas whose not inconsiderable contribution to Celtic history was several years in the past. Peter Grant and Pat McGinlay's commitment to the cause could not be doubted, but both had off days.

The midfield duo of Paul McStay and John Collins was one of the best in the history of the club, but the problem lay in the fact that their style was too similar. In the great team of the late 1960s, there had also been several outstanding midfielders in Bobby Murdoch, Bertie Auld and the outrageously underestimated Charlie Gallagher. They had been great passers of the ball. Therein lay, some thought, the crucial difference between them and the present incumbents. Collins and McStay were great runners for and with the ball, but could be crowded out by an opposition who were determined to defend in depth in midfield and, occasionally, their passes went astray. There was also a problem in delivering the through ball, the defence-splitting pass to a forward who knew exactly what was coming, in the way that Murdoch invariably found Lennox or Johnstone, for example.

Perhaps this criticism of Collins and McStay is unfair. Certainly they retained their popularity with the support. They continued to be selected for Scotland, McStay on seventy-six occasions and Collins on fifty-eight. The crucial difference between the 1960s and the 1990s, some argued, was that Jock Stein had great men in his forward line as well as in the midfield!

For whatever reason, the team stuttered and then ground to a halt in the autumn. October saw a couple of feckless draws against Motherwell and Aberdeen, then an unlucky defeat at Tynecastle before a shocking performance against Falkirk at Hampden which resulted in a 2–0 defeat, not entirely to be explained away by the absence of Paul McStay. By the time that Rangers beat Celtic 3–1 at Hampden in front of a television audience on 30 October, it was clear to all but the blindest of optimists that there would be no sustained league challenge and that, given the absence of backbone from any other team, the title could be handed to Rangers there and then.

This was a sad fact of the dreadful years of the early 1990s. Given that Celtic were seldom in the picture as championship contenders, one might have expected at least a serious challenge from another club. This was rarely forthcoming. Aberdeen had their chance in 1991 when they needed only a draw to win the league on the last day at Ibrox, but failed to do so and thereafter folded tragically, lapsing into a decline almost as spectacular as that of Celtic. Hibs, Motherwell and Dundee United occasionally flattered to deceive, but Rangers invariably had it all their own way.

There was of course no Europe for Celtic in 1994/95. Celtic finished fourth in the Premier League in 1994 and this was not good enough. This was by no means the first time that it had happened, but the fans still missed it. They would have consoled themselves however by saying that any European run would have been short-lived. Certainly those who did represent Scotland in the UEFA Cup, Motherwell and Aberdeen, did not achieve much, lasting barely longer than Rangers had done in the European Cup. This clearly illustrated how far Scottish football had sunk, and how much it needed and still needs a strong Celtic team.

Celtic's league campaign in autumn 1994 was bad enough but worse was to come.The sheer horror of the League Cup final against Raith Rovers on 27 November 1994 put the agonies of supporting Celtic onto a new plane. Celtic had reached the final in a distinctly unspectacular way: 1–0 over Ayr United, 2–1 over Dundee, a singularly inept game at home to beat Dundee United 1–0 and then a pairing with Aberdeen in the semi final at Ibrox. Brian O'Neil, who promised more than he achieved in his Celtic career, scored the only goal of this turgidly unimpressive semi final.

Elsewhere in the competition, Falkirk had disposed of Rangers before themselves succumbing to Aberdeen, but the surprise packets had been Raith Rovers. The Kirkcaldy men, managed by ex-Rangers man Jimmy Nicholl, were a quaint mixture of apparent has-beens like Gordon Dalziel who had made little impact for Rangers in the 1980s, and promising youngsters like Stevie Crawford, Colin Cameron and Jason Dair. They had deservedly reached the Premier League in 1993 – along with Tommy Burns's Kilmarnock – and were unlucky to be relegated in 1994.

Now going well in the First Division, Raith had reached only their second League Cup final by getting the better of Airdrie in a close semi final at McDiarmid Park. Eccentrically, their goalkeeper Scott Thomson had been sent off for the heinous offence of over-stepping the line of his penalty area while carrying the ball and young goalkeeper Brian Potter earned his moment of glory in a tense penalty shoot-out. It was to be the first of two penalty shoot-outs concerning Raith Rovers in this campaign – and the second was to have the direst effect upon Celtic.

Even to an under-performing Celtic team, the team from Kirkcaldy did not seem to present any huge impediment to Celtic's re-entry into the silverware-collection business. Yet the league form was dismal. The last league victory had been against Hibs on

24 September, and the latter part of October had seen three straight defeats including that particularly heart-rending collapse to Rangers on 30 October. November saw three draws, two of them goalless against Partick Thistle at Hampden and Kilmarnock at Rugby Park. The Partick Thistle game in particular was shockingly inept. It was just as well, perhaps, that there was no Europe to bother Celtic this year.

The long-suffering fans, many of whom had had enough and were voting with their feet, (there was an issue too about the high prices being charged at Hampden) looked to the League Cup with a certain amount of desperation to kick-start the season. It was particularly galling to see this depressing turn of events after the euphoria at the start of the season with a new regime and a new manager. It was clear that the damage done by the Kellys would take a long time to clear, and nobody really expected instant miracles from McCann and Burns. Yet a start could be made on 27 November.

The game was to be played at Ibrox as Hampden would hardly have been considered as neutral, according to the Scottish League, for it was Celtic's home ground this season. The final was played on a fine, crisp, late autumn day with just a touch of moisture on the pitch to make it a good surface. The Govan stand had been given over to Raith Rovers fans. This was a touch generous, one felt, considering that the stand held 11,000 people and Raith's home games struggled to reach an average of 3,000! The other three stands were all-Celtic, packed with enthusiastic and noisy fans who believed that this was the day to end the trophy famine. The volume of their support was perhaps a lot more than the play warranted, but the impassioned commitment of them all took neutral observers by surprise.

The teams on that fateful day were:

Celtic: Marshall, Galloway, Boyd, McNally, Mowbray, O'Neil, Donnelly, McStay, Nicholas, Walker, Collins. Substitutes: Falconer, Byrne.

Raith Rovers: Thomson, McAnespie, Broddle, Narey, Dennis, Sinclair, Crawford, Dalziel, Graham, Cameron, Dair. Substitutes: Rowbotham, Redford.

Celtic played in their broadband green-and-white, an outfit that some thought did less than justice to the romance of the hoops. In the first half they were attacking the Broomloan Road end but, after only a minute, horrified even the neutrals in the television audience when Tony Mowbray arm-wrestled the speedy Steve Crawford to the ground. Mowbray was fortunate not to be given a yellow card by Mr McCluskey of Stewarton, but it was a harbinger of things to come as the same Stevie Crawford put Rovers one up in the twentieth minute with a crisp drive after a nervous Celtic defence had conceded an unnecessary corner.

Celtic were level by half time – a fine diving header by Andy Walker – and gradually through the second half began to establish an ascendancy over the Kirkcaldy men. In the last twenty minutes, wave upon wave of pressure rained down on the Raith defence, but veteran Dave Narey (who had made his name with Dundee United) and unashamedly Celtic-daft centre half Shaun Dennis held out. A goal remained elusive until, with six minutes remaining, an Andy Walker drive came off a post and Charlie Nicholas scored with the rebound.

Deliverance was now in sight, or so we thought. Surely Celtic could hold out against this brave and plucky side, who had earned everyone's respect and admiration. But, no. Too much space was given to the dangerous Jason Dair. This young man (a nephew, incidentally, of Jim Baxter, the Rangers and Scotland star of the 1960s) shot, Gordon Marshall couldn't hold on, and Gordon Dalziel scored with his head, although it looked more like his nose, a fact that he subsequently acknowledged, showing with his celebrations that he was still aware of his Ibrox past. Dalziel might just have been offside as Dair shot, but of course the flag would have had to go up instantly. He certainly couldn't have been offside when the ball came back off Marshall.

At that point the initiative was lost. Hard though the supporters tried, they could not rally their team who seemed to sense that doom was hovering all over Ibrox Stadium and about to descend on the green and whites. Raith Rovers on the other hand now had little to lose. They had already proved their point, and Monday's papers would praise them, even if they lost. Extra time provided little in the way of good football as the two teams were absolutely exhausted, and matters led inexorably to a penalty shoot-out, a form of entertainment that Celtic have seldom excelled in since the infamous night in 1972 when Dixie Deans blasted one over the bar in the European Cup semi final against Inter Milan.

Ashen-faced supporters watched as Raith, with the crucial advantage of going first, scored every time. Gordon Marshall's nightmare match continued as at least three Raith penalties looked saveable. Celtic's fifth penalty, taken by Mike Galloway, was almost stopped by Scott Thomson, but trickled over the line. The end was not long delayed, however, for after Jason Rowbotham scored in sudden death, Paul McStay, Celtic's greatest player of the decade, had his penalty saved by Scott Thomson to plunge Celtic supporters into even greater melancholy than their worst enemies could have wished on them.

Yet one could hardly grudge the Kirkcaldy men their one and only triumph in a long and not always distinguished history. Even Jimmy Nicholl, with his Ulster accent and anything but a Celtic sympathiser, expressed a little pity for Paul McStay and the way that the League Cup had been lost. It was however Nicholl's day and they 'danced in the streets of Raith' that night for the first and only time since 1883.

Paul McStay was distraught and would stay like that for the next six months. Perhaps the greatest pain of all that Christmas for the fans was the thought of what that charming, personable and likeable young man and his family must have been going through. Celtic born and bred (his great uncles had played for the club in the 1920s and 1930s) Paul was one of us. The jibes and sneers made at his expense (like the new aftershave to be called 'Paul McStay Mist') cut deep into the flesh of every Celtic supporter, and merely added to the misery that surrounded the club.

McStay would later say in an interview with Mark Guidi in the *Mail Sport Monthly* in March 2003 that, in the context of this match and its aftermath, 'I found out a few things about one or two people. The criticism got personal. I can handle being criticised for my football but it went beyond that and it was too much. It was a trying time and winning that day would have been something positive. My whole world caved in. I felt responsible for everything and it didn't matter how much people tried to console me. I couldn't be calmed.'

For the support, it was indeed 'the dark anguish of the soul' as an earlier chronicler had described the travails of a previous generation.Those who had been young in the early 1960s and who had suffered then were now going through their own version of a mid-life crisis. Veteran supporters recalled another final of long ago against another Fife team with its eerie echoes of the Raith Rovers disaster. This was the Scottish Cup final of 1961 when Jock Stein's Dunfermline were professional enough to grab the Cup from an overwhelmingly superior Celtic team who had done everything but score against an inspired and lucky goalkeeper.

It did seem that life could never be the same again, and that Celtic, homeless and trophyless, were indeed 'finished'. The stake had indeed been driven hard and deep into our hearts on the night of 27 November 1994. Could anyone have blamed Fergus McCann if he had packed up all his money that night and returned to Canada? The sight of the supporters indicated that there were limits to the amount of misery that a person could take, and that perhaps other ways should be sought by each individual to spend their leisure time. After all, a job or a marriage which created so much unhappiness would have been jettisoned long ago.

This state of affairs did pose certain pertinent and pointed questions about the future of Scottish football in general. It was already well known who the winners of the Premier League would be, and we were only in late November. It was the same team that had exited the European Cup in August to an incredulous Greek side called AEK Athens, hardly one of the leading lights in Greece, let alone Europe. It seemed that Rangers were as far behind the rest of Europe as they were ahead of the field in Scotland. It was little wonder that the English perception of Scottish football varied between treating it as a laughing stock and ignoring it altogether.

Yet life had to go on. Tommy Burns, in the *Celtic View* of 5 February 2003, tells the story of how – in the process of contemplating resignation – he was walking to the front door of Celtic Park the day after the final and met an old friend from the Gallowgate. Burns told him that he was packing it in but his friend said, 'Well, there are things needing changed and they are only going to bring in someone else to do it. So why don't you?' Burns stayed. He had, after all, only been in the job for four-and-a-half months. Things might get better.

On the following Wednesday, 30 November, 12,295 brave souls assembled at Easter Road to see what would have been called in happier times 'The Battle of the Greens'. It ended up a dismal 1–1 draw, with Celtic, for a change, coming from behind rather than throwing away a lead. It was nevertheless an excellent example of how bad Scottish football can be when Celtic have a poor team.

There were several touching moments. One was the cheering of Paul McStay by the Celtic fans whenever he touched the ball and the polite, silent respect paid to him by the Hibs supporters. Indeed they reserved all their venom for John Collins who had once plied his trade at Easter Road. Another emotional moment came during the warm-up, when several Celtic players and Burns himself were seen to go over to the supporters and shake hands with the greeting, 'Cheers, big man'. It was a very emphatic way of saying that 'we are hurting every bit as much as you' and that 'we are definitely all in this together'. In spite of the pain, it was a moment which showed why Celtic are, and will remain, a very special club.

On another front, the much promised share issue was launched in December 1994. At this low point in our history, it seemed a particularly inappropriate time to ask people for money, but Celtic supporters found the necessary £620 – the cost of the minimum subscription – and gave as clear an indication as one could possibly expect of their commitment. Something like £20 million was generated by this extraordinary demonstration of loyalty to the club. Not only did it boost the Parkhead coffers, but it also greatly strengthened the link between supporters and club which has been at least a theoretical feature of Celtic since 1888. If there was ever any doubt, we were certainly all in this together now.

An indication of things to come was provided by an entrepreneur from Dublin called Dermot Desmond who spent £4 million on Celtic shares. He was by the end of the season given a seat on the board although everyone was at pains to point out that he was a non-executive director. It did however show how far the club had come since the demise of the Kelly family. Desmond presumably might have bought himself into the club previously, if he had been allowed to do so.

On the playing front, adverse weather in December brought a little relief in the shape of postponements and the festive period did bring a few moments of limited cheer. Paddy Bonner had now recovered from injury and now returned to first-team action replacing Gordon Marshall, who was blamed (unfairly) by many for the Raith Rovers debacle. Then, on Hogmanay, Celtic recorded their first victory in the Premier League for three months, bringing to an end a 'record' run of eleven league games (twelve if we count the League Cup final) without a victory. Falkirk were beaten at Hampden in a hard working, rather than inspired, performance, but it was at least a victory.

The bells for 1995 would surely usher in better times, one felt, and two things happened in the first week of the new year to indicate that an upturn in the club's fortunes was imminent. One was the draw at Ibrox against Rangers on the night of Wednesday 4 January; a 1–1 share of the points made memorable by Paul Byrne's equaliser from a Collins cross. It was a tight game, and a winner could have come at either end in the second half after Byrne's equaliser. It at least earned Celtic some respect and it cannot have been easy for the players, particularly Paul McStay, to return to Ibrox. After all, their previous trip down Govan way had been for the League Cup final.

Another positive sign was the arrival on 7 January 1995 of Pierre van Hooijdonk for £1.2 million from NAC Breda of Holland. Tommy Burns had been interested in him for a while and, though hardly a household name in Scotland at the time, he seemed to have the build to enhance the physical qualities of a rather light-weight forward line. More tellingly, it showed the supporters that McCann's money was not simply going to be used to build a new stadium. Players were to be bought as well.

The stadium was meanwhile progressing, as those who travelled to work every day along London Road or Gallowgate could testify. For a while all had been levelled other than the main stand which presented a bizarre sight in the middle of such a waste land, and historians recalled pictures of St Paul's Cathedral in London after a devastating attack by the Luftwaffe. The surrounding area had been laid waste, but the Cathedral remained.

There was something still very comforting about the continued existence of the main stand. The destruction of the Jungle, the railway end, even the Rangers end, the floodlight pylons and the other features of the old stadium had in some way symbolised the death of the 'old' Celtic. Wicked people had allowed the club to fester and rot. Major restruction was necessary . . . but before that could happen a lot had to be got rid of. It was not unlike an operation to rid the body of a bunion or a rotten tooth or even something more serious.

The patient would survive, but in the short term pain was necessary. 'It has to get worse before it can get better.'

Yet it was difficult also not to recall our great moments at the old Celtic Park – that night in May 1967 when they had come home with that big 'beautifully ugly' Cup. The night, also in May, but this time in 1979 when 'ten men won the league' by beating Rangers 4–2. The defeat of St Mirren to win the league in 1982. The night in 1967 when Vojvodina were shattered in the last minute by Billy McNeill's header from a Charlie Gallagher corner kick. The 2–0 defeat of Real Madrid in 1980. The sheer euphoria of Lennox's last-minute scrambled goal against Morton in 1968 which more or less clinched the league. There were also people's very personal memories of where they stood on their first visit to the great old ground, of match programmes, Macaroon Bars and great players. Perhaps the ghosts of Quinn, Young, Gallacher and McGrory still played there. They certainly still played there in people's memories – and that nobody could ever take away:

> They gave us Jimmy McGrory and Paul McStay
> Johnstone, Tully, Murdoch, Auld and Hay,
> And most of football's greats have passed through Parkhead's gates
> To play the game in the good old Celtic way.

The league campaign continued to fizzle out. The new Dutch player did provide an injection of enthusiasm, but once again the general fecklesness of his team-mates let them down. Occasionally the strong running of Brian McLaughlin, a pocket-sized winger, provided some interest but draws were still more common than any other result. Half the games played ended even and Celtic finished a dismal fourth in the league. Rangers won their seventh successive league title, fifteen points ahead of second-placed Motherwell.

Not for the first time it was the Scottish Cup that the beleagured Celtic support looked to for solace. It was the only Scottish tournament that Celtic had won oftener than Rangers, but as always happens when Celtic are in decline, Rangers were catching up; the Ibrox men now had twenty-six successes compared to Celtic's twenty-nine. In 1995 however, Rangers went out on 20 February at Tynecastle to a Hearts team whose players all happened to click on the same night. Hearts showed that night that Rangers were no great shakes; indeed their European adventures had confirmed that fact.

Celtic were fortunate in that the draw handed them three successive home ties. St Mirren fought hard, Meadowbank were eventually brushed aside but then Kilmarnock put up a hard fight on a Friday night in March when the floodlights (temporarily) failed. There still remained a certain residue of ill feeling between the two clubs about Celtic's perceived poaching of Burns and Stark the previous summer, and this showed itself in a few rough challenges and tackles.

Kilmarnock's lack of affection for Celtic was hardly helped by the charitable award of a penalty when Tom Black was wrongly adjudged to have brought down Brian McLaughlin. It was indeed a soft award, although Celtic were entitled to a break for their midfield superiority. John Collins scored from the spot, and then in a buttock-clenching finale, Celtic survived Killie's late onslaught. Such was the defeatism of the Celtic fans that the conviction remained uppermost until the very end that they would blow it again, but this time, the team held out for a 1–0 victory. It was a game over which the morning newspapers showed a total unanimity. They all agreed that it would have been better if the Hampden lights had stayed out and prevented them from seeing what was happening.

The Scottish Cup semi-final draw sent Celtic to Ibrox and paired them against Hibs. The game was played (as the previous round had been) on a Friday night, 7 April, so that satellite television could screen the match. It was a horrible game with Celtic playing in that hideous strip which was more black than green. They did not look like Celtic. Nor did they play like a Celtic team. Or perhaps they played rather too similarly to the Celtic team of that season and of the recent dreadful past!

Those Celtic supporters in the crowd of 40,950 who were superstitious (and even those who weren't) must have suffered from heart palpitations at one point in the game when a penalty kick at Ibrox at the same Broomloan Road end of the ground came back to haunt us once again. It was indeed a soft penalty, and should never have been given, but the attempt by Andy Walker was weak and well saved by the Hibs goalkeeper, Jim Leighton, of Aberdeen, Manchester United and Scotland fame.

The game fizzled out in a feckless goalless draw with both teams thoroughly deserving the boos and catcalls of their supporters at the end. This necessitated a replay, again at Ibrox, on the following Tuesday. By that time the identity of the final opponents were known. First Division Airdrie beat Hearts in a similarly unimpressive semi final at Hampden on the Saturday. This result effectively ruined what little chance there was of an all-Edinburgh cup final – something that had last happened in 1896 – and which possiblility convinced the Edinburgh papers and their more gullible readers that the Scottish Cup final would be played at Murrayfield.

A glance at the Celtic fans as they disembarked from their buses outside Ibrox on the night of the replay revealed looks of grim determination, tension and pent-up emotion. There was no great optimism, nor singing, other than the odd sporadic chant. It was a serious business. Ibrox, apart from being the home of their Old Firm rivals, was also now the mausoleum of Celtic hopes. Images of Raith Rovers materialized before our eyes, aided by that of Jim Leighton. 'Ah hope we dinnae get a penalty the nicht', said one bleary-eyed punter for whom sleep had become difficult recently.

But the pessimism was this time unjustified. Celtic appeared in a Celtic strip (granted it was that one with the broadbands but it was at least green and white) and this time it was Hibs who had to wear fancy dress. Huge empty spaces appeared, particularly in the Hibs section, and the crowd was 8,000 down on the first match – a reflection perhaps on how highly both sets of fans valued their team at that moment.

For Celtic there was no Pierre Van Hooijdonk. Celtic would miss him, but on the other hand there had been quite a few lacklustre performances by Pierre of late and perhaps a change of personnel might help. It was hardly new blood, but it was the worthy Willie Falconer who scored the first goal after picking up an excellent through ball from Paul McStay. Before half time, Celtic went further ahead, this time with a fine curling shot from the edge of the box by John Collins.

Two goals up, and Celtic should have been in easy street, but this was 1995, the year in which Celtic did not make life easy for their supporters. Hibs pulled one back – a scrappy unsatisfactory affair with Paddy Bonner looking at fault for not being decisive enough – and for a while an equalizer looked likely. This might have brought extra time and – yes – a penalty shoot-out with all its horrendous possibilities, but the clincher in fact came at the other end.

It was a glorious one too scored by Phil O'Donnell, who would become that much maligned, much injured underperformer, occasionally referred to as a hypochondriac by the disgruntled support for his perceived malingering: 'I spend more time in the toilet than he does on the park'.This was still Phil's first season and he treated himself to one of his few moments of glory in a Celtic jersey as he rose like a bird to head home a Rudi Vata free kick. Phil celebrated this success by heading off his own line a few moments later, and the final whistle blew with Celtic well on top and the relieved supporters in rare good humour.

There was a moment of comedy too. Darren Jackson would join Celtic two years later, and indeed earn a deserved place in our affections, but in 1995 he was far from being the darling of the hoops. This was mainly due to his tendency to exaggerate injuries and other things. Here he was seen, with blood dripping from his nose, to be alleging to referee John Rowbotham that he had been punched by Peter Grant. As if Peter would do anything like that! Such was Jackson's reputation for play acting that Rowbotham refused to be convinced. Television pictures that night were however distinctly uncomfortable for Mr Rowbotham and lovers of Peter Grant, but Darren Jackson spent the rest of the game being booed by the Celtic fans as he continued his self-pitying whingeing and his vendetta with the blessed Peter.

Thus Celtic were into another cup final, their first Scottish Cup final since 1990 and their opponents were Airdrie. Airdrie – a team that no longer exists in its original manifestation as Airdrieonians after the club went out of business in summer 2002 following prolonged financial problems caused mainly by the construction of an all-seater stadium, which they could not afford and never fill. As we now know a new club, Airdrie United, has arisen to take its place.

Like Third Lanark, a club that went to the wall in 1967, the demise of Airdrieonians caused a certain amount of sadness among those who loved the Scottish game. Their old ground at Broomfield, with its quaint cricket-style pavilion in the corner, had been the scene of many a battle. It was also a nursery for a considerable number of fine players, some of whom like Bob McPhail in the 1920s and Ian McMillan in the 1950s had gone on to play for Rangers, there to cause many a heartache for Celtic fans.

But it was not for these reasons that Airdrie were disliked in the 1990s. They had a poor disciplinary record and a small, but unpleasant band of supporters who tended to ape the worst of the

Rangers fans in their singing of sectarian songs and anti-social behaviour. Crucially for the existence of the club, such morons tended to alienate the very many decent Airdrie supporters, who were embarrassed at such behaviour by a small minority. They were indeed a small minority, but there was now no silent majority to counteract them.

Alec McDonald, their manager in 1995 and a Rangers hero of the seventies, was respected for his football knowledge – but his fan club among fellow professionals would not have been a large one. One particular piece of childishness earned Airdrie more than a little notoriety. Referee Davie Syme (ironically no great hero at Celtic Park either) had made a clear mistake, but an honest one, in awarding a penalty to Dunfermline in a League Cup semi final against Airdrie at Tynecastle in 1991. Dunfermline went on to win the game (after a penalty shoot-out) and Airdrie had no forgiveness in their heart. They were apparently unable to accept that Mr Syme could, like the rest of the human race, make the occasional mistake. Airdrie's captain made a point of not shaking hands with Syme at the start of the next game that he officiated with them.

Such incidents, as well as an appalling number of yellow and red cards, did not endear Airdrie to the rest of Scotland, but here they were in the Scottish Cup final of 1995. They were no strangers to the occasion – in fact they had been there in 1992 (more recently than Celtic!) and had also put up a creditable performance against Jock Stein's Celtic in the 1975 final. They even claimed to have one or two supporters who still recalled their only Scottish Cup success in 1924!

Celtic's comfortable (in the end) victory over Hibs in the semi final was on 11 April. The cup final was to be played on 27 May. This meant a wait of over six weeks in which it was extremely difficult not to recall the previous cup final of that season and another First Division team called Raith Rovers (who had in the meantime won the First Division to regain their Premier League status.) The strain of waiting was hardly helped by the team's continuing awful per-formances in the league.

Defeats were sustained at the hands of Aberdeen, Hearts and Partick Thistle. But there was one bright moment when, in the last Old Firm game of the season, Celtic beat Rangers 3–0, the goals coming from Van Hooijdonk, the Albanian Rudi Vata and an own goal. Yet even this victory has to be qualified. Rangers had clearly given up for the season, having won the championship by fifteen points from second-placed Motherwell without even considering Celtic as serious challengers. Celtic in fact finished fourth behind Hibs and were a good eighteen points adrift of Rangers. But any win over Rangers is a satisfying one, and it did work wonders for morale.

However spirits were once again cast down in the last league game of the season, at Tannadice on 13 May, the day that relegated Dundee United bade their temporary farewell to the Premier League. This was indeed sad for a team who had played in the top tier of Scottish football since 1960, had won the Scottish Cup a year previously and appeared in the UEFA Cup final of 1987. Dundee United were a side for whom Celtic fans had respect and admiration for. We were distressed at the demise of the Tannadice men but what was of more import to Celtic fans in the run-up to Hampden was that Peter Grant had damaged his knee ligaments.

This looked like a serious blow. If there was any player who knew what Celtic meant, it was Peter Grant. Peter had a sad habit of missing big games. He had missed, for example, the 1988 Scottish Cup final through injury, and his presence in the League Cup final this season would surely have made a difference. Now it seemed that Peter would miss this final as well, and as Tony Mowbray was already out of contention through suspension, and Brian O'Neil with an injury, Celtic's team was a long way from what manager Tommy Burns would have had in mind.

Illogically the Scottish Cup final was to be played at Hampden. The League Cup final had of course been played at Ibrox as Celtic had been using Hampden as their home ground for league games (hardly a lucky ground for only six out of eighteen had been won!), but the SFA put its foot down and said that Hampden would be the venue for their Scottish Cup Final. Airdrie did not protest.

Ironically, both teams were homeless at the time of the final. Celtic Park was of course being redeveloped (and beginning to reveal a massive and impressive north stand) and Airdrie were between grounds – Broomfield having been sold and New Broomfield not yet ready – and operating from Portakabins. The game itself was a difficult one to call. Celtic, in theory, should prevail for even in a bad season (and in playing terms Celtic had showed little improvement from the previous season) they must have better players than the team which finished fourth in the First Division. But this was the Celtic of the nineties; nervous, insecure, unsteady, battered and vulnerable. The condition of the players mirrored that of the fans.

It is hard to put into words just exactly how much this game meant to Celtic fans. 1951 and 1965, two previous Scottish Cup occasions where Celtic had to win – and did – were recalled by the older members of the support. This was of little real comfort to those lucky ones who had tickets for the now much diminished Hampden and the less fortunate ones who prepared to brace themselves for a television ordeal. Some had suffered so much watching the Raith Rovers tragedy last November (all sorts of psychosomatic disorders were reported by supporters) that they simply could not face watching the game and headed for the hills like people anticipating the onset of nuclear war.

A boost was given to fans by the increasingly optimistic noises coming from the Parkhead camp on the fitness of Peter Grant. There was the definite feeling that Peter should be with us, even if half fit. Peter provided some kind of stability, Peter would hurt along with us if we lost and would rejoice with us if we triumphed. Peter, in this sense, transcended the word professional. He was a lot more than that! His fitness however remained in doubt until the very morning of the match. How delighted we were to see Peter take his place in the Celtic team as the teams ran out! Possibly even more than Tommy Burns, Peter was a jersey player, arguably the best known jersey player of all time. It was a shame that Peter had a few limitations in his game, yet no one can argue that what he lacked in ability and occasionally self-restraint, he made up for in commitment and enthusiasm for the cause. After a defeat, no one would hurt more than Peter. After a victory, Peter Grant would be the first to share our joy.

The Duchess of Kent was the guest of honour at Hampden for the Scottish Cup final. She had had no great obvious history of being a football fan, although she had frequently done the honours at the All England Lawn Tennis Championships at Wimbledon watching a sport she clearly loved. Hampden Park was anything but her natural habitat, but she was an attractive well-dressed woman. The anti-royalists of the Celtic support hurled their scorn at her as she came out to be presented to the teams, with 'The

Soldiers' Song' in full cry. It was here that Airdrie scored a massive propaganda victory as every one of their players, led by captain Jimmy Sandison, kissed her as they were introduced.

Kissing royalty is simply not done (and rarely even contemplated) in Presbyterian Scotland, and this act raised a few eyebrows, although the good lady was not fazed and even looked somewhat flattered by this show of affection. The Celtic players however were more polite than gallant and contented themselves with a handshake – apart that is from veteran physio Jimmy Steele, Celtic's special guest, sadly no longer in the best of health, who enjoyed his special minute of being kissed by royalty. The late Willie Maley, manager and in some ways the maker of the club, had been a great lover of royalty. He would have loved to have met the Duchess, but what would he have made of the kissing?

The teams were:

Celtic: Bonner, Boyd, McKinlay, Vata, McNally, Grant, McLaughlin, McStay, van Hooijdonk, Donnelly, Collins. Substitutes: Falconer, O'Donnell.

Airdrie: Martin, Stewart, Jack, Sandison, Hay, Black, Boyle, Smith, Cooper, Harvey, Lawrence. Substitutes: McIntyre, Smith.

The referee was Les Mottram of Wilsontown and the crowd was a meagre 36,915, thanks to the ongoing reconstruction of Hampden. (The press had not been slow to point out that Ibrox or even Murrayfield would have allowed in a bigger crowd.) The day was fine, but the standard of play was poor, reflecting the tension that hummed visibly and audibly round the ground with even Celtic's more experienced players, like Paul McStay and John Collins, affected quite clearly by the desire not to let the fans down again.

Since Pierre van Hooijdonk's arrival at the turn of the year, opinions had been divided about him. More arguments were heard about his value to the team than about any player since perhaps John 'Yogi' Hughes in the 1960s (not to be confused with the defender of the same name in the 1990s), as the support were divided into the pro-Pierre faction and his detractors. True, the big Dutchman did give a certain amount of strength and weight to an otherwise unimpressive Celtic attack, but his presence had not cured Celtic of their infuriating habit of drawing games that they should have won comfortably and Pierre's total of seven goals for half a season was hardly impressive. There were days as well when Pierre had looked out of sorts, lethargic and not really in the mood.

But 27 May 1995 was the day that Pierre made his lasting contribution to Celtic history. Celtic, playing towards the Kings Park end of the ground where congregated most of the anxious support, started brightly. Mark McNally, that earnest but otherwise uninspiring central defender, playing his first full game for six months in the desperate situation brought about by the unavailability of Mowbray and O'Neil, missed a good chance as early as the fourth minute. This came about when the hard-working Tosh McKinlay took a corner kick on the right and provided McNally with a free header. A sharper, match-fit McNally would surely have scored.

Thomas 'Tosh' McKinlay had been one of Tommy Burns's buys. He joined Celtic in November 1994 for £350,000 from Hearts, replacing Pat McGinlay who had gone to Hibs the day before. Tosh had played for Dundee before his move to Tynecastle and so, after his first Old Firm game, he became one of the few players who had played in all three Scottish city derbies in Dundee, Edinburgh and Glasgow. Only a fortnight before signing he played a major part in helping Hearts to a 1–0 victory over Celtic. Sadly, when he joined the club, he had already played for Hearts in the League Cup and was therefore cup-tied for the final against Raith Rovers.

But he had made a difference for Celtic, particularly after the New Year, with his crosses from the left. Four minutes after McNally's unfortunate miss, a pinpoint cross from the now inspirational McKinlay saw van Hooijdonk head home. It was a magnificent goal – somehow typically Celtic, indeed McGroryesque, in its execution and much celebrated by the now relieved and noisy support. It was a particularly gratifying moment for Tommy Burns who had actually brought both players to the club. With either or both of them on board, there would have been no Raith Rovers disaster.

One would have thought that this might have been the start of a barrowload before half time, enough to render the second half irrelevant, but this was 1995. Celtic had never been good at defending a narrow lead. The traditional style of play and the demands of the fans militate against such tactics and 1994/95 had been particularly bad for Celtic taking the lead and then allowing the other team to equalise. Jokes were made about the Celtic supporter who had to shoot his dog, because it kept throwing away its lead or 'What is the difference between Celtic and Cardinal Winning?' 'Well, the Cardinal is winning.'

As it was, Celtic remained very much on top for the rest of the first half, but clearly lacked enough class players to finish the job. Wee Brian McLaughlin, for instance, was extremely annoying to watch. A hard worker, a good runner and a tricky player – but not a good finisher nor one adept at delivering an accurate cross. He was unkindly likened by one of the television commentators (no less a person than Alex McLeish) to a jigsaw puzzle – because he went to pieces whenever he got into the box!

Half time came and went with the score still at 1–0. Van Hooijdonk had been injured and was replaced by the workmanlike Willie Falconer. It was Falconer who crossed for John Collins to give him the chance to put the game beyond Airdrie, but Collins – not having one of his better games for Celtic – pulled it wide of the target. The rest of the second half was long and painful, with more eyes on the clock than on the game, particularly as there were numerous stoppages for injuries and petty fouls. Simon Donnelly was taken off and replaced by the more experienced Phil O'Donnell, who had scored for Motherwell in the 1991 Scottish Cup final, but still there was no sign of the second goal that would have killed Airdrie.

Indeed, much of the play was in the Celtic half, very surprising given the apparent gulf in class between the two teams. Airdrie more than once won the battle of the midfield and pressed diligently, occasionally getting the better of Boyd, Vata and McKinlay. Disturbingly, Paddy Bonner was not having a good day, fluffing a few cross balls and generally showing a great deal of hesitation. Bonner, deservedly a Celtic hero, had now won his place back from Gordon Marshall, but there did remain doubts about his fitness. He must not let us down today, we prayed.

But one man stood out. Peter Grant. Ignoring the residual pain in his knee, he ran tirelessly, shouting, cajoling and earning an even bigger place in the hearts of the Celtic faithful than he had previously. For one reason or another, Peter had experienced more than his fair share of pain (both physical and emotional) in his Celtic career, made all the worse for his repeated, and transparently honest, statements that he was a Celtic supporter. Twice he went down injured (once the result of a deliberate and cynical kick by an Airdrie man who knew exactly what he was doing) but both times he got up and shrugged off the pain, determined to get back into the fray.

But this was Peter's day: several clean-as-a-whistle tackles (one in particular when Lawrence was in the clear), always on hand to mop up problems, co-ordinating the defence and generally a source of inspiration as he guided this ordinary Celtic team to their thirtieth Scottish Cup triumph.

The last few minutes were agonising as Airdrie strove manfully for the equalizer that would take the game into extra time. If only Collins had put that one away at the start of the second half . . . if only Celtic had been a shade more direct . . . if only Pierre hadn't had to go off . . . all these thoughts tormented the soul of every living Celt. Down on the bench, life was just as tense and several times, Burns, a deeply religious man, was seen to raise his eyes to heaven or even to turn his back on the play, and stare into the main stand to find inspiration or solace from his wife, perhaps.

The agonies were shared in the nation's living rooms as carpets were worn away, children snapped at, dogs put out to enjoy the summer sunshine in the garden. Refined wives and daughters were appalled at the tension-ridden atmosphere and the expletives: 'Kick it, ye **** !' being the advice to Celtic defenders, as the finer points of the game were forgotten.

Three minutes of added on time had been played before referee Les Mottram put Celtic fans out of their misery. The final whistle followed a certain amount of Airdrie pressure, including a corner kick on the right at the King's Park end of the ground. 'Please God, not another 1955' prayed the old-timers – a reference to the goal scored from a corner forty years previously by Clyde in the last minute to draw that Cup Final. Fortunately, not this time, for Celtic were awarded a goal kick, a decision that was cheered ecstatically by fans behind the goal.

The joy at the final whistle was out of proportion to the way the team had played, but nothing could gainsay the fact that we had won the Scottish Cup. Paul McStay in particular was relieved, for he had borne unfairly the burden of the League Cup final, and it spoke volumes for his character that he came back from that horrendous

Sunday of six months previously. The Duchess is seen on the video asking Jim Farry for the name of the Celtic captain, and then quite clearly says 'Paul, well done . . .' before handing over the famous old trophy.

There is probably no greater sight in football than the green-and-white scarves raised aloft to the strains of 'You'll Never Walk Alone' or 'We are Celtic supporters, faithful through and through'. This was one of the great days in Celtic history, so reminiscent of 1965 when the Scottish Cup was won in similar circumstances. But one question was now being posed by Celtic fans. Was this the stepping stone to greater things? Everyone knew that two years after that famous day in 1965, the European Cup was brought back to Britain for the first time. Was history about to repeat itself?

It was hard to address oneself to that question, for the ecstacy could not entirely disguise the fact that this still was a very ordinary Celtic side with a great deal to do if they were to catch up with Rangers who had now (effortlessly and without any real challenge) won the title for the past seven years in spite of being, by top European standards, a distinctly ordinary team. And in any case, a new factor entered the equation.

The following morning stories appeared in the newspapers which indicated that the working relationship between Burns and McCann was not what it could have been. In particular, Burns seemed upset about the paltry amount of money available for new players. Did this mean that the new success was about to implode on itself? Was the old Celtic habit of self-destruction about to appear again, even at this moment of triumph? Was either Burns or McCann about to leave the club, Tommy after having given us our first trophy for six years and Fergus after having saved the club from ruin?

However, a more sober assessment led one to the conclusion that the press were up to their old mischief-making tricks again, and that the 'story' did seem to be an effort to take the limelight away from Celtic by giving undue emphasis to a few things that had been said, perhaps unwisely, by the men concerned. It was hardly the first or the last time, after all, that journalists with no news to report had had to make it up. What was unusual about this one was its timing – but in the event, nothing came of it other than a public declaration of mutual support in midsummer. Burns and McCann worked together for another two years.

What supporters could do this year was enjoy their summer for the first time in six years. Celtic supporters find it hard to relax on a Spanish beach unless their team has won at least something the previous season. This year the sangria tasted so much nicer, for there was no need to dodge any football conversation with the English folk in the same hotel who earnestly supported Plymouth Argyle or Port Vale and who always politely said 'I've always preferred Celtic to Rangers' to cheer us up, occasionally adding some banal nonsense like 'My wife's a Catholic' or 'My grandmother is Irish'.

Now we could regale then with stories of Paul McStay, Peter Grant and Pierre van Hooijdonk. Celtic were back in the land of the living.We could look the present in the eye and forward to the future. The Kelly regime had gone. Had they ever thought to consider what they had done to us? And how did they feel now?

3

1995/96: So Near

1 995/96 was the season in which Celtic almost made it. At long last, for the first time since they actually won the championship in 1988, a realistic challenge for the Premier League was forthcoming from Celtic. They finished up only four points behind Rangers, and most independent observers agreed that it was Celtic who played the better football. Yet it was also Rangers who beat them in the League Cup and the Scottish Cup, albeit narrowly on both occasions. Ironically in the Premier League, only one game was lost (as distinct from Rangers who lost three times) but it was the sheer number of drawn games – eleven – that proved to be Celtic's downfall. Nowhere was this more starkly delineated than in the simple statistic that Celtic could not beat Rangers when they opposed each other directly – and the Glasgow giants were now so far ahead of everyone else that Old Firm matches assumed even more importance than they had hitherto.

In the four head-to-head league games, Rangers won once and the other games were drawn. On all three occasions the consensus of opinion was that Celtic were a shade better on the day (and once in particular more than a shade) than Rangers, but bad luck, good goalkeeping and a few chances that should have been snapped up all combined to give Rangers an undeserved point on each occasion. There was also the phenomenon of what some might call a slave mentality, so reminiscent of the early 1960s, and indeed the recent past, where Celtic teams were paralysed into believing that Rangers were better than they were – where in fact they weren't!

But there were many plus points from this season as well. One was the gradual development of the new Celtic Park. The north stand, holding 27,000, had been officially opened at a pre-season friendly against Newcastle United in August. It was an imposing structure, built, reportedly, at a cost of £18 million. The two-tiered edifice now dominated the skyline of the East End of Glasgow, an impressive indication of prosperity in the middle of what remained a depressed environment. In the old days (pre-1966) when the original 'Jungle' – with its leaking roof and cinders for terracing – was in situ, that particular structure with its general decadence was difficult to get excited about, but it did somehow reflect the general poverty and deprivation of the area. Did this new structure now betoken affluence for the team and its supporters?

The team were now therefore back home after their year long sojourn at Hampden. Work was continuing at both ends of the ground. This may have made it difficult for the players given this slightly surreal situation, but for supporters it was encouraging to see the stadium slowly taking shape, the most positive benefit being that the new ground would be bigger and better than Ibrox – and deliberately so! There was also a great sense of being there at the beginning of a new era for the club. Seeing everyone seated at Celtic Park was a novel experience.

The turf had also been relaid the previous spring. In a move which attracted little attention in Scotland, although a great deal in Ireland, shamrocks were planted in the first sod on 10 April 1995. The sod of turf in question had been dug up in a place called Mullaghduff the night before. It is a tiny fishing village in the west of Donegal and Bonner's Bar in Mullaghduff now proudly displays the spade with which the sod was dug up. This was a vague, in fact distinctly tenuous, symbol of Celtic's roots, but club historians would recount how in March 1892 before the present Celtic Park was opened, one Michael Davitt, an ex-Fenian and later a colleague of Charles Stuart Parnell, had planted shamrocks where the centre spot would be.

This move in 1995 was perhaps part of a propaganda exercise to link Celtic more to her roots in Ireland, and to do more to attract supporters from that island. Certainly it was a feature of the late 1990s and the early twenty-first century that more and more Irish buses were seen in the bus park. There always had been a large support from Ireland for big games and a trickle for league games, but now there seemed to be much larger numbers making the trip across the Irish Sea from Donegal, Derry, Sligo, Belfast and other parts of the Emerald Isle. Indeed buses from England also became a feature of attendance at Celtic Park, and the Celtic crowd was now a polyglot one with Glaswegian accents mixing with Geordie, east-coast Scottish with Birmingham or London, and Irish with Highland.

The start of the season was also enhanced by the presence of the Scottish Cup. For the sake of public relations, photographs were taken of the team with the Cup in front of them and the new north stand behind. There was a feeling that the good days were coming back, if they weren't actually here yet. Celtic and silverware should go together, it was felt. The supporters were now entitled to expect some sort of payback for the long years of supporting a team which had produced very little in recent memory.

A further important development was that there were now the makings of a settled squad. The arrival of Jackie McNamara from Dunfermline at the end of September for a fee of £650,000 made a huge difference to the team. The fee was not excessive and Jackie was an interesting and creative player, the son of a Celt of the same name. McNamara senior had played forty times for the team in the early seventies, although he is better known for his contribution to Hibs and for his left-wing political sympathies, which earned him the nickname of Boris! Jackie junior played on the right (of the pitch, that is, not the political spectrum!) balancing Tosh McKinlay on the left with powerful attacking play. The midfield was further bolstered by the arrival of Morten Wieghorst from Dundee at a cost of £600,000, although he was hardly required and indeed played very few games that season. Collins and McStay were still there and up front the twin foreign strikers of the Dutchman Pierre van Hooijdonk and the German Andreas Thom forged a productive partnership.

Andreas Thom (soon to be called Andy) was signed from Bayer Leverkusen for £2.2 million at the end of July. He had been capped by Germany, and was looked on as being the ideal foil for van Hooijdonk. In particular he was expected to finish off the van Hooijdonk knock downs. He did have the unfortunate tendency to be injured, and has the misfortune to have a book named after him for this reason. Apparently some denizens of the north stand have a tendency to either arrive late or to leave early, sometimes to the extreme annoyance of other spectators. This book (about the

1997/98 season) is entitled *The Andy Thom Experience* because Andy also found it difficult to last ninety minutes!

But there had been two much-publicised failures in the transfer market in summer 1995. One was David Ginola, a French internationalist forward, who later became notorious when he played for Tottenham Hotspur for diving and claiming penalties. The despicable Ginola had seemed all set to sign for Celtic, but then suddenly joined Newcastle United, cheerfully admitting that he was using Celtic as a bargaining pawn in his negotiations with the Geordies! Small wonder that in the pre-season friendly between Celtic and Newcastle, when the new north stand was unveiled, Ginola was booed mercilessly by the home crowd.

Celtic also came off second best in a tussle over the Yugoslav Gordan Petric. He had played for Dundee United and certainly looked competent enough, although hardly in the millions of pounds category. Nevertheless defenders were needed and Petric looked all set to sign . . . when suddenly he opted for Rangers instead. Rangers's interest had been late and low-key and motivated, it appeared, less by any real admiration for the player than by a desire to win an early point in the Glasgow propaganda battle. It reminded us of 1989 and the filching of Maurice Johnston, a move designed to make Celtic look mean and unambitious.

This manoeuvre by the Rangers management certainly succeeded as Celtic's defence was much criticised throughout the coming season, although not always with cause. John Hughes (no relation to the John Hughes of the 1960s, but given the same nickname of 'Yogi') had been bought from Falkirk for £380,000 (less than a quarter of what Petric would have cost) to team up with Tom Boyd. Celtic fans will always love a wholehearted player and forgive the occasional lapse, so Hughes was a favourite. He had his moments of weakness, but it must be stressed that of the crucial eleven games that were drawn, six were goalless and three finished one apiece, something that indicated a shortcoming in attack as opposed to defence.

The third plus point to come out of the 1995/96 season was the rebuilding of the relationship, so important in all teams, but particularly in the case of Celtic, between players and fans. That the team had won back the respect of the fans was seen in the last game of the season on 4 May 1996, when, after an easy 4–1 victory over Raith Rovers, the team embarked on a lap of honour in front of a packed stadium. And this was for a team which had yet again lost out to Rangers in all three Scottish domestic tournaments! As one Kirkcaldy fan was heard to say, 'If this is what happens when they lose a league, what will they be like if they win?'

The start of the season also saw a new phenomenon that became known as the Celtic huddle. Apparently, the players spontaneously decided that they should do this publicly just before the start of the game to show an ethos inspired by Alexandre Dumas's book, *The Three Musketeers*, of 'One for All and All for One'. It certainly attracted attention, admiration and even imitation – sometimes in mockery, it must be said, but if imitation is the sincerest form of flattery, then Celtic were much flattered. Before long, rugby teams, cricket teams and even amateur dramatic groups throughout Scotland and the world were doing the same thing.

But what did they say to each other in that huddle? Peter Grant solemnly informed everyone on television one night that, 'It's like the Freemasons. We never tell', and indeed it has remained a secret. Possibly it was one of these very straightforward and frank team talks along the lines of 'Lets get stuck in!' or perhaps, as some supporters believed, it was a resurrection of the ancient, tribal, blood-curdling Fenian chant:

Up the long ladder and down the short rope!
To hell with King Billy and God Bless the Pope!
We'll meet you tomorrow, we'll tear you in two
And we'll send you to Hell with your Red, White and Blue!

Whatever it is that they say to each other, it has remained one of the many attractive idiosyncracies of the new Celtic from its inception at the start of the 1995/96 season.

There was also at least one major piece of injustice suffered by the club, and this is something apart from refereeing decisions that went the wrong way. Celtic might well have won both the league and the Scottish Cup had it not been for a piece of administrative incompetence which led a few years later in 1999 to the sacking of a high ranking official of the SFA. The Jorge Cadete affair has been skilfully dealt with in Tom Campbell's excellent book, *Celtic's paranoia . . . all in the mind?* and it did have a significant impact on Celtic's performances in the latter part of the season.

The saga began just after the turn of the year. The management team of Tommy Burns and Billy Stark, irked by the failure to score against Rangers in the New Year game, began to pursue an interest in Sporting Lisbon's Jorge Cadete. Cadete would of course be remembered by the fans as the man who scored both goals for Sporting Lisbon and put Lou Macari's Celtic out of Europe in early-November 1993. Negotiations proceeded and, by the end of February, with a considerable part of the season still to go, Celtic thought that they had landed Cadete. He was duly paraded at Celtic Park with the obligatory Celtic scarf before a game with Partick Thistle on 24 February the day after he 'signed' and was seen on television looking at the replica of the 1967 European Cup which (as he would naturally have been expected to know) was won in Lisbon. Mercifully we were spared 'the only team I ever wanted to play for' and 'a dream come true' sort of cant, (no doubt we would have got it if he had had a better command of English!) but Jorge did look happy to be with us and to be eagerly anticipating his active participation.

He would make his debut, we were told, as soon as the 'papers came through'. However they took a long time to arrive, and it was not until Monday 1 April that he was allowed to make his debut for Celtic. This was a live television game. Cadete came on as a sub-stitute when Celtic were already thrashing a poor Aberdeen side 4–0, and scored with his first kick of the ball! His belated debut meant that he had already missed several league games since the day (23 February) that Celtic thought they had signed him. Two of these games had been draws – one of them had been the Old Firm encounter at Ibrox, and the other a dismal goalless performance against Motherwell. Had Cadete been available for selection, Celtic would have had another attacking option and the results in both games might well have been different.

Scottish Cup regulations also meant that as the formalities had not been completed by 23 March, Cadete was not eligible to play in the Scottish Cup semi final of 7 April. This was particularly hard and indeed inconsistent, for he had been allowed to play in the league on 1 April! The opponents in the semi final were Rangers and the game was lost by two goals to one. Once again the presence of Cadete might have made a difference.

It is of course facile to claim that the apparent incompetence of Jim Farry, the chief executive of the SFA, was the *only* thing responsible for Celtic losing the league and the Cup that year. But it was certainly a factor and Fergus McCann felt sufficiently perturbed about the matter to pursue it relentlessly and obdurately with the eventual result that, years later in 1999 and long after the damage had been done, Farry was sacked by the SFA for his failure to expedite the arrival of Jorge Cadete.

There are three possible explanations for this curious affair. One is the widely believed one that Farry 'had it in' for Celtic in the tradition of George Graham and other former SFA secretaries who simply did not like either Celtic, their supporters or the man who was in charge of the club. This is possible, but unlikely, although as far as Celtic supporters are concerned, conspiracies, secret handshakes and rolled up trouser legs are seldom far from their consciousness – and not always without justification!

Another possible reason is sheer incompetence, as if Farry simply forgot all about Cadete's papers – again an unlikely scenario given his administrative experience and ability. Indeed it is hard to believe that Farry or his staff would have forgotten about a matter of such magnitude with such a large amount of money involved. The media would have ensured, one would have thought, that this matter did not slip the memory.

The most likely possibility lies in Farry's legalistic and pettifogging mind. He had frequently been lampooned on the satirical football programmes on radio and television for being a master of doubletalk and a paragon of pedantry. He did enjoy making an easy task complicated, apparently, and a situation like this – dealing with a high profile transfer to Scotland from a foreign country and involving bodies like UEFA and FIFA – was one that he did not wish to rush, even if pressurised by Celtic. In fact, that was possibly another facet of his character; he enjoyed the fact that McCann was compelled to wait for him. It gave him a feeling of power.

For whatever reason, Cadete's clearance did not arrive until it was too late and Farry deserved his comeuppance, much delayed though it was. Ironically, by the time that Farry was fired, Cadete had long since left Celtic Park, having failed the club badly (although not necessarily by his playing performances on the field) and clearly being unable to deal with the emotional intensity of a club like Celtic in a country with a climate and culture far removed from his own. In this of course, he would hardly be alone. Indeed a feature of Celtic's foreign imports at this time tended to be that, although generally speaking they were more gifted players than those who played for Rangers, they lacked emotional and mental stability. Words like fruitcake were used more than once to describe some of them.

But 1995/96 opened with the League Cup, the tournament that still sent a shiver of horror down the spine of supporters following last year's Raith Rovers fiasco. A competent enough 3–0 win at Somerset Park over Ayr United heralded the season, but then the draw for the next round gave Celtic a home draw . . . but against, of all people, Raith Rovers! By coincidence the first league game of the season a few days earlier on 26 August was at Stark's Park, Kirkcaldy against the same opponents, so Celtic now had ample opportunity to exorcise the ghost.

The league game resulted in a 1–0 victory. It was a fine warm afternoon and a good, hard fought, game won by Pierre van Hooijdonk's header late in the second half. The League Cup match, played eccentrically the following Thursday 31 August at Celtic Park could not have been more dramatic. Celtic Park was a strange sight for its first competitive game of the season. The old stand on one side, the new north stand on the other and behind both goals – nothing but workmen's cabins and caravans! Thus there was nothing to stop the wind, and the wind blew a phenomenal amount of litter onto the park. Half time for example was spent watching an army of yellow-oilskin-clad stewards clearing the pitch of chip bags, cigarette packets and newspapers discarded by environmentally unaware Glaswegians!

The game was a good one. A goalless first half did credit to both teams, but then a fine strike by Pierre van Hooijdonk seemed to have won the game for Celtic. Tony Rougier's free kick, however, brought Raith back into the game and the body language of the Kirkcaldy dugout and their players seemed to betoken confidence. We now had extra time and everyone in the 27,546 crowd was aware that the dreaded 'penalty shoot-out' words were waiting in the wings. Fortunately, a Simon Donnelly strike with very little time left was enough to win the day, although Jimmy Nicholl, the manager of Raith Rovers, made a bizarre complaint that Celtic had not returned the ball properly to his team after an injury to a Celtic player. In fact Celtic were returning the ball to a Raith defender, but van Hooijdonk 'intercepted' the ball and headed it out of play near their own corner flag. Raith then took their throw-in but promptly lost possession, the ball came to Donnelly and he scored.

Any Raith Rovers complex had thus been dispelled but the League Cup dream ended in the next round when Rangers came to Celtic Park on Tuesday 19 September. It was one of these annoying Old Firm games where there was very little between the teams, but Rangers got the goal through Ally McCoist. It was late in the game, and Marshall looked a little at fault for failing to deal with the cross which was headed home by McCoist. Extravagant and provocative celebrations then followed, deserving of a booking and doing little to endear McCoist to the home crowd, who were worthy of a commendation for their restraint.

But if there was any comfort to be gained from the League Cup exit, it came in the thought that Celtic were now at least on a par with Rangers as far as ability was concerned. All that was needed was luck and a killer instinct – two things that are by no means unrelated, but as yet making no appearance at Celtic Park. In fact Rangers went out of the League Cup in the semi final to an Aberdeen side who went on to lift the trophy, beating Dundee in a dull final. Amazingly, it would be one of only two trophies won by Aberdeen in the 1990s – a stark contrast to their glory days in the 1980s, and an indication of how seldom provincial clubs in Scotland could expect to win anything.

Another sore blow was to come Celtic's way when Rangers returned to Celtic Park on league business at the end of September, only eleven days after the League Cup defeat. Once again there was little to separate the teams, but it was Rangers who got the goals in a 2–0 defeat, courtesy of Cleland and Gascoigne. Celtic huffed and puffed, particularly in the second half, but no goals came, the defensive-arc formation utilised by Rangers proving very impressive and sadly very obvious to those on the top tier of the north stand. In addition there seemed to be the psychological problem of coping with Paul Gascoigne, which reminded older supporters about similar problems with Jim Baxter in the early 1960s. Gascoigne was a high profile and talented player . . . but he was by no means unbeatable, unless the opposition considered him to be so! Rangers second goal that day was a case in point, for Gascoigne ran unmolested almost the length of the field as several Celtic defenders seemed to run away from him, when a tackle would not have been out of the question.

Celtic had already been involved in a remarkable league match at Aberdeen on Sunday 10 September with a lunch time kick off for the benefit of viewers on Sky Television. Celtic were two down after ten minutes, courtesy of a Boyd own goal and a crisp strike from Aberdeen's Eoin Jess, reputedly the target of both Celtic and Rangers. Yet Celtic fought back and by half time they were ahead! Fine goals by John Collins and Andy Thom levelled things, then as the eventful first half was drawing to its conclusion, a Thom shot was spilled by Aberdeen's Theo Snelders, Collins was on hand to net the rebound, and incredibly, Celtic went in 3–2 ahead. Equally incredible was the second half. There was no further scoring, although there might have been had Celtic not had to play with ten men, losing John Hughes after his second booking.

The Rangers reverse at the end of September would turn out to be the only league defeat of the season, but there was little time to dwell upon it, for Celtic were now deeply involved in Europe. The first round of the Cup Winners' Cup involved Celtic in a long and arduous trip to Georgia to play Dynamo Batumi. The Foreign Office had to be consulted about the wisdom of this trip to a politically unstable land (the birthplace of one Josef Stalin) where exotic diseases like dysentery, and long forgotten ones like diphtheria, abounded. Celtic took their own food, but returned with a 3–2 victory, Andy Thom scoring two fine goals.

It was Andy who scored another two in the second leg at Celtic Park as Celtic romped to an easy 4–0 victory, the other goals coming from Simon Donnelly and Andy Walker. This was fine and betokened a certain amount of progress, but it was noticed that after each European game there was an adverse reaction on the home front. The return from Georgia, for example, was followed by a feeble 1–1 draw against Motherwell, and the Rangers disaster came only two days after the return leg. The Rangers reverse may have happened anyway, but the loss of points to Motherwell could have been avoided, if the game had been move to a Sunday (as would happen in future). Playing a game in a distant foreign country on a Thursday meant that the team did not get back until late on the Friday. A poor performance on the Saturday was hardly surprising, therefore.

Much more demanding opposition was forthcoming in the next

round of the Cup Winners' Cup when Celtic were drawn against the formidable Paris St Germain, quite clearly one of the best teams on the continent. This time there was an adverse home reaction even before they went! Celtic carelessly lost two points to Hibs at Celtic Park – in spite of playing some brilliant football – on the Saturday before they went to France. They then compounded the felony by performing very disappointingly at Kilmarnock on the Saturday after Paris and ending up with a goalless draw. But why were Celtic denied a penalty when two Kilmarnock players pushed John Collins to the ground with only minutes left? In between times, the team had gone to Paris on 19 October and emerged with respect and credit after a 1–0 defeat. In fact, a late rally might just have produced a vital away goal, but it was not to be.

The return leg at Celtic Park was widely recognised as being one of the best games of football seen there for many years, although unfortunately most of it came from the visitors. Paris St Germain won 3–0, playing superb football, yet Celtic had their moments as well, thrilling the appreciative crowd with some fine play. But they had no answer to Patrice Loko, whose two goals before half time effectively killed what little chance Celtic had.

So once again, Celtic saw the exit door in Europe long before Christmas, this year on 2 November. Rangers would also flop in the European Cup before the year was out, but Celtic did at least have the consolation of knowing that they went out to a fine footballing side. The respect of the supporters was retained, and there was a feeling that the team could only learn from what they had seen of Paris St Germain. Both teams were given a great round of applause from a sporting Celtic crowd, who thus maintained their reputation of appreciating good football, even if it did come from their opponents.

After this, the form of the team steadily improved as the players got to know each other better and to operate as a unit. With Europe off the horizon, they displayed an enthusiasm and vitality that the denizens of Celtic Park had not seen for a long time. The feeling developed that the team were going somewhere. It was encouraging to see the very obvious team spirit that Tommy Burns was clearly working hard to foster, with players covering for each other, reading each other for passes and the form of the two playmakers Paul McStay and John Collins being very impressive indeed.

There was a disappointing goalless draw against Raith Rovers at

Celtic Park on 8 November, the game being spoiled by the ultra-defensive tactics of the Kirkcaldy side. As time ticked away, and Celtic's forwards became more and more desperate, Raith's two central defenders Shaun Dennis and Ronnie Coyle (ironically both Celtic-daft) booted the ball time and time again into the north stand, knowing that it would take a long time to come back! Other than that, Celtic's form until Christmas was very good, with particular praise being earned for a 4–0 thumping of Hibs at Easter Road on 9 December. The visit to Rangers on Sunday 19 November will be much remembered for the goal that never was, according to the coverage on STV. Rangers seemed to score but the 'goal' was disallowed. Television was so busy playing back the 'goal' that it failed to notice that the referee had chalked it off! Thus the whole nation was conned by overzealous attention to playbacks!

Not that it mattered all that much, though, for the game finished 3–3 with several more close things at each end, and a brilliant van Hooijdonk equaliser from a McKinlay cross late in the game. It was a splendid contest with both teams thoroughly deserving their ovation at full time. The next occasion on which the teams met was at Celtic Park on 3 January. This was a different story in two respects. One was that it was goalless, (a rarity in Old Firm fixtures) and the other was that Celtic had all the pressure, outplaying Rangers for much of the game, but unable to score!

That they did not score was due to several factors. One was sheer bad luck, another was occasionally inept finishing – but the main factor was the performance of Andy Goram in the Rangers goal. 'Andy broke our hearts': Tommy Burns argued these words would be a fitting epitaph for the match, and Goram certainly had the ability to spread himself wide and stop Celtic scoring in one-on-one situations. Like all good goalkeepers, he also enjoyed more than his fair share of luck. Conversely, Celtic players began to feel that they had no luck, an understandable but fatal condition when words like jinx and destiny creep into a footballer's psyche.

The problem did not lie in the inability of the players, nor in the commitment and leadership of Tommy Burns. From the New Year game onwards, the team stepped up a gear and played enough good football to warrant becoming champions. But they lacked the one quality that is the hallmark of all league winners: consistency. January 1996, for example, saw fine away victories at Kirkcaldy,

Aberdeen and Tynecastle, before an infuriating loss of two points to Kilmarnock at Rugby Park on 20 January. (Kilmarnock away thus lived up to its reputation throughout the 1990s and indeed into the new century as one of the Old Firm's more difficult fixtures.) Yet even that represented progress, for Rangers had horrified their fans by going down 3–0 to Hearts at Ibrox on the same day. Somehow it was all the more galling because they had not been able to take full advantage of a Rangers slip-up.

There was a remarkable game against Hibs at Celtic Park on 3 February. It had been a niggly, unpleasant contest, but Celtic did well to come back from being a goal down and win 2–1. Jim Leighton, that sprightly veteran of Scottish football (and in 1996 far from finished, for he still had a few Scotland appearances to come) suffered an injury and Darren Jackson, still much reviled by the Celtic Park faithful, took over in goal. That was until things became complicated and, at one point, the referee Mr Roy erroneously allowed the game to proceed when Hibs did not have a goalkeeper! Leighton was ready to return, and Darren Jackson took off the goalkeeper's jersey and took up his outfield position. The referee however did not immediately allow Leighton to return. It needed the stand-side linesman to flag and point out the illegality of all this, because the rules of football stipulate that there must be a goalkeeper – and Hibs at that point had no one wearing the goalkeeper's jersey.

Celtic were now hard on the heels of Rangers, but should have beaten Falkirk on 10 February. There they met an old friend called Maurice Johnston who quite clearly fouled Jackie McNamara in the penalty box, but got off with it to earn the Bairns an ill-deserved 0–0 draw. It was now obvious that Celtic would have to beat Rangers at Ibrox on 17 March. A draw would simply not be good enough.

Meanwhile the Scottish Cup had also seen a certain amount of progress with the defeat of a team called Whitehill Welfare from outside Edinburgh who were given the use of Easter Road for the day. Then Raith Rovers (whom Celtic saw a lot of in those days) came to Celtic Park to be competently dealt with. After that there was a very tense game against strong-running First Division leaders Dundee United at Celtic Park in the quarter final on Sunday 10 March.

This game was televised live and, for a long time, it looked as if Celtic would be eliminated from the competition. In the first half the unimpressive home side lost a goal and might well have lost a player as well. Gordon Marshall brought down the dangerous Craig Brewster and a penalty kick was awarded. There was a strong case for the dismissal of Marshall on the grounds that Brewster was denied a clear goalscoring opportunity. But the referee showed a little wisdom and mercy, Marshall stayed on and although he managed to save Owen Coyle's penalty kick, Coyle scored with the rebound. United finished the half well on top.

Celtic did play better after the restart but, as the second half progressed, it looked less and less likely that Celtic would score, such was the organisation of Dundee United's defence with whom manager Billy Kirkwood had clearly worked hard. But we had been here before. We recalled the Scottish Cup Finals of 1985 and 1988 between the same two teams when apparently hopeless causes had been turned around.

To the chagrin of the Tannadice men, it happened again – something that showed a degree of character in the Celtic players. A free kick lofted into the penalty box with only minutes left on the clock found the head of Pierre van Hooijdonk, then, in the very last minute when we had settled for a replay which would have been no more than the Taysiders deserved, Andreas Thom picked up a fine pass from Jackie McNamara to run through and score the winner. This sent the Celtic Park stands into delirium and reduced the small but gallant pocket of Dundee United supporters to despair.

What made this occasion all the more poignant for United was that they were now in the First Division, less than ten years after they had contested a UEFA Cup final and vanquished teams like Barcelona. All admirers of the Tannadice club were distressed at that, but would be delighted when they returned to the top flight at the end of that season, albeit only after a play-off with Partick Thistle, another team that all real lovers of the game had a soft spot for.

The Sunday following the Dundee United quarter final saw the crunch league match at Ibrox. Rangers were five points ahead of Celtic, but seemed to have the more difficult run-in. A Celtic win would certainly give them the psychological advantage, maximise the pressure on Rangers and reduce the points' gap to only two. The television audience once again saw an excellent game between the two old rivals with Celtic doing well to come back from being a goal down at half time. It was John Hughes who scored the equaliser, but it was not enough. Jackie McNamara was harshly sent off, just to make things more difficult. The final ten minutes saw a flurry of chances for both sides, any one of which might have gone in, but it was not to be. 1–1 was the final result, a scoreline that suited Rangers far more than it did Celtic, as it maintained the five point differential between the sides.

Celtic then (as frequently happens in the wake of a bad or indifferent result against Rangers) stumbled badly the following week with a goalless draw at Motherwell (although there seemed to the spectators nothing wrong with a good goal scored by Pierre van Hooijdonk in the second half) while Rangers won at Falkirk. This made the lead seven points, a gap that looked well nigh unbridgeable with only six games left. Then came the night of Jorge Cadete's much delayed debut at Celtic Park on Monday 1 April against Aberdeen, who were a pale shadow of the great Dons teams of the past. Two goals each by Simon Donnelly and Pierre van Hooijdonk were added to by Cadete's debut goal in a fine Celtic performance. As this game was shown live on terrestrial television, the nation was mightily impressed – but it all seemed too late for Celtic.

Not for the first time, it was the Scottish Cup that represented Celtic's best chance of an honour. The semi final had paired Celtic with Rangers and Hearts with Aberdeen. Hearts beat the Dons on Saturday 6 April at Hampden, and the following day the Old Firm met at the same venue. Once again, it was heartbreak for Celtic who played just as well as their opponents, but it was McCoist in the first half and Laudrup in the second who scored the goals at vital points of the game to give Rangers the advantage. McCoist's goal came just before the interval, when he pounced on the rebound after Marshall failed to hold a Robertson drive. Laudrup scored in the second half following a charge up the pitch at a time when Celtic were beginning to get on top of the Rangers defence.

But this Celtic team did at least fight and had they played as well all through the game as they did in the last ten minutes, then the outcome would have been totally different. Morten Wieghorst had been brought on at half time to replace the ineffective Brian McLaughlin but hard though they tried, Celtic could not break down the Rangers defence until the eighty-first minute when a low Jackie McNamara cross found the head of the diving Pierre van Hooijdonk and Celtic were back in the game. The supporters, some of whom had shamefully already broken ranks and gone home, now became more animated and the team, sensing an equaliser, surged forward.

Two chances came Celtic's way, and both fell to the unfortunate Simon Donnelly. One was a McNamara cross which he headed over, and the other was a clear shot on goal which he skied over the bar. This was hard on the youngster who was already struggling to live up to the expectations of the support and the media. It was a serious blow to his confidence from which he took a long time to recover, but it was an even more serious blow to the club who now faced a season without silverware.

Yet just as we were about to despair, there was a hint of a lifeline in the league campaign. On Wednesday 10 April, Rangers went down, for the second time that season, to Hearts. That game was at Tynecastle and kicked off quarter-of-an-hour earlier than Celtic's home game against Kilmarnock. Once again, history repeated itself when, as in January, Kilmarnock denied us a win on a day when Hearts had beaten Rangers. Killie in fact scored first, but when van Hooijdonk equalised late in the second half, the crowd, listening to BBC Radio Scotland and spurred on by the possibility and latterly the certainty of a Rangers defeat, did all they could to lift Celtic to a victory which would have reduced the gap to two points. Sadly, it did not happen, and Rangers stayed four points ahead.

This required Rangers to lose twice to teams other than Celtic, as the quota of four league games between Celtic and Rangers had now been used up. Had Rangers been only two points ahead, who knows what might have happened, given the pressure that would have been on them as they stumbled towards eight-in-a-row? The Kilmarnock game was once again an example of the historical, even primeval, Celtic Park death wish. The game could and should have been sealed up in the first half, but such was the psychological atmosphere in the ground resulting from a defeat at the hands of Rangers three days previously, that the fans were dispirited and the players, sensing the all-encompassing depression, became demotivated and lacked the ability to up their game.

Ironically and gallingly, Celtic, with the pressure now off them and with nothing to lose, finished the season in style. A fine win at Easter Road over Hibs was followed by beatings of Falkirk, Partick Thistle and Raith Rovers, in all of which four goals were scored. The Partick Thistle game was particularly praiseworthy, as the team were down 2–1 at half time against a Thistle side fighting for their Premier League lives, but eventually triumphed 4–2. Sadly it was not enough, and the end came when Rangers beat Aberdeen at Ibrox on Sunday 28 April to win the title for the eighth consecutive year. Once again, we (and the rest of Scottish football) had cause to rue the collapse of Aberdeen, for Celtic needed the Dons to do better against Rangers.

The game against Falkirk on 20 April was remarkable for its half time guest. It was Peter St John, the writer of that enchanting ballad 'The Fields of Athenry', and he sang it to a very appreciative audience, who joined in. Those who did not know the words would find them in the match programme! The press raised an eyebrow or two about this, for it seemed to sit ill with the pious stuff coming from Celtic Park about 'Bhoys Against Bigotry'. Was not this an Irish rebel song? It most certainly was, and Celtic fans enjoyed singing it. The club was able to argue that it was in tune with its traditions, for the Irish potato famine of 1845 and 1846 was the reason why most of the forefathers of the current supporters had ended up in Scotland. In addition, the song itself contains no incitement to violence, and is in fact a fine romantic ballad. But:

> for you stole Trevelyan's corn
> That the young might see the morn

and

> against the Famine and the Crown
> I rebelled, they brought me down

did seem to be full-blooded denunciations of the British Empire and all its works, something that the Celtic Park crowd clearly revelled in that day!

For Celtic, there was much to be happy about in the form of the team as the season ended. There was little wrong with the defence or the midfield, in which Paul McStay continued to excel. The cause for concern was the forward line, which had too many off days, as was indicated by the amount of goalless draws – six in all in the league campaign and the fact that Celtic scored eleven goals fewer than Rangers. The problem seemed to be the lack of variety in the attack with too much emphasis being put upon the aerial power of Pierre van Hooijdonk. Pierre's partner (until the belated arrival of Jorge Cadete) was Andy Thom, but the earnest German did tend to fade away, or get injured late in the game and necessitate a substitution. The wing-back play of Jackie McNamara and Tosh McKinlay was often encouraging (not least because they were both Scottish), but the purists and the romantic among us yearned for an out-and-out winger to give the Celtic forward line the required variety. For a while it had appeared that Brian McLaughlin might give us just that, but he was slightly built and soon began to reveal a disturbing tendency to run into trouble and lose the ball once he had done the difficult bit of winning it and beating his direct opponent. Sadly his career at Celtic Park was beginning to fizzle out.

A player whose Celtic career was now over was John Collins. Next season he would be playing for Monaco. Collins had played six seasons for the club, having joined Celtic from Hibernian in 1990. He had been a marvellous player, but was very unfortunate in that he played during a difficult period in the club's history. His 217 appearances included 47 goals, and it was noticeable that in all the finger pointing and stone throwing that went on in the bad days of the early 1990s, seldom was Collins blamed by the fans. In many ways the model professional, the man from the unlikely provenance of Galashiels, deep in the rugby-playing territory of the Borders, fully deserved the fifty-eight Scotland caps that he eventually won.

On the face of it, 1995/96 had thus been a tolerably successful season for the club, but being second in Scotland is tantamount to being last. There was also now quite clearly in our collective psyche the disturbing thought that Rangers were now only one title short of Celtic's record breaking nine-in-a-row run of 1966 to 1974. 1996 was the year that Celtic almost won the Premier League. Some argued that they did enough to win and that they played, over the piece, better football. This claim is not without foundation, and was certainly backed up by quite a few representatives of the media in addition to the testimony of supporters of other teams. Yet Celtic failed for three easily identifiable reasons. One was the failure to beat Rangers in head-to-head games, something which spilled over into the cup competitions. Tommy Burns clearly had some work to do on the psychological aspects of managing Celtic. Another was the traditional Celtic inability (a feature of the club since 1988, and possibly even

1888) to kill teams off when they were ahead, and the third reason was the old one of not getting a refereeing decision at a crucial time.

Blaming the referee is of course the oldest football excuse in the book, and hardly confined to Celtic fans. Other teams also feel cheated and deprived from time to time. It was of course the late Jock Stein who, however much he fulminated against the likes of Mr Davidson from Airdrie, pointed out that blaming the referee is simply not good enough. It is up to Celtic to be so far ahead in the game that a refereeing decision is of no relevance. One recalled several shocking decisions given against Celtic in Stein's day, but as the team were already a few goals ahead, refereeing incompetence or even bias simply was of no consequence.

Yet season 1995/96 was close enough to be a heartbreak – and the heartbreaks continued into the summer, when two further blows were visited upon us as signs of Rangers apparently unconquerable supremacy and arrogance. The semi final defeat left only Hearts between Rangers and the Scottish Cup. The final on 18 May was one of the most one-sided in recent years as a sub-standard Edinburgh team (who had twice registered good results against Rangers that season and of whom more was expected) collapsed this time against the Ibrox men who, without taking life particularly seriously, won 5–1. For Celtic supporters, there was a further source of anguish in that Gordon Durie scored a hat trick. Hitherto the only players to score a hat-trick in a Scottish Cup final had been Celts: Jimmy Quinn in 1904 and Dixie Deans in 1972. Gordon Durie was not a bad player, but it was hard to link him in the mind with the august company of Jimmy and Dixie. It was another example of the woe that was inflicted on Celtic fans in that period.

Another particularly painful blow came in the summer. June 1996 was the month in which 'football came home' to England for the European Championships and Scotland, with Tom Boyd, Tosh McKinlay and John Collins on board, were involved. Craig Brown's side were drawn in the same section as England, and lost heartbreakingly to the host nation at Wembley. Just after the hapless Gary McAllister missed his infamous penalty, Paul Gascoigne of Rangers ran up the field and scored a virtuoso second goal for England. The jeers and sneers of the Rangers supporters returned, even though this time they were directed against all of Scotland, rather than just at Celtic.

4

1996/97: 'A Celt through and through'

I f 1995/96 was the year in which Celtic almost made it, the following year, 1996/97, must be considered a failure. It certainly was so considered by Fergus McCann, because Tommy Burns was sacked at the end of it. Burns had been manager of the club for three years. Rumours had surfaced from time to time that he did not like McCann, or that McCann did not like him, but hard though the press tried, no permanent rupture of the relationship had been achieved. In some ways, Burns had done well, and the team were certainly light years better in 1997 than they had been in 1994 but his only trophy was the Scottish Cup of 1995. Tommy was still retained in the affection of the fans but three years was considered long enough to land at least one championship. Tommy had failed to deliver; Tommy therefore had to go.

It was not simply that he had failed to win the title, it was that Rangers did so and had now won it nine years in a row to the distress of everyone connected with Celtic. The press had not been slow in summer 1996 (after the European Championships in England had finished) to point out that if Rangers won the league again, they would equal the nine-in-a-row achieved by Jock Stein's team in the late 1960s and early 1970s. It was hardly calculated to pour balm on the nerves of Burns and his team as they prepared for the new season.

There was the usual pre-season optimism from Celtic Park. Although John Collins was no longer with the club, having decamped to Monaco, it did seem that a fine squad was being assembled at Celtic Park. New signing Jorge Cadete had impressed in his necessarily truncated debut the previous season. Surely more would be forthcoming from him in this campaign. Further proof of Celtic's intentions came on 31 May 1996 when they bought an Italian called Paolo di Canio from AC Milan, who was given a four-year contract worth £3 million. The size of the transfer fee is in doubt; the figure of £1 million was quoted by some but di Canio in his autobiography cites £800,000, a suspiciously low figure for a man who had won a *scudetto* with Milan.

Di Canio's autobiography is a fascinating read, and although some or indeed all of it may have been ghosted by a professional writer, there can be little doubt that the real di Canio is in there. There is, of course, as in all football autobiographies, more than a little self-justification and a fair sprinkling of vitriol and spite, but Paolo comes across as a likeable, albeit roguish, character with a propensity to attract controversy and conflict wherever he goes. Whatever he cost Celtic that summer, he was recognised as a top player by those who watched Channel Four's Italian football coverage on Sunday afternoons. It certainly seemed that he and Cadete could solve the chronic goalscoring problem that was bedevilling the club (particularly against Rangers) and deliver, at long last, a championship. The goalless draw, the curse of last season, had to be brought to an end.

All of this meant that Celtic now had four high-profile foreign players competing for places in the forward line: Van Hooijdonk, Thom, Cadete and di Canio. They seldom all played in the same game and when they did, most notably in the UEFA Cup game against Hamburg at Celtic Park, it was not a success, because there were too many quality forwards and not enough class in other areas of the side. In theory it seemed a good idea to have so many players competing for a place in the team, but the problem with these four was that none of them were as emotionally committed to the club as one would have liked, and with the exception of Andreas Thom, all suffered from emotional problems and caused Tommy Burns and the club more than their fair share of heartaches. Thom was different in the sense that he was a total professional, but his problems were related to his propensity to pick up injuries.

To tighten up the defence, Celtic paid a club record fee of £4.5 million to Bolton Wanderers for centre half Alan Stubbs. He would be a good player for the club, even though his commitment in his first Scottish game at Pittodrie seemed a trifle excessive when he was sent off. He was prone to injury, however, and had a tendency to feature in the tabloids rather too often in the context of either him or his wife wishing to go back home. He would eventually get his wish and return to England in 2001 to play for Everton, the team that he supported as a boy and of whom he was an unrepentant lover. He would have the misfortune to suffer (and thankfully recover) from serious illness in the shape of testicular cancer. Later on in the season, the defence was supplemented by Enrico Annoni from Roma, a powerful defender and a likeable fellow but one who never quite left his mark on Celtic Park in the way that was expected.

The development of the ground had now made considerable progress, and the structure now known as the Lisbon Lions stand at the east end of the ground (what used to be called the Rangers end) was in place to supplement the magnificent north stand. The other end would not be ready for another two seasons yet, but temporary uncovered seating had been put in place there with cagoules on offer in case it rained! It was clear that when the stadium was completed it would be one of the best in Britain, if not Europe.

Celtic's first competitive game that season in fact was against Kosice of Slovakia. This was in the qualifying round of the UEFA Cup (Scotland's poor record in Europe now meant that Scottish teams had to play in this round) and in the first leg on 6 August, Celtic did well to hold them to a 0–0 draw in spite of a red card being shown to Simon Donnelly. The return leg at Celtic Park was unimpressive and stayed at 0–0 for an incredibly long time, given the constant pressure from the home side, until a very late goal by Jorge Cadete saw Celtic through over the ten man Slovakians. It was a close and horrifying call against a team who were anything but the elite of Europe.

Celtic's European adventure that year was short lived in any case. The next round paired them with Hamburg and in both legs they lost 2–0. The game in Glasgow was a poor Celtic performance with the 45,412 crowd stunned into silence after an early goal from which the team never recovered. The second leg in Germany was a real horror story – well in the tradition of Celtic in Europe in recent years – as the team finished the game with only nine men on the field, after central defenders John Hughes and Malky Mackay were dismissed.

This completed a miserable trio of midweek September defeats. On the Wednesday between the Hamburg matches, Celtic had exited from the League Cup after extra time at Tynecastle to a Hearts team short of four first-team men, all of whom had been sent off against Rangers at Ibrox the previous Saturday. In spite of this apparent advantage, Celtic once again blew it to continue their melancholy tradition in this particular competition. Granted it was a good game, and Celtic had been a little unlucky not to finish the game off within the regulation ninety minutes, but it was becoming clear that Burns and Celtic had more than a few problems in winning games that should have been there for the taking. It was also now a horrifying statistic that season 1982/83 (fourteen years before) had been the last time that Celtic had won the League Cup. Clyde and Alloa had provided few problems in the earlier rounds of the tournament, but Hearts, even without the four first-team regulars, had been too strong!

To a Celtic fan, this sort of thing is unacceptable and already mutterings were beginning to be heard on supporters' buses and in the towering stands of Celtic Park that Tommy Burns was not the man for the job. Yet, as happened in the 1960s with Jimmy McGrory, it was hard to get angry with Burns, for he was transparently a Celtic fan, through and through, and just as upset about recent performances as any of us. His skills in the field of public relations were excellent, and he never failed to be anything other than a perfect representative and ambassador for the club.

But it was certainly Rangers who won the propaganda battle during the season, and several other seasons as well. The controversy centred on Paul Gascoigne, known to one and all as 'Gazza'. This undeniably talented footballer, of Geordie extraction, was always good for newspaper copy and seemed quite prepared to do anything to keep himself in the limelight. In his days with Newcastle United, Tottenham Hotspur and Lazio, there had been no lack of focus on him, but now in the sometimes culturally impoverished country called Scotland, little else appeared on the back or front pages of the tabloids, it seemed, than Gazza.

Funny hairstyles, tears, songs, fights, imitation-flute playing, drunkenness, wild parties, wife beating – these and many more centred on Gazza. On one occasion in a game against Aberdeen he blatantly head-butted an opponent in the chest, an incident somehow missed by the referee, and there were other incidents on the field as well. It did not seem to matter how bad the news was, he would invariably manage to be at the centre of it, providing masses of copy for the greedy tabloids. In this of course one can see the parallel with a naughty schoolboy who would do anything, no matter how juvenile, to be at the centre of attention. Then, on occasion, he would complain that the media would not leave him alone! In common with the British royal family, some of whom were at this time behaving very badly, there was a failure to recognise that it was the media who created and sustained him.

Yet Gascoigne was not an entirely detestable character. There was apparently a kind side to him, and he did not lack a sense of humour. There was, for example, the occasion when he picked up a referee's yellow card which had fallen on the ground and proceeded to 'book' the bemused official. The referee however failed to see the funny side and yellow-carded him for real. Respectable Rangers fans of course were embarrassed by some of Gascoigne's behaviour, especially by the alleged wife beating, which alienated quite a few of their female supporters. But not them all, sadly. The cult following did not diminish, and Rangers were shrewd enough to keep him on the front and back pages of the newspapers, for no other reason than that it kept Celtic off them! Gascoigne was good copy, no matter how offensive some of his behaviour would become.

A feature of Celtic's season was the amount of red cards given out to players. Some were justified, others weren't, but it was undoubtedly a fact that team discipline was not what it could have been. In particular, it was hard to be sympathetic to a player who was sent off for a second yellow card. A professional football player should surely have enough self-restraint, control and sheer common sense to prevent this from happening.

In the league, Celtic had a mountain to climb if they wanted to stop the nine-in-a-row nightmare from becoming a reality. The title simply had to be the priority. In fact, from September onwards, there was no real doubt about that, for the club was out of Europe and the League Cup. Consistent form was essential if Celtic were to wipe the smirks off the faces down Ibrox way and wipe Gascoigne and his antics off the back page.

In fact, the initial league games in season 1996/97 were not all that bad. A 2–2 draw at Pittodrie on the opening day was acceptable, given that centre half Alan Stubbs had been sent off harshly for a last-man offence, and then there followed five straight victories, and convincing ones at that. Hibs and Dunfermline were put to the Celtic Park sword five times and Raith Rovers four times, and the two away games at Kilmarnock and Dundee United had seen narrow, but deserved, wins. In the Rugby Park encounter, di Canio, in his debut game in the Premier League scored a wonder goal, and it was also the Italian who made the late winner for the victory at Tannadice after Dundee United had equalised. The victory was all the more praiseworthy for the fact that Celtic finished the game with ten men, Brian O'Neil having been sent off for reasons that were hard to fathom.

But reality set in on 28 September when the team went to Ibrox and lost miserably 2–0 to goals by Gough and Gascoigne. This was painful considering that the defeat came in the wake of the League Cup and UEFA Cup exits at the hands of Hearts and Hamburg. It was as if the players no longer believed that they could win at Ibrox, and the simple reason why Celtic did not win the league in season 1996/97 was that they lost four times to Rangers. It was the first quadruple in Premier League history between the Old Firm, and it showed the psychological gap that existed between the sides.

In all four games, Celtic had cause to complain not only about poor refereeing, but also sheer bad luck. In the September encounter, a case could have been made for the ordering off of three Rangers players. Di Canio was brought down in the penalty box early on by Richard Gough for what looked like a last-man offence. Perhaps it was because it was a last-man offence, with a red card the automatic punishment, that referee Willie Young affected not to see the incident. In addition to that, Jorg Albertz appeared to stamp on Brian O'Neil, and the luckless O'Neil also seemed to be kicked on the ankle by Gascoigne. As well as that, Celtic hit the post and came close on several other occasions. To make the job even harder, Tosh McKinlay was sent off, admittedly within the letter of the law, for two offences, although neither seemed to merit a yellow card.

On a Thursday night at Celtic Park in November, a dreadful mistake by the ill-starred O'Neil – who had suffered so much at Ibrox – allowed the talented Brian Laudrup to give Rangers an early lead and what proved to be the only goal of the game. Then Van Hooijdonk missed a penalty. In January 1997, a linesman (later proved to have a Rangers-supporting connection, albeit with the Celtic-sounding name of McBride) disallowed a good 'goal' by

Cadete at a time when the game might at least have been drawn. It was never made clear whether the 'goal' was disallowed for offside or for handball but, on either count, the television replays of the incident made it abundantly clear that the linesman was wrong. Rangers then got two late goals to make the final score 3–1.

In March, Rangers's only goal was scored by Brian Laudrup but it came after a clear push on Enrico Annoni. Malky Mackay was sent off in the second half, and Paolo di Canio, claiming extreme provocation, was seen by everyone challenging a Rangers player, Ian Ferguson, to a fight at full time. Rangers celebrated their victory by provocatively mocking the Celtic huddle, and full-scale violence was not far away from Celtic Park that dreadful Sunday afternoon.

Supporters had cause to feel aggrieved on all these counts individually, but then again no game is ever decided on one piece of bad luck or one refereeing decision, however outrageous. Celtic simply lacked the confidence to look upon Rangers as equals, even though they possessed players who were every bit as good. Therefore they were dependent to an overwhelming extent on good refereeing, something that they did not always get.

The four league defeats by Rangers were perhaps the main reason why the luckless Tommy Burns had to go. There is little point in complaining about refereeing, however unhappy one may feel about it. There are more positive responses to injustices. In 1965 Jock Stein inherited a Celtic team that had suffered more than once the previous year from dodgy decisions against Rangers in particular. Stein did two things about that. One was his physical presence and aura on the touchline which 'cowed referees into fairness' as someone put it, and the other was his ability to instil into the team a determination that quirky refereeing decisions need not matter, as long as the team is winning by a sufficient margin. In neither of these two areas was Burns proficient, and the team therefore became over-dependent on that ill-defined, but important, quality that we call luck.

There was also, after the November and the March defeats at the hands of Rangers, a marked failure to bounce back quickly. This is the ability to overcome a disappointment and win the next game, or the next series of games. In November, the team were so traumatised by their defeat against Rangers (not helped by having, ten days later, to watch on television Rangers winning the League Cup against Hearts at Celtic Park) that they drew the next home game against Hearts and then lost to Motherwell at Fir Park. It was the knock-on effect, the domino theory, the sympathy vote, the house of cards; call it what you will, but it indicated a lack of backbone.

In the Hearts game, di Canio having equalised with a penalty, ran to grab the ball to take it back to the centre spot, got himself embroiled in a violent altercation with a Hearts player and was red carded. No punches were thrown but arms were raised and the referee was technically correct. It was an action which hinted at mental instability on the part of di Canio. Insanity some might have said, and sadly, a great deal more of this was to be exhibited.

Similarly, after the loss of the March game to Rangers (and a feckless display against bogey team Kilmarnock a few days earlier) the team then went on two occasions to Fife, with the title not yet completely lost, and drew with Dunfermline and then Raith Rovers, who were by now almost relegated. To be fair, the Dunfermline game had seen a spirited fightback from being 2–0 down at half time, but Cadete rather spoiled the party for himself by throwing his jersey into the crowd at full time, having been specifically told not to.

Indeed, one of the valid criticisms that could be laid at Burns's door was the lack of discipline. Red cards were shown to Celtic players on fifteen occasions throughout the season, something that really ought to have been addressed. It is fine to take the view that the players were well motivated, but no player, however talented, can serve the cause by having an early bath. Still less can he help if he is sitting in the stand for the next few games serving a suspension. It could of course be argued that some of the red cards were unjustified, but not all of them.

The league was lost by five points, a narrow enough margin to be annoying, in that one Old Firm victory and a general tightening-up of games against lesser opposition might have made all the difference. Excuses could be made for Tommy Burns in that he had tremendous injury problems. Not one player played in every game of the season and the manager had to call upon no fewer than twenty-eight players for league games, some of them very inexperienced youngsters like Chris Hay, Stuart Gray and a man who seemed to have arrived from Ancient Rome, Mark Anthony.

Burns had also signed a midfield player, David Hannah, from Dundee United for a knockdown price. This man, while lacking in real class, nevertheless performed manfully for the team, and the quirky among us were to point out that Hannah was the first palindrome (a name spelt the same backwards as forwards) to play for the club! Or was he? There had been a Robert Hannah who had played for the club in the 1970s, although only as a substitute.

Injuries are, of course, part of the game, and one must qualify any talk of an injury crisis at Celtic Park or Ibrox by the realisation that these clubs have the ability to buy their way out of such temporary difficulties. If one wishes to talk about an injury crisis, one should note what happens at the likes of East Fife and Forfar, where a trawl of the Junior and amateur ranks is the only feasible solution. Injuries at big clubs bring opportunities as well as problems. Nevertheless the toll taken by absent players, whether due to injury or suspension, did mean that the team seldom had a settled look about it. Alan Stubbs, bedevilled as he was by repeated rumours about him, or his wife, not being happy and wanting to leave was also a repeated cause for concern. Phil O'Donnell also continued his miserable run of luck with injuries, and questions were now being openly raised about his value to the club.

One great Celtic career was being slowly brought to an end by an ankle injury. The player was Paul McStay who announced his retirement in mid-May 1997, after taking part in only twenty-one first-team matches during the season. He played in the first league game at Aberdeen, but was then more or less out until the New Year, and limped off the field at Stark's Park, Kirkcaldy in early April to finish his career. For more than fifteen years, he had delighted Celtic followers. Since his debut in 1982, this clean-cut young man had been an admirable role model for Hoops' fans everywhere. He was hard-working, talented, an excellent passer of the ball, a fine goalscorer and thoroughly deserving of his seventy-six caps for Scotland and his nickname, the 'Maestro'. His career had witnessed quite a few spectacular triumphs and a fair share of disasters, but they were seldom his fault. Indeed in the dreadful days of the early 1990s, it had often seemed that McStay was all that Celtic had in the way of genuine talent.

He played 677 times for the club, and won league titles in 1982, 1986 and 1988, the Scottish Cup in 1985, 1988, 1989 and 1995 and the League Cup in 1982. It was scant reward for such yeoman service, but McStay will go down as one of the greatest Celts of all time, even though he had the misfortune to be with the club at such a desperate time in its history. In 1992, he gave the impression of imminent departure by throwing his jersey into the crowd at the end of the game on the last day of the season, but was persuaded to stay because of 'my love for the club and because I was comfortable in that environment.' Paul always retained his dignity, and retains a love for an institution that is so much part of his heritage. Great uncles Willie and Jimmy – heroes of the club in the 1920s and 1930s – would have been proud of this man.

It was therefore fitting that the club had recognised McStay with a testimonial match – against Manchester United – on 12 December 1995. Although ground reconstruction restricted the crowd to 37,000 it was estimated that the player picked up in the region of £400,000 from the game, a tidy sum by any standards but one that reflects his massive contribution over the years. After the match, which Celtic won 3–1, McStay said, 'It was brilliant, unbelievable, a very special and emotional night for me.'

Peter Grant was also on his travels having missed a large chunk in the middle of the season through injury. Grant was a tremendous servant to the club, and he had deputised as captain for Paul McStay for part of the season. His departure to Norwich City was a cause of sadness, not least on the part of the player himself. Peter Grant was and is a genuine Celtic supporter, and is delighted, when the opportunity presents itself, to return to Celtic Park to support the team that he adores. And, like McStay, the club marked his unstinting service by arranging a testimonial. It was against Bayern Munich on 22 January 1997, and 40,000 turned up to witness a 2–1 victory for the German giants. But on a very special night the result was immaterial and Grant, who had never been one of the best paid players at Celtic Park, earned around £400,000. He was moved to tears by the waves of emotion pouring down from the stands and was heard to say, 'You can take me to heaven now.'

It was as late as 7 May 1997 before Rangers actually clinched the league. Their form during the run-in was anything but satisfactory for their supporters, as they lost to Dundee United, Kilmarnock and Motherwell. Their nine-in-a-row came against Dundee United at Tannadice on a Wednesday night, two days after they had lost the opportunity to win it at Ibrox against Motherwell on the holiday Monday. This stuttering progress to the title was a further cause of anguish for the Celtic fans, because it showed that Rangers could have been beaten had Celtic enjoyed the breaks at key moments.

The Premier League was therefore for the ninth year in a row a disaster area, but the final nail in the coffin of Tommy Burns came in the Scottish Cup. It was ironic because in this competition, Burns had arguably one of his best moments as Celtic manager. But there was neither lasting nor tangible success and Tommy had to go, something that he now seems to recognise.

The competition started in January with a 5–0 thumping of Clydebank in a game played at Firhill because Clydebank, already on a slow and painful road to extinction, had no home ground. Then came a trip to Easter Road on Monday 17 February for a game which a Phil O'Donnell goal seemed to have won until a late and dubious penalty converted by Darren Jackson gave Hibs an undeserved equalizer. The replay was won comfortably enough at Celtic Park by two goals to nil, the counters coming from O'Donnell and di Canio.

This brought Rangers to Celtic Park for the quarter final on Thursday 6 March. A game was played on that absurd day of the week (not for the first time that season) to satisfy the demands of Sky Television, which paid a substantial amount of money into the coffers, and was thus able to determine such matters. It was something that was bitterly resented by supporters, many of whom travelled long distances from places like Ireland and England and found it difficult to get to Glasgow on a Thursday night. Regrettably, television money talked louder than the fans.

By the time the cup match came around, Celtic had already lost three times to Rangers, had not beaten their Old Firm rivals since May 1995 and in consequence did not face this game with any great confidence, particularly as the media kept using words like hoodoo and jinx. On the other hand, such runs have to end sometime. Rangers, held to a draw at Pittodrie the previous Saturday (while Celtic had competently dealt with Hearts) were without the charismatic Paul Gascoigne. They seemed to be struggling, under a certain amount of pressure from their own support to deliver nine-in-a-row. In addition, they had no real answer to the question frequently posed by Englishmen and Europeans, 'If you are all that good, why don't you do better in Europe?'

In what is arguably their favourite competition, Celtic rose to the occasion and won comfortably. Two goals were scored within the first eighteen minutes. The first was from defender Malky Mackay who headed home a fine di Canio cross, then the Italian converted a penalty after Cadete was brought down by Joachim Bjorklund. For the rest of the game Celtic, with Paul McStay outstanding and ably supported by the earnest McKinlay and McNamara, were never seriously threatened. Penalties were claimed by both sides, but none were given by Mr McCluskey of Stewarton, although the two claims by Celtic both looked more convincing than the one he had given earlier.

But Rangers never came close to scoring in open play. In terms of performance, this was a thoroughly professional Celtic side, and the frustration of Rangers and their fans was obvious from early on in the second half. Yet, even with a two goal lead, it was difficult to relax, for Celtic were still capable of losing any plot. Not this time, though, and di Canio notes in his autobiography that he had never heard anything so loud as the crescendo of noise as full time approached and victory began to look secure. Celtic Park resounded for a full twenty minutes after the final whistle in response to such brilliance and the euphoric hope was expressed that not only the Cup but the league too might yet be acquired.

That was on a Thursday night, and by the Saturday, the radio and the press pundits, who three days before were talking about hoodoos and jinxes, now jumped ship and were confidently predicting that this could at long last be Celtic's season! So genuinely impressed had they all been by this excellent performance that a league and cup double was on the cards. For a short while Celtic's star burned brightly, and although still trailing in the title race, they could, it was felt, still catch up with a Rangers side who were now dispirited and anxious.

Sadly this did not last long, for Celtic, having gained a little psychological advantage, proceeded to throw it away in their next league game against Kilmarnock. They then lost to Rangers in the league the following Sunday. But the Scottish Cup now saw Celtic in the semi finals with Falkirk, Kilmarnock and Dundee United. There did not seem to be anything there that could not be handled, and the semi final at Ibrox against Falkirk, which was played on the brilliantly hot spring day of 12 April, was a great opportunity. Celtic were without Paul McStay, who had already played his last game for the club, but they had recently acquired a new forward in Geordie Tommy Johnson signed from Aston Villa for a fee of £2.4 million.

The red-haired Johnson, a transparently honest and immediately likeable character who had made his debut the previous week as a substitute, at once made himself popular with the fans when he scored in the semi final. This happened when he prodded home a loose ball more than half way through the second half, and it looked as if that would suffice for Celtic. But another chance immediately afterwards was squandered, and then came the moment that, in retrospect, sealed the fate of Tommy Burns. The Celtic defence failed to mark beanpole defender Kevin James at a corner kick and the Bairns equalised with only five minutes left.

This was disappointing, but there did not seem to be any reason why Falkirk could not be conquered in the replay on Wednesday 23 April. This time the weather was different with heavy rain, and the crowd of 35,879 (considerably down from the 45,261 of the first game) saw one of the more grizzly of Celtic's many Scottish Cup horror stories. McGrillen scored for Falkirk in the middle of the first half, and then, hard though Celtic tried for the rest of the half, they could not get an equaliser. Alarmingly, as the second half progressed and the rain intensified, (conditions in which better and more spirited Celtic teams of the past would have been expected to thrive) several of the players wearing green seemed to throw in the towel and become disheartened in a way which Celtic supporters will never accept of their team. Van Hooijdonk had now gone. He had been away since the beginning of March and his presence was sadly missed.

Chances did come, but were not seized upon and large sections of the Celtic support had already evaporated by the time that the referee brought things to an end. Falkirk were jubilant (not without cause) but the Celtic support were plunged into a depression so complete, comprehensive and lasting that there was now no one left, apart from the ultra-loyal Paolo di Canio, to argue for the retention of Tommy Burns as manager.

The rest of the season was played out in a surreal atmosphere. Rangers, as it turned out, stumbled more than once on the run-in, but Celtic were too far behind and too demoralised to do anything about it. The league had now been lost nine times in a row, and thus the record of Jock Stein's teams had been equalled by Rangers. If Rangers were to win the Premier League in the following season, that record would be shattered. The pain was intense, and there were those who felt that Celtic could never do it now, such was the slave mentality which overwhelmed everyone at the club at the very thought of Rangers. Even when the team could on occasion beat the Ibrox men, as in the Scottish Cup quarter final, they immediately threw it all away by stumbling at the next hurdle. Some supporters exhibited signs of clinical depression as marriages and relationships were put under unbearable strain.

The axe fell on Tommy Burns on Friday 2 May 1997, when Rangers were still some points short of winning their ninth successive title. Ironically it was the day after New Labour under Tony Blair had won the general election to end eighteen years of Conservative rule. It had been a landslide victory, bringing to an end an era of corruption, sleaze and misuse of power. The thought occurred, 'Would we ever see a New Celtic doing something similar?' Certainly, it was a valid parallel, given how poor Labour had been at one point during the dreadful Thatcher years. Labour had come back when many people thought that they wouldn't. Whither Celtic?

A further political ingredient was added to the pot as some supporters went to Celtic Park that fine evening to do nothing other, it seemed, than to swell the ghoulish crowd of those already there doing nothing other than lamenting what had happened. A van passed along London Road. It contained the defeated Scottish National Party candidate who was – via his loudspeaker – thanking all those people who had voted for him. He then turned on his music and the environs of Celtic Park were treated to that dreadful dirge, 'Flower of Scotland', which includes the words 'When will we see your like again?' Indeed, when were we going to see the likes of Jock Stein or Willie Maley again?

It was impossible not to be sorry for Tommy Burns. Ironically with three full seasons under his belt, he was the longest-serving Celtic manager of the 1990s. He had of course won the Scottish Cup in 1995, but that was all. Crucially, he had failed to land the championship. He can be considered unlucky in several respects. One was that he was manager in a time of flux. His first season was the Hampden season and the next two were played against the backdrop of the redevelopment of Celtic Park. His relationship with the chairman was described as 'up and down' with many arguments. Yet, was there anything surprising about that? Both were dyed-in-the-wool Celtic supporters, and if one keeps one's ears open at Celtic Park on any match day, it will be obvious that Celtic supporters seldom agree.

Burns himself claimed to have known for some time that the axe was going to fall on him, having come across 'some papers' that contained the views of 'certain people'. (*Celtic View* 5 February 2003) He said that 'it was a constant fight at Celtic Park' under McCann and then adds cryptically, 'So many of the issues were nothing to do with football and it was these factors which led to my demise'. What these factors were we can but guess, but it is difficult to imagine Tommy being shown the door, if the Scottish Cup (or preferably the Premier League) had been landed at the end of the 1996/97 season. In the eyes of the fans, at least, Tommy had been sacked for his failure to prevent Rangers winning nine-in-a-row.

Where Tommy was at his unluckiest was in the emotional instability of three of his foreign signings. Van Hooijdonk, di Canio and Cadete, (the 'three amigos' as they came to be known), while players of undeniable ability nevertheless gave him more grief than any manager is entitled to expect. Perhaps he would have been better advised to use the money on Scottish talent, for playing ability is not enough. There must also be a genuine commitment to the club and its supporters.

On the other hand, although there were many young Scotsmen who would have played their heart out for Celtic, and who certainly had the correct attitude, talent was hardly in superabundance in Scotland either. One of the side effects of the Celtic–Rangers ingathering of foreign stars at the expense of home-grown youngsters was the decline of the Scottish national team, now well on its melancholy way to becoming the laughing stock of the rest of Britain.

Jorge Cadete was the one who came closest perhaps to being the personality goalscorer that is the *sine qua non* of all good Celtic teams. His tally of thirty goals was certainly impressive (although it pales into comparison with what Henrik Larsson would later produce) but he always claimed that the stumbling block was not Tommy Burns but Fergus McCann. He had clearly made up his mind that he was going to go at the end of the season, and when he scored in his last game, a meaningless fixture against Dundee United, he kissed the grass – a theatrical, but sadly empty, gesture.

In later years he owned a pet canary called 'Fergus'! He also appeared on Portuguese television's equivalent of *Big Brother*, and continued to express his undying love for Celtic and the fans. It sounded good when we read it in Scottish newspapers on quiet days, and it really was such a pity that such rhetoric had little basis in reality. He would, for example, claim that he paid the £400,000 transfer himself just to join Celtic and that at the meeting with McCann he was 'tired' and omitted to get a hitherto verbal promise to up his salary written down as a legal and binding document. All this begged the question of why he did not employ an agent or a lawyer.

In addition, he added bizarre charges that McCann had described Portugal as a banana republic, and cut the ground from under his own feet in his claims about how much he loved Celtic when he complained that Leeds United tried to buy him during the season but McCann upped the asking price to £7 million! When he returned to Celtic Park in February 2003 to do the honours for the half-time lottery, he asked Martin O'Neill for an opportunity to rejoin the club. It was a pity that the much-loved Celtic fans, Burns and even McCann were so short changed by this talented but flawed Portuguese genius. Yet his appearance that day for the Paradise Windfall draw was greeted with a surprising amount of warmth from some fans who clearly allowed themselves to forget the downside of Jorge Cadete.

Van Hooijdonk continued with his undeniable and lamentable ability to get into trouble and to fall out with people in his later career, but he will always be remembered with affection for his goal in the 1995 Scottish Cup final as well as the two goals for Feyenoord which removed Rangers from the UEFA Cup in February 2002. His remarks about his salary of £7,000 per week being all right for the homeless, but not for a top footballer, are less easy to forgive and forget, as well as being a blatant lie and an insult to a section of the community that Celtic were meant to be all about.

On 9 March 1997, the Sunday after Celtic had beaten Rangers in the Scottish Cup quarter final, Pierre was transferred to Nottingham Forest. He had taken no part in the victory over Rangers, his last appearance being as a substitute on 1 March in a league game against Hearts at Celtic Park. It was inevitable, given the trouble that he had caused and was continuing to cause, but nevertheless supporters were sorry to see him leave. The transfer and fee are described, cryptically and enigmatically, in *Rothman's Football Yearbook* thus: 'Forest sign Celtic's Dutch striker Pierre van

Hooijdonk for £3m rising to a possible club record £4.5m'. This meant, presumably, that Celtic would receive a cut of any future transfer deal. Van Hooijdonk, Cadete and di Canio had been dubbed the three amigos. With Van Hooijdonk's departure, we were left with the 'gruesome twosome'.

Paolo di Canio was undeniably world class, and possibly in terms of pure ability the best that Celtic have had for some time. Since his arrival from AC Milan in August, he had won the hearts of all fans, and particularly the ladies. His goals were frequently memorable and he had the happy knack of scoring them at crucial times: for example in a hard-fought match at Pittodrie on Boxing Day, it was Paolo who, late on, sprung the annoying Aberdeen off-side trap to produce the goods.

Some of his touches were sheer theatre, like the times he wore golden boots which he would sell for charitable purposes after the game. He charmed the tea ladies at Celtic Park with all the finesse of the traditional Italian Romeo. Like Tommy McInally, Charlie Tully and Jimmy Johnstone of bygone years, he was the cheeky chappie with whom the fans could identify. Had he stayed a little longer, he might indeed have been the propaganda counter blast to Paul Gascoigne. It was a shame that he was not as much of a team player as he could have been, for Celtic immortality beckoned.

He did develop a special love for Celtic, and if we can believe some of the things he said in his autobiography, he immediately embroiled himself, rather unwisely, in the Protestant–Catholic struggle in the city of Glasgow. He also claims that he was particularly attached to Tommy Burns who on at least one occasion managed to persuade di Canio not to walk out of the club. On another occasion he claimed to have developed with Burns an almost Pentecostal ability to understand someone else's language! Tommy spoke broad Glasgow much too fast for someone like Paolo with his, as yet, imperfect knowledge of English. But it didn't matter for di Canio understood him anyway!

His Achilles heel however was his disciplinary record. Quick to lose his temper and rather too ready to use his fists, Paolo did himself few favours in this respect. Later in England, he earned notoriety by being red carded when he pushed a referee over after disputing a decision, but he also on another occasion won the respect of everyone by refusing to score a goal when an opponent was injured. He was a curious mixture of petulance and chivalry. Is there something quintessentially Italian in all this?

Without doubt, Tommy Burns was also unfortunate in coming up against a Rangers team who knew how to win, particularly in the direct matches between the two. In Burns's three seasons, twelve league games, one League Cup tie and two Scottish Cup matches were played between the sides. Burns managed to win only three of these games, although luck was never with him. Andy Goram was without doubt the luckiest goalkeeper alive on more than one occasion and Andy's good luck was Tommy's bad luck. But championships are not won by luck.

In addition, Rangers did have one player of undeniable class. This was Brian Laudrup whose wing play was outstanding and whose behaviour on the field was so impeccable that he earned the reluctant admiration of Celtic fans. Yet the annoying thing was that the rest of the Rangers team were not all that good, as was evidenced by their poor record in Europe where, arguably, they were even worse than Celtic. But in Old Firm games, there could be little doubt that Rangers had the edge and the confidence that comes with having won so many games in the past.

There was also the undeniable fact that Rangers were a team which had been built up over the last nine seasons with a great deal more money spent on it than had been on Celtic. They were a team who played expecting to win, and usually did. It was of course like that in reverse when Jock Stein was manager of Celtic. The title-winning sides of 1973 and 1974, for example, were not necessarily great teams, but they had the victory ethos instilled into them.

It was indeed difficult not to feel the pain of Tommy Burns. A Celt through and through, a deeply religious man, a family man and someone who had been a great player in his time for the club, Burns was a man with whom the supporters could identify. Like Jimmy McGrory and Billy McNeill before him, he had failed at Celtic Park as a manager . . . but no one could find anything bad to say about him. It was often said about McNeill that he was 'too much of a supporter to be a manager'. Perhaps this was also true of Tommy Burns.

On Sunday 4 May Celtic played a league game at Easter Road against Hibs. It was a television game, and ironically Celtic played well and won 3–1. After the match Paolo di Canio gave an interview in which he lamented the loss of his friend Tommy Burns and hinted that Celtic might not see too much more of his good self either. It was typical di Canio. Unaware that he himself was at least partly responsible for the fall of Burns, Paolo exemplified the anguish of Celtic in these days. Loads of potential and ability, but unable to deliver at the crucial moments, Paolo could easily have been one of the greatest Celts of all time, on a par with Kenny Dalglish, Henrik Larsson and even Patsy Gallacher, but he would sadly soon be on his way.

The pain continued to be intense but perhaps it all came home to Celtic fans on 24 May, the day of the Scottish Cup final. This year's big event was contested by Falkirk and Kilmarnock. All the clichés about 'family finals' that had last been used in 1991 when Dundee United and Motherwell contested the final, were trotted out, and 'How nice it was to see two teams like. . . .' Such statements are of course deeply offensive to Celtic (and Rangers) supporters, implying that the Old Firm supporters have no families, but there was an added poignancy to this occasion if you were a Celtic fan.

One could of course head off to a golf course or a cricket field, take the family shopping, or do something else altogether. Or one could sit and watch the game on the box. In all truth, it was honest, wholesome entertainment won 1–0 by Kilmarnock, but it was difficult to cope with the ghosts of Celtic past who kept intruding, as they always do on Cup Final day, unbidden, but not unwelcome: McAvennie, McGarvey, Aitken, McGrain, Dalglish, Lennox, Murdoch, Auld, McNeill, McGrory, Gallacher and Quinn . . . and other heroes of bygone days. Sounds of sobbing could be heard now and again from behind the couch. These were undeniably the shades of Celtic of long ago. When would they ever rise again?

Yet there was humour as well; grim, black, gallows, yet defiant humour. T-shirts often appear on supporters' bodies to indicate the mood of the moment. On this occasion, I saw in Glasgow that summer a supporter wearing a T-shirt with the lettering 'Nine-In-A-Row? What's all the fuss? We did it first 1966–74!' Hope would as always spring eternal, and the first task for the directors was to find a new manager.

5

1997/98:
'That nightmare phrase, ten-in-a-row'

The end of the 1996/97 season had seen Celtic supporters in a sombre and puzzled mood. Sombre because Rangers had now equalled the nine-in-a-row run of league titles from 1966–1974, and puzzled because there seemed to be a general lack of direction at Celtic Park. The previous summer of 1996 had seen Celtic buoyant in spite of their failure to win anything and reasonably confident that life could be turned round soon under Tommy Burns. But 1997, with its grievous loss against Falkirk in the Scottish Cup semi final, had brought a real and lasting depression. Burns of course had to go.

In the middle of June came the surprise announcement that Jock Brown had been appointed general manager. This was a surprise for several reasons, not least because it came, as it were, out of the blue. In the first place, we were not really sure what general manager meant. It was along the lines of what Terry Cassidy did for the old board – an unhappy precedent if there ever was one – namely a role as front man for the administrative side of the club. Gradually Brown's function would become clearer. Using his legal background, Jock would negotiate contracts and deal with the day-to-day business of the club, but would play no part in team selection or tactics.

This seemed to many to be a positive move, and we were encouraged by the news that former manager and playing legend Davie Hay would be Jock's assistant. Jock Brown was a well-known character in the game, having been a commentator with both Scottish Television and BBC Radio and Television. Less happily, he had been seen at the side of players when contracts were being thrashed out, something akin to the role of the dreaded agent. But he had certainly been a good commentator, enthusiastic and knowledgeable. Initially it seemed to be a good appointment, albeit that he had no obvious Celtic pedigree.

This last point needs to be examined. He would indeed become very unpopular and that unfortunate phrase 'not Celtic minded' would be applied to him. But, this was not heard at the outset and indeed only became an issue when it became clear that he and Wim Jansen did not get on. But Wim Jansen still lay in the future and, for now, Jock Brown's appointment was a popular one. His early interviews on radio and television were impressive and he seemed to be dignified and professional, conscious of the difficulties that lay ahead in the rebuilding of Celtic, but determined to make an impact.

The phrase 'not Celtic minded' needs to be analysed. It can be roughly translated as 'not being a Roman Catholic', and Jock Brown was certainly not of the Roman persuasion. In fact, he came (like another Jock of many years before, one Jock Stein) from a Protestant background in Lanarkshire and his family had Church of Scotland connections. In addition to that, it emerged (years later, in a bizarre tabloid revelation) that Jock's brother Craig, who was then manager of Scotland, left messages on the answering machine of a female friend in Kirkcaldy, interspersed with Rangers songs like 'Hello, Hello, We are the Billy Boys'.

Jock Brown insisted that his favourite team was Hamilton Academicals (until, that is, he started to work for Celtic) but that now he had a job to do. Certainly he seldom appeared dressed in anything other than a green blazer and tie, and for the rest of the summer enjoyed a very high profile indeed, endearing himself to the fans by his constant appearances on television and by his general affability and good nature.

But he did from an early stage antagonise the media. Journalists, always jealous of one of their own who has done better than they have, lost no opportunity to do him down, even in circumstances in which no blame could reasonably been laid at his door. It was, of course, the media that stirred up the Celtic-minded nonsense. Any antipathy towards Brown did not originate from the fans. Celtic supporters have proved time and time again that they will accept anyone no matter their background – otherwise there would have been no Jock Stein, no Kenny Dalglish and no Danny McGrain, to name three from the recent past – unless and until things go wrong and the media step in to aggravate the situation.

In early July 1997, 53-year-old Wim Jansen was paraded as the coach/manager. Only the 'anoraks' among us knew much about him, although we older ones might have recalled that dreadful night in May 1970 when Feyenoord, with Jansen on board, beat Celtic in the European Cup final. He had also been a member of the Dutch World Cup squads of 1974 and 1978, and played in the final on both occasions although both games were lost to the host nations, West Germany and Argentina. Wim, who sported a shock of curly hair, had solid coaching credentials gained in places such as Belgium, Holland and Saudi Arabia, although in a reference to his career in Japan the phrase 'the second worst thing to hit Hiroshima' revealed the depths to which the gutter press were prepared to sink in terms of taste to get a cheap jibe at Jansen and Celtic's expense.

Jock Brown made a major mistake by misleading the media when he let it be known that Jansen had been Celtic's only target. This was barely credible, although one also had to discount most of the unlikely candidates peddled by the press. Jock would have been better to keep his counsel on this one. As to who the others were we can but speculate, but the usual suspects – Bobby Robson and Guus Hiddink – were mentioned. And one of Scotland's quality newspapers carried an 'exclusive' that the new Celtic coach was going to be an obscure Portuguese fellow called Artur Jorge. This may have even been a piece of disinformation from a Celtic source to discredit the press. If that were so, the press would certainly have their revenge.

Jock and Wim had two major and immediate problems to deal with: Jorge Cadete and Paolo di Canio. Cadete may have been suffering from some kind of mental illness, whereas di Canio only gave the impression that he was. Neither seemed willing to return to Scotland for the start the new season. It was reminiscent of the *Iliad* of Homer when the great hero Achilles has fallen out with his leader Agamemnon and refuses to fight for the Greek army, preferring to sulk in his tent instead. Celtic's problem was that there were two of them, both fine players and worth bothering about.

Brown went to Portugal to see Cadete in an attempt to persuade him to return – a mission that was never likely to succeed, given that some sort of mental paralysis seemed to have taken over Jorge and his lady friend. When Jorge and Jock met, the good lady apparently stayed in an ante-room, eavesdropped on the conversation and now and again shouted advice to Jorge, the main thrust of it being that she did not want to go back to that wild northern country called Scotland. By February 2003 when Cadete returned to Celtic Park to draw the half-time lottery in a game against Livingston, this lady seemed to have been deposed and replaced by another. It was no coincidence that he seemed to be now more pro-Celtic, even to the extent of wishing an unlikely resurrection of his career in green and white, and appearing repeatedly in the media to tell all Portugal and all Scotland how much he loved the Celtic!

In the circumstances of 1997, however, Jorge was always going to be a dead loss. The irony was rich after the struggle that Celtic had had to persuade the authorities to allow him to make his debut in 1996. In later years of course Jorge would tell us that he had to pay his own transfer fee, that he signed for Celtic for a wage of less than £20,000 a month (oh dear!), that McCann welshed on a verbal promise to pay him more and that he now had a pet canary called Fergus. It was a relief when the club received £3 million for him when he was transferred to Celta Vigo.

Di Canio behaved in a similar manner. He threw tantrums, refused to turn up for a pre-season tour of Holland, mourned obsessively for the departure of Tommy Burns and at the same time told the world how much he loved Celtic and the fans. Paolo of course claims in his autobiography that the *casus belli* was a verbal promise made by Fergus McCann during the previous close season that his contract would be renegotiated in the summer of 1997. If this were the case, then di Canio, with all his worldly wisdom, ought to have insisted that a clause to this effect should have been written into his contract, instead of relying on a vague statement from a man who he said spoke to him no more than three times in the intervening year. Perhaps the real cause of di Canio's unhappiness was that he felt he was the best player at Celtic Park and should be rewarded accordingly.

It has to be said that Jock Brown handled this one badly, even if di Canio's account of browbeating and bullying should be taken with a pinch of salt. Repeatedly Brown said that di Canio would not be sold, even on the day before the actual sale. When Celtic persuaded Sheffield Wednesday to pay £4.5 million for Paolo on 6 August 1997, Jock argued that it was a trade and not a sale because Regi Blinker was coming in part exchange. Such specious nonsense fooled nobody, but be that as it may, there was no Paolo di Canio at Celtic Park.

But there was a Darren Jackson. Jackson was one of the characters of Scottish football, having made his name with Dundee United and Hibs. A sum of £1.25 million was paid to Hibs for his signature. He was like Gordon Strachan of the previous decade in that he was almost universally detested by supporters of other teams. This was not necessarily a bad thing, and although some people were not happy about the move, most Celtic supporters welcomed him as an honest and determined professional, if perhaps a little past his best.

More enthusiasm was engendered by the arrival of Craig Burley from Chelsea for £2.5 million. Craig was Scottish and had a good reputation, and was unhappy with Chelsea for dropping him from the 1997 FA Cup final team that beat Middlesbrough. We knew that Burley would fit in at Celtic Park, because his attitude was right from day one. There was also a low-key signing from Feyenoord for the modest sum of £650,000; a character with his hair in dread-locks by the name of Henrik Larsson. He was obviously well known to Wim Jansen, who had managed him briefly at Feyenoord in 1993, but at this stage he was simply a stranger with a funny hairstyle to most of the fans. A Swede, apparently. And a Frenchman called Stephane Mahe, a left back, signed from Rennes for £500,000.

Murdo MacLeod was to be Jansen's assistant, having originally been appointed reserve-team coach. This was an excellent choice for MacLeod was very popular with the fans after his glorious playing career in the 1980s, although his background was, like Brown's and Jansen's, other than 'Celtic minded'. It was even rumoured that he had begun his football career with the Boys Brigade! But Murdo had the ability to get on with Jansen and, with his extensive background of playing, coaching and commentating in Scotland, would pass on his invaluable local knowledge.

The season started calmly enough with a trip to Cardiff to meet Inter Cable-Tel in a qualifying round of the UEFA Cup. The game was played at Ninian Park, the home of Cardiff City and as that was the ground where Jock Stein had met with his fatal heart attack in 1985, an impressively dignified minute's silence was held for the man who still meant so much to the club. No sign of any future squall was apparent as supporters saw Wim Jansen and Jock Brown sitting together on the team bus, chatting amicably and waving to the fans. The team beat the Welsh part timers very comfortably and completed the job at Celtic Park a week later.

The first game of the domestic season was at Easter Road on Sunday 3 August. It was a live television game with a lunchtime kick off, and Celtic elected to start the new season by playing poorly. Hibs scored first. Malky Mackay equalised, then Celtic decided to bring on a substitute, one Henrik Larsson. Television cameras zoomed in on this figure with the dreadlocks, and the Rangers fans watching in the pub all jeered at this apparent effeminate who did have, it must be admitted, with that hairstyle the look of a fairly attractive female from the neck upwards.

Almost immediately, the luckless Larsson gave the ball away to Chic Charnley. Chic had once played for Partick Thistle (he would do so again after his sojourn at Hibs) on a Saturday while blatantly supporting Celtic on a Sunday and other days of the week. Charnley, who would have given his eye teeth to play for Celtic, immediately showed us what we had been missing by scoring a great goal from the Larsson mistake. Celtic were now 2–1 down, and with so many in the team unfamiliar with their colleagues, found it hard to string passes together and Hibs finished this game well on top. The season was not off to a good start. The following day Rangers beat Hearts, and Celtic were already three points adrift. That nightmare phrase, ten-in-a-row, began to raise its ugly head.

So who was this strange-looking chap called Larsson whom Jansen had signed? He was the son of a Swedish mother and a merchant-sailor father from the Cape Verde islands off Senegal. He had been brought up in Sweden, suffering racist taunts for his mixed origins in that supposedly tolerant paradise but had silenced his tormentors by his ability to play football. He played for two teams with similar names – Hogaborgs and Helsingborgs – then moved to Feyenoord where after a good start, his career faltered under manager Arie Haan. Wim Jansen had been his first manager at Feyenoord and clearly thought he could do a job in Scottish football.

For Celtic, things deteriorated the following week when Dunfermline Athletic pulled off a rare victory at Celtic Park, in spite of Celtic having been a goal ahead at half time. Alarmist words like crisis were already being aired, but then McDiarmid Park, Perth became axiomatic to the proceedings. Celtic went there in the League Cup in midweek, played absolutely dreadfully and were indebted to a highly dubious extra-time penalty (which Simon Donnelly converted) as hands were wrung and teeth were gnashed at such an insipid performance. All sorts of ex-players and experts were now wheeled in to television studios to explain the problem with Celtic. But then, the skies cleared as quickly as they had darkened when Celtic returned to St Johnstone on league business the following Saturday and, with the aid of a brilliant Larsson diving header, registered a fine 2–0 victory. Perhaps, there was something in that Swede with the dreadlocks after all!

This was in fine time for the club's European campaign (the second leg of the second qualifying round of the UEFA Cup) against Tirol the following Wednesday. Celtic were 2–1 down from the first leg, but in a terrific return match at Celtic Park, forged ahead, then allowed Tirol to catch up, then scored two late crucial goals to give themselves a 6–3 victory on the night, 7–5 on aggregate. The game had resembled a game of basketball where a goal seems to be scored every five minutes, and the defending was deplorable, but Celtic were through. Their reward (and it was quite a reward in terms of media interest) was a tie against Liverpool.

This was put on the back burner, however, until after the game against Rangers that was due to be played on the night of Monday 2 September. It wasn't played that night because of the accident involving Princess Diana in Paris on the night of Saturday 31 August. This event seemed to plunge the country (or at least the southern half of it) into disproportionate and hysterical grief. The supine, sycophantic Scottish authorities were emotionally bullied into postponing football matches and this included the Old Firm clash. Even a Scotland international game the following weekend was delayed from Saturday to Sunday because players like Ally McCoist made the faintly ludicrous statement that they were uneasy about playing on the day of the funeral.

It was probably just as well for public relations that the Old Firm game was postponed, however much we deplored the pathetic caving in of authorities to such bogus moral blackmail. It would have been difficult to see the Celtic supporters respecting a minute's silence in front of television cameras with the Rangers fans there to bait them. In any case, few Celtic supporters could be expected to share the apparently all-engulfing grief for the good lady. The suggestion that she had been assassinated by the British Secret Service was one that was not categorically dismissed out of hand and, all in all, it was perhaps better that the game wasn't played until November.

Celtic's next two games were thus both against Motherwell – one in the League Cup at Celtic Park and the other at Fir Park in the league. The League Cup tie was unimpressive, but a good Larsson goal was enough to see Celtic through, and led to a semi final tie against Dunfermline in the League Cup. Celtic had been given an additional boost when Dundee United earned everyone's gratitude by putting Rangers out the previous night.

The Saturday league game at Fir Park was frankly a shocker. Celtic deserved much credit for rising above the fouling and vicious tackles from a Motherwell side once synonymous with good football. Less impressive was Celtic's defending. It was Marc Rieper's debut (this Denmark international with nearly fifty caps had recently been signed from West Ham United for £5 million) and he was clearly struggling to adapt to the Scottish game. Alan Stubbs, alongside him, had a similarly unhappy time and Motherwell's two goals were eminently preventable. Celtic, however, with two goals from Burley and one from Donnelly won the day.

There followed the games against Liverpool. They naturally generated a great deal of emotion and hype as supporters recalled the European Cup Winners Cup semi final of 1966 between the two clubs. Celtic should really have won that tie in 1966, but in the second leg at Anfield the linesman could not believe the speed of Bobby Lennox and made the decision that a perfectly legitimate goal was, in fact, offside. The media discussed endlessly the passionate nature of the two groups of supporters, both of whom sang 'You'll Never Walk Alone' with such relish. Indeed the pre-match singing before the Celtic Park game was arguably the most awe-inspiring sight at the ground for many years, certainly since the stadium had been revamped.

Before the two games, the feeling had been expressed that Celtic did not have much hope. In retrospect, it does seem that the games came too early for this new and fast-developing Celtic team. The difference was not in ability, nor class, but in confidence. This was shown twice during the first leg at Celtic Park on 16 September when Celtic started off in awe of the Liverpool players and allowed young Michael Owen (who would later confess in his weaker moments that he was a Celtic supporter) to take the lead. Gradually Celtic's confidence grew, and McNamara equalised with a tremendous strike and then Simon Donnelly converted a penalty. This should have sealed a famous victory, but Celtic in the most heartbreaking of circumstances lost a late goal when the whole team seemed to be afraid of Steve McManaman and allowed him to run through and make the final result 2–2 without even having to avoid a tackle.

At Anfield two weeks later one goal would have sufficed for Celtic. But it was not to be. It was a physical game which finished goalless, allowing Liverpool to go through on away goals, but the consensus of opinion was that Celtic deserved better. Indeed Celtic had the better chances against an unadventurous Liverpool team. In the first half a lob from Simon Donnelly went agonisingly wide, and then with time running out Henrik Larsson was inches away from getting a touch on a hard-driven cross. Celtic were out of Europe at the end of September. There was nothing unusual about this, but this year there was the definite belief that they were developing into a good team, a fact acknowledged by English journalists. The Liverpool games had indeed come too early for Celtic.

One is normally very suspicious about statements like 'an exit from Europe allows more time to concentrate on the domestic tournaments'. It sounds as if a club is making the best of a bad job. In fact this time it was true. Building a side, particularly after the frantic circumstances of the summer and the demands immediately thrust on the new manager, does take time and slowly, gradually, Celtic began to develop into an outfit that had to be taken seriously.

Before the Liverpool games, Celtic had beaten Aberdeen and Dundee United. Aberdeen were in the middle of that phase in their history when they were Celtic's 'rabbits' and could do nothing against green-and-white jerseys. (Yet the previous week the same Dons had fought back well to earn a draw against Rangers at Ibrox.) This particular day against Aberdeen at Celtic Park, Larsson began to show how good he really was – if we hadn't suspected that already – by scoring two fine goals, one of them a devastating free kick. The following week at Tannadice, Celtic's two first half goals from Donnelly and O'Donnell were too good for a hard-working United side that pulled one back but never really looked like adding to their total.

The month of October saw three good league victories over Kilmarnock, Hearts and St Johnstone with consistent performances from Burley and Larsson in particular, and if that weren't enough to be going on with, they also qualified for the final of the League Cup. The lily was gilded when Scotland's international team (beating Latvia at Celtic Park with several Celtic players on board) qualified for the 1998 World Cup finals. The euphoric feeling now grew that this could be Celtic's season, a feeling that began to gain ground even at Ibrox when Rangers lost – for the second time that season – to Dundee United at Tannadice on 25 October.

Celtic's hardest game during this part of the season was actually against Hearts. The Tynecastle men were in cracking form and the possibility of it being they, rather than Celtic, who would end the run by Rangers was not discounted until very late in the league campaign. Indeed quite a few Celtic fans, shamefully, would confess to close personal friends in moments of weakness that they would settle for just such a scenario. On this autumn day at Tynecastle, however, Celtic rose to the challenge and in a game eerily reminiscent of that played at Tannadice a few weeks earlier, scored two goals without reply, then after Hearts pulled one back, were able to ride out the storm in a manner that gave their supporters few qualms.

That game was on 18 October and Celtic fans were already on a high because, on the previous Tuesday, a Craig Burley goal had been enough to see off Dunfermline and put Celtic into the final of the League Cup. The goal was masterly in its execution and owed a great deal to Henrik Larsson. A cross from the right found the Swede in the penalty area. A less intelligent man might have turned and blasted the ball over the bar, but with four defenders closing on him, he tapped the ball back to Craig Burley who hammered it home. The Pars had one chance late on when Jonathan Gould saved from Hamish French, but it was Celtic who were into the final to play Dundee United on 30 November.

Thus October ended with Celtic just ahead at the top of the league and Wim Jansen deservedly winning the manager-of-the-month award. November would bring a few disappointments, but at the end of it, Celtic would confirm themselves not only as potential champions, but also have something tangible to mark their undoubted resurgence.

November did indeed have its moments. Two things happened off the field. One was the arrival of Paul Lambert from Borussia Dortmund for £2 million, quite clearly one of Celtic's best-ever signings. For some considerable time before and after this move, the tabloids tried to stir things up with hints about Brown and Lambert not getting on, and saying that Brown did not think much of Lambert's ability, but if this were true, there was no evidence to back it up.

The other, less happy, development was the departure of David Hay from the backroom staff after a public and hardly subtle dispute with Jock Brown. Hay might well have said that he wanted more money, but the underlying cause did seem to be a personality clash. This was a shame because they had cooperated effectively to arrange contracts for the likes of Henrik Larsson, and their good work was beginning to bear fruit on the park. It was generally felt that both Brown and Hay might have tried a little harder for each other or waited a little longer, but it may also have been something deeper than that going back to the days when Brown was a commentator and Hay was a manager. However the departure of Hay annoyed Jansen and MacLeod and further isolated Brown. Such things do not matter so much, in the eyes of the fans, so long as the team is doing well. November, as we have said, brought a mixture of good and bad, but as the month went on, the good began very definitely to outweigh the bad.

After a comparatively easy 2–0 win over Dunfermline on 1 November, Celtic went to Ibrox to meet Rangers, played badly and lost 1–0. A couple of days before this, a story had leaked to the press about a training ground bust up in which Tosh McKinlay had allegedly head-butted Henrik Larsson. There is of course nothing necessarily unusual or even anything sinister about such training-ground spats. In 1957, before the famous 7–1 League Cup final win over Rangers, Tully and Evans had come to blows and then gone on to play the game of their lives. But this may not even have been a fight. In fairness to McKinlay it has to be acknowledged that he was under a great deal of pressure as his position in the Celtic team was less than secure, and more often than not he was consigned to the substitutes' bench.

Tosh had never played the game anything less than enthusiastically for all the teams whose colours he had graced: Dundee, Hearts and Celtic. He had deserved the plaudits for his part in the 1995 Scottish Cup win, and had looked particularly good in the 1995/96 season. But sadly he was now being blamed for the poor start to the season and had lost his place to the temperamental Frenchman Stephane Mahe, although ironically he was still in the Scotland squad, if not necessarily in the starting eleven. This hardly excuses what he did to the player who was now being looked to more and more as the man on whom Celtic depended. The matter was eventually smoothed over and McKinlay's action was apparently forgiven by Larsson, but Tosh's Celtic Park career never got back on the rails after this. Rangers fans sang his praises:

> Oh Tosh McKinlay,
> Tosh, Tosh, Tosh McKinlay
> He put the heid
> Upon the Swede,
> Oh Tosh McKinlay

The game at Ibrox that saw the sending off of Stephane Mahe as well as a defeat was bad enough, but worse was to follow the following week when Celtic lost at home to Motherwell. This time it was Regi Blinker who shot himself and rest of the team in the foot. His contribution to the cause at Ibrox the previous week had been absolutely negligible and here he was ordered off in the first half for needlessly using the elbow on an opponent! This was crazy, sad stuff and it seemed that all the good work at the start of the season would be blown away.

Things looked grim in the following midweek when Rangers came to Celtic Park to play the game postponed because of Princess Diana's death. In a remarkable encounter, with numerous yellow cards dished out, Rangers went a goal up. It was scored by Marco Negri very soon after Paul Gascoigne had been sent off. Ironically, Gascoigne's red card, however overdue it was in terms of previous encounters, seemed a little harsh, but Rangers had scored immediately and clearly held the upper hand. Celtic tried everything they knew to get back into the game, and desperation was beginning to replace what little skill there had been in the first place. A goal simply would not come, and it appeared very much as if the players had given up, returning to the previous mindset that Celtic are not allowed to win Old Firm encounters. Then, just on full time, a Jackie McNamara cross found the head of Alan Stubbs to set Celtic Park ablaze.

'So there's a God after all' someone said, and from then on for some considerable time, Celtic seldom looked back. Dundee United were despatched at Celtic Park in the league the next Saturday. Then on Sunday 30 November at Ibrox Stadium against the same Dundee United in the League Cup final, Celtic regained silver and a belief in themselves. The teams were:

Celtic: Gould, Boyd, Mahe, McNamara, Rieper, Stubbs, Larsson, Burley, Thom, Wieghorst, Blinker. Substitutes: Donnelly, Annoni, Lambert.

Dundee United: Dijkstra, Skoldmark, Malpas, Pressley, Perry, Pedersen, Olofsson, Zetterlund, Winters, Easton, Bowman. Substitutes: McSwegan, Dolan, Andersson.

It was, quite simply, the best football that Celtic had played for a very long time. Goals came from Rieper and Larsson before half time, then Burley scored in the second period to kill off what little chance there was of a United revival. But what really thrilled the fans was the superb play of the likes of Morten Wieghorst and Regi Blinker, the latter clearly out to atone for his recent disappointments and disgrace. A nice touch was shown at the end when the three substitutes – Donnelly, Annoni and the recently signed Lambert – were all brought on to share the triumph. It was, all in all, like the good old days.

It almost beggars believe that, on 30 November 1997, this was only the second piece of silverware that Celtic had won in the 1990s! But there was certainly a spring in the step of everyone connected with the club for some time after that. It had given the players confidence that they could win other competitions and had cheered up the supporters. Even if (perish the thought!) Rangers did win ten-in-a-row, there would be something to savour.

Thus were the dark pre-Christmas days enlightened by the thought of the green-and-white ribbons on that handsome (although occasionally diminished and despised) League Cup trophy. But sterner and more onerous tasks lay ahead. The next game was a trip to Kilmarnock. The supporters were on a high and songs of triumph reverberated around Rugby Park that cold day of 6 December with even the Kilmarnock stands quite blatantly displaying the green banners of the infiltrators. But the whole thing was a massive disappointment, and the game ended goalless with Celtic clearly unable to fulfil the expectations of their followers. It was the sort of thing that had happened all too often in the past few seasons, when a success had not been consolidated, and an advantage had been thrown away.

No excuses were possible about injuries, and the team had lost ground to Hearts and Rangers in the league. An opportunity was immediately given to the players to redeem themselves on the distant fields of Pittodrie the following Wednesday night. Aberdeen supporters are frequently amazed at the number of Celtic fans who seem able to travel to their city. Here on a Wednesday night in December, the Celtic fans simply took over the place.

There was an added attraction in the reappearance in the starting line up of Darren Jackson, following a life-threatening operation and treatment for hydrocephalus, a serious brain illness. Darren had appeared on the substitutes' bench on a couple of occasions, but this was his first start since his illness. He celebrated with a stunning goal, in which he rounded the goalkeeper to put Celtic two up after Larsson had opened the scoring. Jackson's illness had won the supporters' sympathy and his fine performance at Pittodrie guaranteed that whatever he had done in the past, he was now very much a Celt and welcomed as such.

In truth it was a poor Aberdeen side, but any away victory is welcome, especially, one feels, at Pittodrie where the home side do often raise their game. The following day, Celtic's new signing, Harald Brattbakk, arrived from Rosenborg (now that Rosenborg were out of the Champions League). His scholarly, clerical appearance belied the fact that he was a proven goalscorer in Norway, and he was to be blooded in the Saturday game against the strong-going Hearts, then at the top of the league. Indeed the Tynecastle men earned the plaudits of many in the press, understandably delighted that a team outwith the Old Firm might take the title. Questions were asked however about their staying power. Would they still be there at the end? Certainly the Hearts support were there in strength that day but must have felt very disappointed at their team's negative strategy of defending in depth and hoping for a break. Harald Brattbakk was brought on as a substitute late in the game, but it was Burley who broke the deadlock, following some fine work from the now mightily impressive Henrik Larsson.

It was an excellent victory for Celtic and was followed the week before Christmas by a 5–0 thrashing of the other Edinburgh side. Hibs were totally outclassed and had caved in long before the end. But we were brought down to earth with a bump the following week against St Johnstone at McDiarmid Park. Crucially for this game, Larsson was injured and Celtic struggled. St Johnstone scored midway through the second half, and in spite of a late pounding of the Perth goal in the last few minutes, Celtic could not equalise.

Thus 1997 drew to a close. It had been a remarkable year for the club. The impression among the support was that Celtic were not quite there yet, although things had certainly moved in the right direction. The League Cup final had been a tremendously rewarding experience, the support had been lifted, Liverpool had almost been defeated, there was in the words of that dreadful cliché 'a buzz about the place'. But it remained to be seen whether Celtic could concentrate their resources and get the benefit of their new signings in time for the end of the season . . . and kill off the spectre of ten-in-a-row that haunted Christmas and New Year celebrations.

Rangers were of course the visitors on 2 January. The St Johnstone defeat meant that Rangers were now four points ahead of Celtic, with Hearts wedged in between. A Rangers win at Celtic Park would give them a seven-point cushion, something that might be difficult to deflate with less than half the fixtures remaining. In addition to this, Celtic had failed to beat Rangers in the last ten league games, and a failure to register a victory here would reinforce that old inferiority complex. A draw at the very least was imperative, and at half time this looked like the probable outcome in a game that was fast and furious, but short on skill and class. In the second half, however, Celtic gradually took command and Andy Goram was certainly the busier keeper. The stands and the millions watching on television at home and in the pubs began to feel that we had been here before many times, and that Goram would save Rangers again.

Not this time, though. In a breathtaking all-Scottish move, Lambert found McNamara who sent a defence-splitting backward pass through to Burley to angle the ball home. This was in the sixty-sixth minute, and twenty heart-stopping minutes later, Paul Lambert showed how right Celtic had been to spend money on him by thundering home a shot from twenty-five yards. This had followed a prolonged spell of Celtic pressure, and the inability of Rangers to clear their lines properly. Celtic Park and those looking on in pubs and clubs erupted at such brilliance while Rangers supporters quietly evacuated both places in a tacit admission that their team had lost on the day to a better side.

Lambert was of course an established Scotland internationalist and the winner of a European Cup medal with Borussia Dortmund in 1997. He had arrived in Dortmund via St Mirren and Motherwell, and his return to Scotland was more to do with genuine homesickness and a desire to play in his native country than any offloading of him by the European champions. His last game for the German giants was a very emotional occasion and the fans demonstrated their genuine affection for him. He had been a success wherever he played. And he seemed to be beginning the right way with Celtic.

The victory over Rangers reduced the gap at the top to a single point but Celtic then proceeded to infuriate their fans by playing dreadfully to draw at Motherwell in the next game. Jackson missed a penalty, which could have won the game, but Darren's miss was sadly in tune with the rest of this inept performance. It was not dissimilar to the game at Kilmarnock after the League Cup final. Celtic now had shown that they could raise their game to win crunch matches, but what did not seem to be getting through was the realisation that all games are important ones in the quest for the title.

The next game was against Dundee United at Tannadice, but it was postponed from Saturday 17 January until Tuesday 27 January. In the meantime, Celtic had advanced to the next round of the Scottish Cup thanks to a routine defeat of Greenock Morton, a club that had fallen on hard times and were soon to fall on worse. Dundee United would have cause to complain of bad luck against Celtic many times. On the occasion of this rescheduled match, United were arguably the better team, but as was the pattern many times in games between those clubs, United first went ahead, Celtic then equalised and then with time running out grabbed a late and arguably lucky winner. It did however show that Celtic had some kind of character.

January ended well for Celtic, who did not play on Saturday 31

January as their game against Aberdeen was moved for the benefit of television to Monday 2 February. But those who listened to the nail-biting commentary from McDiarmid Park discovered that a talented St Johnstone side could beat Rangers as well as Celtic. Celtic's competent victory over Aberdeen on the Monday, after the Dons had taken an early lead, put them level on points with both Rangers and Hearts at the top of the league.

Incredibly, after the weekend of 7–8 February, all three teams were still level. Rangers surprisingly could only draw with Dunfermline, a team they had thumped 7–0 on their previous trip to Ibrox, and then on the Sunday the whole nation saw Celtic throw away two points on live television. Hearts equaliser was undeserved and scored in added-on time that was over and above what was due, but the real culprit was Harald Brattbakk who was profligate of several opportunities, and one absolute howler in particular, to kill the game. This was at a time when Celtic were looking comfortable after Jackie McNamara had put them ahead just before half time.

But for the rest of February Celtic hit top gear and gained a supremacy over their two rivals. There was first of all a narrow but decisive Scottish Cup win over Dunfermline at East End Park, and then two Celtic Park thrashings of Kilmarnock and Dunfermline before a tight victory over Hibs at Easter Road. The Kilmarnock game was remarkable. Not only was another section of the stadium now open (the south-west corner) but also Harald Brattbakk as if to say sorry for his shocker at Tynecastle scored all four in the 4–0 victory – but it could easily have been eight! Twice he hit the post and, on at least two other occasions, he missed tolerably acceptable chances.

By the time that Celtic edged it over Hibs at Easter Road at the end of February, the other challengers had lost ground. Rangers first dropped two points against Kilmarnock the Tuesday night after Celtic beat Killie 4–0. Then Rangers and Hearts faced each other, and the resultant draw was perfect for Celtic. February thus finished with Celtic two points ahead of Hearts and four ahead of Rangers.

Nine games remained, and the smart money was now on Celtic. The Scottish Cup intervened the following weekend (all three title challengers won, Rangers luckily in a replay against Dundee) but then the weekend after that, Celtic seemed to be making great strides towards the championship. On the Saturday, Hearts drew and Rangers lost. The Sunday saw Celtic yet again on television, where they were almost constantly that season, and at half time were well on top of a mediocre Dundee United.

The Achilles heel however reappeared as they were only one goal ahead. It was a fine goal scored by Simon Donnelly, who was having a good season, and there should have been more. How often had we said that this season and indeed throughout the 1990s? Unbelievably, Celtic came out in the second half, lost the plot, allowed Dundee United to take the initiative and conceded a goal. This gave the Taysiders a draw, and Hearts and Rangers the chance to hang on in the race for the title.

On 21 March, all three teams won by the odd goal, Celtic doing well to take three points at Pittodrie, but the 28 March encounter between Celtic and Hearts at Celtic Park meant that, yet again, something had to give. This was a poor game and neither team frankly deserved anything other than the 0–0 scoreline, which very accurately reflected the standard of play. Meanwhile at East End Park, late Dunfermline pressure was not converted into an equaliser and Rangers gained two points over both Celtic and Hearts with a 3–2 victory.

With six games were left, Celtic were two points ahead of Hearts and three ahead of Rangers. It was still anybody's title, and at this point, two other factors entered the equation. One was the Scottish Cup. All three teams were in the Scottish Cup semi finals, Hearts to play Falkirk and the Old Firm to play each other at 'neutral' Celtic Park. Hampden's renovations were still ongoing and Celtic won the toss for the game to be played in the East End of Glasgow, although the main stand at Celtic Park was to be populated by Rangers supporters!

Celtic's progress to the Scottish Cup semi final had been impressive without ever being brilliant. Competent wins over Morton, then Dunfermline, preceded the remarkable quarter final at Tannadice which included incidents like United's manager Tommy McLean being sent to the stand for arguing with a linesman after his own team had scored! This was the stuff of soap opera but nothing in comparison with Celtic's late winner, an own goal scored by Eric Pedersen after Harald Brattbakk had missed a Larsson cross. It transpired later that Eric's wife had had a baby that morning. Mother and baby were both doing well . . . but father less so.

The other factor was that, by this time, everyone knew that there was trouble behind the scenes at Celtic Park. It had been remarked upon that Jock Brown and Wim Jansen were nowadays seldom seen together, and when they were, looked ill at ease in each other's company. Speculation had been going on for some time. Indeed as early as 4 February Jock Brown – in his weekly 'Jock Talk' column in the *Celtic View* – had admitted that he and Wim were not the best of pals, but that he still thought Wim was the best man for the job and so backed him to the hilt. This had been in response to a few stories in the press where Jock's mischievous enemies were capitalising on the alleged rift.

Now, in March, Wim Jansen acknowledged on a website that he and Jock Brown did not get on, and that he might be leaving at the end of the season. On television he admitted that there was a get-out clause in his contract, but he assured us he would be here until the end of the season at least. The newspapers seized on this and made the most of it. It was archetypal, primeval, predictable Celtic self-destruction at a time when the team simply did not need it. How far this was a piece of mischief making on the part of the press no one will ever know, but the two protagonists must surely be condemned for not patching things up for public consumption.

It is like this in a marriage, one feels. Not every marriage is made in heaven and anyone who says rubbish like 'fifty years and not a cross word' is of course a liar. The skill lies in controlling things and not involving a third party. Once a third party enters the scene, be it lover, mother or therapist, the marriage is doomed – and the children will suffer. In this case it was the Scottish press that was the third party, and the children were the players and fans of Celtic.

The version of the dispute that was put out for public consumption was that an impasse had been reached. Brown claimed that he asked Jansen for a plan for next season. Jansen said that before he could do that he would have to know how much money he would have to spend on new players. Brown's reply to that one, presumably, would have been along the lines of 'I can't tell you that, until I see your plans' and it could have gone on like that for some considerable time. In fact there was more to it than that. It was simply a power struggle, at a time when infighting was the last thing on earth that we, the fans, needed.

Before the semi finals of the Scottish Cup were played, Rangers, who made a good start to April, stole a march on the other two in the title race and beat a poor Hibs side 3–0 at Ibrox. They were thus level on points with Celtic although they had played a game more and had an inferior goal difference . . . but it did put pressure on the Celtic team.

In both semi finals, the real action happened late in the day. At Ibrox, Falkirk equalised against Hearts in the eighty-fifth minute, but then Hearts replied with two goals. The Old Firm semi was played the following day in a frenzied atmosphere, an atmosphere enhanced by the game being played at Celtic Park rather than at Hampden. The toss of the coin to determine whether the game would go ahead at Celtic Park or Ibrox was about all that Celtic won, for their display was a sore disappointment to the fans. Celtic had chances, failed to take them, Stubbs was injured and taken off and then Rangers scored in the seventy-fifth minute. This was a defining moment for Celtic . . . and on this occasion they failed to live up to the challenge. Rangers scored again, and although Burley grabbed a goal in injury time, the game had gone from Celtic.

An exit from the Scottish Cup is always painful for Celtic and their supporters, particularly if the opponents are Rangers. In this case there was no time for self-pity, for this year the league championship was even more vital. Celtic had to play their game in hand at Kilmarnock the following Wednesday. Hearts too were in action that night at Motherwell. Celtic's game was played in wet conditions, and it was one of the many games that season won by the sheer strength of character of the players and the enthusiasm of supporters rather than skill. Larsson and Donnelly both scored fine goals to Kilmarnock's one, and Celtic custodian Jonathan Gould had a great game at the other end as a spirited Killie side strove for an equaliser at the death. Hearts drew that night, so Celtic were now three points ahead of both Hearts and Rangers.

But the weekend of 11–12 April was derby time. Hearts went to relegation-threatened Hibs on the Saturday, and as is the way of the world and fixture quirks, Celtic found themselves facing Rangers for the second Sunday in a row. Hearts disappointed their fans by going down 2–1 to Hibs, but were given a lifeline, albeit a tenuous one, by the events at Ibrox the following day.

It was once again another profound disappointment for Celtic fans. Rangers had undoubtedly taken great confidence from their triumph in the Cup only seven days previously. In short, Rangers showed the world that they knew how to beat Celtic. Yellow cards were distributed liberally by Hugh Dallas, and Bjorklund of Rangers was very lucky to receive only a booking. There was little between the teams in terms of ability – if anything Celtic had more of the ball – but it was Thern and Albertz who scored the goals at crucial points, and in the league table, Rangers were now equal on points and marginally ahead on goal difference.

Thus with four games to go, excitement (if it hadn't done so long ago) reached fever pitch in Glasgow in a way that would be hard to parallel in all the long history of these two teams. There was now severe pressure on Celtic in one of the most crucial seasons in their 110-year history. Ten-in-a-row for Rangers would diminish the achievement of the great Jock Stein team of the sixties and seventies and Celtic fans felt that this must not be allowed to happen. Hearts were still in with an outside chance but, after their defeat by Hibs, needed both Celtic and Rangers to blow it.

Celtic had the easier run-in. They had three home games against Motherwell, Hibs and St Johnstone and an away trip to Dunfermline, whereas Rangers had to visit Aberdeen, Hearts and Dundee United and play Kilmarnock at home. Television companies grabbed two away games, one for each side: Celtic at Dunfermline and Rangers at Aberdeen. They would be played on a Sunday and quite a few people questioned the fairness of all this, in that it did give the team playing on the Sunday the advantage of knowing how the opposition had done. On the other hand, it could put a lot of pressure on them. And in any case, it didn't really matter whether you complained or not, as television money now ruled the roost.

Saturday 18 April tipped the balance slightly in Celtic's favour. Celtic chose to play well, competently dispatching Motherwell 4–1 with goals coming from Burley and Donnelly who scored two each, after Motherwell had taken an early lead. Rangers presumably had listened to the radio commentary of that game with some dismay. Sunday saw them at Pittodrie where an undercurrent of hatred towards the Ibrox team had existed for well over two decades.

Aberdeen's mediocre season would be much boosted if they could beat Rangers. In that task they were much helped by Amoruso who committed a violent indiscretion and was sent off. Stephen Glass scored for the Dons, and then Aberdeen treated their fans and the watching Celtic supporters on television to a display of football which in other circumstances would have been derided as negative, poor and the sort of thing which deters people from coming to football matches. It was possession stuff, but it worked, particularly after the premature departure of the distraught Lorenzo Amoruso. Seldom have Aberdeen been so popular with the Celtic fans, and after the 1–0 victory, the position now was that Celtic, with three games to go, were three points and three goals ahead.

But then the following weekend, the pendulum swung back slightly towards Rangers, not yet completely nor decisively, but significantly nevertheless. It was Glasgow versus Edinburgh. Hearts finally blew up by losing 3–0 to Rangers at Tynecastle. It was perhaps predictable but sad all the same that a provincial team like Hearts should hold their own against the big two for most of the season but then disappoint at the death. Under their shrewd manager, Jim Jefferies, they had proved that they could do it on occasion (they would win the Scottish Cup that year by beating Rangers in the final at Celtic Park) but the bottle and the psychological belief had been sadly missing at crucial times in the league. This was despite a crop of excellent players, many of whom – including Neil McCann, David Weir and Colin Cameron – would go on to greater things at bigger clubs.

Such philosophical ramblings about the condition of Scottish football were of little concern however to the 49,619 Celtic fans who endured a tantalising and frustrating afternoon at Celtic Park watching their favourites draw 0–0 with Hibs. True, there were one or two decisions that went against the home side, but a team challenging for the championship should be so far ahead of relegation candidates that standards of refereeing do not matter. Celtic, in truth, were feckless and nervous, bearing little resemblance to the team that had so competently disposed of Motherwell the week before.

Hibs in fact defended well, but Larsson and Donnelly both missed chances, and the players were not helped by the waves of self-doubt pouring out from the stands. Yet, Hibs did not score either (nor had they looked vaguely capable of doing so) and the game ended goalless. This draw, and Rangers's win in Edinburgh that day, meant that Celtic were only a point ahead of the Ibrox men with two games to go. Celtic's advantage in goal difference was also cancelled out in what was now a two-horse race and the closest two-horse race there had ever been.

For the next weekend of 2–3 May, Rangers were scheduled to play

Kilmarnock at Ibrox on Saturday while Celtic went to Dunfermline on the Sunday. Kilmarnock had already played a large part in the campaign of 1997/98 and would continue to do so. The Ibrox game was given a bizarre twist when it was announced that the referee was Bobby Tait, who had specially asked for this game as a retirement present, for he was a Rangers supporter and wished the last game of his career to be at his spiritual home! It was recalled that Tait had allowed Hearts an overgenerous amount of time to grab a late equaliser against Celtic in February, and the wisdom of the authorities was questioned . . . to say nothing of their probity!

It was one of life's supreme ironies that Tait (who refereed the game very fairly and honestly, it has to be said) allowed some minutes of injury time here as well, and that his final act as a referee at Ibrox was to point up the field to signal a goal for Kilmarnock! Ally Mitchell thus earned a place in Celtic's Hall of Fame along with Albert Kidd, who had finished off Hearts for Dundee in 1986. The game was nerve wracking to those listening on the radio, but with time wearing away, the score was 0–0.

Radio listening is the most heart-rending way of all to follow a game, and there are limits to how much one can take of the high tension involved. A walk in the garden or round the block with the dog was called for, timing it so that we arrived back at exactly the full-time whistle. The arrival at the house was followed by a grab for the television remote-control and the announcer talking about 'Remarkable events at Ibrox!' So, they had scored – I knew that Tait would give them more minutes – I had all my excuses ready before I realised that the goal had been scored not by Laudrup, nor Albertz nor McCoist but by someone called Ally Mitchell!

This meant that Celtic were still a point ahead and had two games left, whereas Rangers had only one. Celtic then could do it at Dunfermline the next day. In fact, Rangers seemed to be admitting that it had slipped away from them and that Celtic would be worthy winners. It certainly looked that way at half time on that warm day at East End Park with Celtic a goal ahead – a crisp strike from the excellent Simon Donnelly after some fine work by Henrik Larsson.

Celtic's fans were full of anticipation and Rangers fans presumably switched off their television in favour of some gardening or even talking to their wives. But as happened time and time again throughout the 1990s, Celtic could not finish the game off. The second half dragged on, but a second decisive goal would not come. Celtic were denied a clear penalty when Larsson was pulled down, a few other decisions went the wrong way and Celtic became more and more frustrated.

Well inside the last ten minutes, Craig Faulconbridge entered the fray as a Dunfermline substitute and earned his one and only moment of glory in an otherwise totally undistinguished career. The tiring, yet still confident Celtic team, impatient for the final whistle, conceded a free kick. A long ball came across the penalty area. The newly arrived Faulconbridge had perhaps a little more energy than others on that hot day, and he was a big lad. He rose and without connecting cleanly was able to head a looping ball that just beat Jonathan Gould. East End Park was silent apart from the token home support, most of whom in any case prefer Celtic to Rangers. The Pars had equalised, but there were still seven minutes left to play. Celtic threw everything at that Halbeath goal, but it would not happen for them. Full time came and many Celtic supporters collapsed head-in-hands as if they had been defeated.

The pessimism, though severe and widespread, was premature and unwarranted. Over the weekend, Celtic had in fact gained a point over Rangers. Celtic were now two points ahead. Very quickly, we worked out that with Celtic playing St Johnstone and Rangers going to Tannadice to play Dundee United, there were nine possible outcomes. A Celtic win finished the matter, as indeed did both teams drawing or losing. In addition a Celtic defeat would now not matter as long as Rangers only drew. What spelt disaster was a Celtic draw or defeat . . . and a Rangers win.

The week before the event was a long one with lifelong atheists admitting to prayers and promises to attend church every Sunday as long as. . . . The author recalls reading about the siege of Masada in AD 73 when the Jews threw themselves off their rock fortress rather than surrender to the Roman army. This must have been in his mind on the Thursday night when he vividly dreamed that Rangers were 4–0 up at Tannadice, and that St Johnstone had scored a late winner. The whole Celtic support on the upper tier immediately threw themselves down into the Janefield Cemetery rather than face the horrors of ten-in-a-row!

Rangers announced all sorts of plans involving helicopters to cover the miles between Glasgow and Tannadice in the event of their being successful, so that the trophy could be presented in front of their fans. It was of course a very good propaganda exercise for them. From Celtic Park came nothing other than the usual pre-match clichés and a nervous silence. Paul Sturrock, the likeable manager of St Johnstone, now happily recovered from what had appeared to be a heart attack was in the middle of all this. The one time Dundee United striker (and in the opinion of many Dundonians, the best player of all time at Tannadice) revealed that he had received all sorts of cranky letters from nutcases on both sides with abuse and the occasional threat.

Indeed, St Johnstone had played a significant part in this year's championship, having defeated both Celtic and Rangers. They were not to be despised, but neither were Dundee United, under the stern management of Tommy McLean with elder brother Jim in the background. The Brothers Grimm, as they were affectionately nicknamed.

The Celtic Park stands were jam packed with 49,701 inside and thousands outside begging for tickets. Many of the dispossessed offered hundreds of pounds for a brief, and employed emotional blackmail with pieces of cardboard telling everyone that they had come from Galway, Cornwall or Caithness to see this game. Eventually, the unsuccessful ones were compelled to listen to the roars of the crowd and the commentary on BBC Radio Scotland, without doubt an even more gut-wrenching scenario than actually being inside.

Celtic could not have got off to a better start against a St Johnstone side weakened by injuries and suspensions. Henrik Larsson scored a crisp goal from the edge of the box in the first minute, taking everyone by surprise. There were however another eighty-nine minutes to go, and no one needed reminding of the Celtic self-destruct mechanism which worked along the lines of failing to score another goal, then allowing the other team back into the game to equalise. This would have been deadly, especially as transistors informed us that Rangers were one ahead at Tannadice, then two . . . whereas Celtic were only one up over the Saints.

The excruciatingly painful second half crawled on, with supporters paying as much attention to the clock as they did to the actual game. We were somewhat assuaged by the news that a chap called Zetterlund had pulled one back for Dundee United, but that was still only 2–1 and we knew that one lapse of concentration, one goal from St Johnstone would kill all Celtic hopes and plunge us into the sort of Stygian melancholy that would be unimaginable in its ferocity, intensity and permanence.

But the Angel of Deliverance was at hand. The hard working Simon Donnelly was withdrawn and replaced by the scholarly looking Harald Brattbakk. Harald had been much reviled, and sometimes deservedly so, but today he would be forgiven. Only eighteen minutes remained when Jackie McNamara sent over a ball and Harald ran on and scored.

Words fail the historian as he describes the scenes at the final whistle, not only at the ground but also in living rooms in Scotland and all over the world. Contemporary accounts of Armistice Day in 1918 say that there was of course celebration and jollification, but a more common emotion was sheer relief that it was all over. Quick witted as ever, Celtic fans immediately chanted, 'Where's yir chopper noo', to the tune of 'Chirpy Chirpy Cheep Cheep' (by Scottish group Middle of The Road); this, of course, was designed to mock David Murray's plan immediately to fly the 'league winners' back to Ibrox from Dundee by helicopter for a celebration. The wilder elements in the Celtic support would party for days (there is the true story of a Fife teacher who did not reappear in his classroom before the Wednesday, and even then with a severe dose of what he termed the 'shakes') but the quieter ones were far more restrained. We thanked God and went to bed that night, able to experience the quiet and gentle drifting off to sleep that comes to a man who is content and happy. Never again would we have to listen to jibes that ended up with '. . . in a row'!

The war is over. The rebels have won! Dominic Keane, Fergus McCann and Brian Dempsey celebrate in March 1994 after ousting the old board.

Pierre van Hooijdonk with the Scottish Cup in May 1995, following his winning goal in the final against Airdrie.

A delighted Paul McStay lifts up the Scottish Cup in 1995.
In the background on the left is the Duchess of Kent,
who presented the trophy.

Peter Grant in action against Aberdeen at Pittodrie. Brian Irvine is the Aberdeen player and Tommy Burns looks on in the background.

Who's that with Tommy Burns and Fergus McCann? The 'Big Yin' shows his true colours.

Heard the one about the Italian, the Dutchman, the German and the Portuguese? Messrs di Canio, van Hooijdonk, Thom and Cadete celebrate a goal against Kilmarnock in August 1996.

December 1997. Fergus McCann, Wim Jansen and Jock Brown pose with the Scottish League Cup. Sadly relationships between all three men would not always be quite so amicable.

'He's the man'. Henrik Larsson tells everyone that it was Harald Brattbakk who scored the second and decisive goal in the game against St Johnstone, which clinched the Premier League in 1998.

Kenny Dalglish and John Barnes enjoy the winter sunshine in Portugal in January 2000. Disaster however was just round the corner . . .

8 February 2000, disaster looms as Barry Wilson scores the first goal for Inverness Caledonian Thistle.

19 March 2000. In the middle of the disaster and carnage that was 2000, Celtic managed to salvage the Scottish League Cup by beating Aberdeen 2–0. Tom Boyd looks happy and relieved.

A pensive looking Alan Stubbs.

22 September 2001. Bobo Balde and Robbie Winters of Aberdeen in an SPL clash at Celtic Park.

Martin O'Neill celebrating in typical style at Celtic Park in August 2000.

6 April 2002. Celtic have just received the SPL trophy after beating
Livingston 5-1, and Johan Mjallby is a happy man.

Two fans with a passable resemblance to Martin O'Neill and John Hartson
enjoying themselves in the heat of Seville.
Sadly the result was a disappointment.

1998/99: Paradise Lost

The Roman writer Tacitus notes that after the Roman invasion of Britain in the first century AD, 'Britain was conquered and immediately thrown away'. In a similar way, Celtic won the Premier League in 1998 and then immediately threw it all away. The league was clinched on 9 May, and the celebrations were long, loud and totally deserved, as traditional Celtic strongholds like Croy and Garngad resounded to the sounds of triumph that did not die away until well into Sunday and even later. All sorts of celebrations took place, and a feature, as always, was the amount of closet Celtic supporters who had been in hiding for the past nine years but who now felt able to re-emerge into the world.

On Monday 11 May, Wim Jansen, in a move that stunned many Celtic fans but came as no surprise to others, resigned. The reason was his ill-disguised inability to get on with Jock Brown. Supporters sided with Wim, and certainly the press spared no effort in their attempts to blacken the name of Jock Brown even more than they had done previously. Brown was vilified and accused of being either the enemy within or a Trojan horse. He was simply not 'Celtic-minded' they said, whatever that fatuous phrase might mean. But then again the Dutchman Wim Jansen could hardly be accused of being Celtic-minded either!

The Celtic party were in Lisbon (of all places, the scene of their greatest ever triumph in 1967) when Wim Jansen broke the news. They were there to play a friendly against Sporting Lisbon. How the players reacted is not known. It can hardly have been a surprise to them either, but it was at the very least disorientating to be the heroes of the hour on the Saturday, and then have their boss quit two days later! It was a situation almost without parallel, even in the frenzied world of football.

There are indeed two sides to every dispute. It does indeed, as the Scots proverb says 'Tak twa tae mak a fecht'. It remains appalling that neither of the two men, earning as they did huge salaries, seemed to make the slightest effort to get on for the sake of the club. In any walk of life, there will always be those with whom one would not wish to share a pint on a Saturday night. Nevertheless, sometimes one has to swallow one's spittle and get on with it and at the very least establish a *modus vivendi*. The sad thing was that although Jock apparently won this battle, in that he stayed while Wim didn't, he too was forced out only five months later after sustained pressure from fans and the media. This need not have happened if a greater effort had been made to get on with Jansen.

In addition to the personality clash, of course, there might have been another factor, namely that Jansen felt that he needed more money to buy players for an onslaught on Europe, now that Scotland had been conquered, and that Jock Brown as the front man for Fergus McCann was the man who had to say no, or at least not yet. If this was the case, then the episode hardly reflects credit on McCann, for this was surely no time to be parsimonious. The team had done well, but very nearly blew it towards the end of the season and clearly some strengthening was called for.

The supporters might have been appeased if a new man had appeared immediately. Murdo MacLeod apparently offered his services to Brown. This would have been an immensely popular choice. One or two photographs of Brown and MacLeod with their arms round each other with the league championship trophy and the League Cup in attendance would put things right. Murdo – a non-Catholic incidentally but no one ever said that he was not Celtic-minded – was an immensely popular figure with the support, and more importantly he was associated with success both as a player and an assistant manager. Sadly, it was not to be.

MacLeod had of course played a key part in last season's success. He had been a fine player for Celtic in the early 1980s, and had picked up a great deal of experience in his subsequent coaching and managerial career with Hibs, Dumbarton and Partick Thistle. There would be very few men who knew the Scottish scene better, and he had of course also played for a top German club, Borussia Dortmund.

A certain amount of grim, although scarcely disguised satisfaction, was still evident at Celtic Park the week after the winning of the league. To make life even better Hearts had beaten Rangers to lift the Cup thus ending the Tynecastle trophy hoodoo that had haunted the Jambos since the weekend of the Cuban Missile Crisis of 1962. The media were very impressed by the new Celtic Park, now three-quarters completed, and remarked on what a good job Celtic had done in hosting the Scottish Cup final.

Celtic's need to appoint a new manager was not exactly forgotten about, but was now buried under a great deal of hype surrounding the 1998 World Cup. This was an immensely successful affair in France (Scotland might have qualified for the later stages but for a disgraceful, yet archetypal, performance in the last group game against Morocco) but by the time that France lifted the trophy well past midsummer's day, Celtic had still not appointed a new manager. *A fortiori* they could not buy new players either. It was frustrating as the new season approached ever nearer, and the rumbles of disquiet began to be heard even louder.

It was as late as 17 July that the new manager was announced. He was Dr Josef Venglos, an amiable fellow, but unknown to everyone bar the most pedantic of football fanatics. His problem was that he just did not look like a Celtic manager. He was 62 years old, (not that age need be a problem, for Willie Maley had won the Empire Exhibition Cup in 1938 at the age of 70) distinguished looking, erudite, urbane but a favourite uncle rather than one able to take on such an awesome club. His mid-European accent made him appear like a participant from of those documentaries about the Second World War where survivors told stories of how they defied the Gestapo and lived through the Nazi occupation.

Venglos had been a player with Slovan Bratislava when they played Celtic in the European Cup Winners' Cup of 1963/64. He did not play in either game, but had observed Bobby Murdoch's penalty kick at Celtic Park and John Hughes's brilliant individual goal that had won the tie in Bratislava. Other than that, he had had little direct contact with either Celtic or Scotland. Venglos had a good managerial pedigree with the Czechoslovakia national team and was assistant manager when that country won the European

Nations' Cup (as it was then known) in 1976. He also had a brief, and unsuccessful, spell in charge of Aston Villa in the early 1990s.

It was also painfully obvious that he was not, nor anything like, first choice. The sheer length of time it took to appoint him made that fact obvious. Names like Gerard Houllier, Joe Kinnear, Egil Olsen and even Martin O'Neill had been mentioned, (sometimes authoritatively by the press, sometimes as sheer invention to fill a barren back page) as well as almost everyone currently employed in the Scottish game, but Dr Jo it was. The club did make the effort to appoint an assistant with knowledge of the scene in Scotland and Eric Black, the head of youth development at the club, was promoted to assistant manager while retaining his responsibilities for young players. Black had been a member of the great Aberdeen side of the early 1980s and indeed had scored against Real Madrid in the final of the European Cup Winners Cup in Gothenburg in 1983.

The supporters were distinctly unhappy about all this. They could hardly have been otherwise. They were in a cleft stick, by no means for the first time in the 1990s. They wished to protest at this ham-fisted way of running a football team, but did not want to be seen as disloyal to the men on the field who were after all league champions and still heroes. And they did have a ready made target on whom to vent their frustrations. It was of course none other than Jock Brown, who had driven out Wim Jansen and then had taken an inordinate length of time to appoint a successor. There was another public relations own goal when news leaked out that Venglos was only being offered a one-year contract, enough to see the club through to the departure of Fergus McCann who had always said he would depart in March 1999.

As early as the Champions League qualifier on 22 July 1998 at Celtic Park, supporters were holding up letters that spelt out an uncomplimentary message to Jock Brown. Yet that was less distressing than the result itself – a dismal 0–0 draw against St Patrick's Athletic, a team of Dublin part timers. It was already clear that there was a considerable malaise among the playing staff.

On the positive side, though, the stadium was now more or less completed after some further work in the summer. The temporary seating behind the west goal (the old railway end or Celtic end) had gone and been replaced with a massive structure that became known as the Jock Stein stand. For good or ill the club was also part of the brave new world of Scottish football, otherwise known as the Scottish Premier League, or SPL. The top ten clubs had broken away from the Scottish Football League to form an autonomous structure with the intention of maximising revenue from the sale of television rights and sponsorship. At first the new body was a great success and was able to negotiate a four-year rights' deal with Sky Television worth £45 million in the summer of 1998. The downside from the point of view of fans was that many of the live games on Sky were scheduled for the ludicrous kick-off time of five past six on a Sunday evening.

Fergus McCann invited Jock's widow, Mrs Jean Stein, to unfurl the league flag in front of the stand named after her husband before the game against Dunfermline Athletic on 1 August, an occasion that was spoiled when a few boneheads decided to boo McCann. This was a clear indication of unhappiness over what had happened in the summer, but nevertheless bizarre considering that the capture of a league title was being marked.

What the gentle Mrs Stein made of all this we can but imagine, but the booing did in some ways symbolise a turning point for Fergus McCann. He had always said that he would leave after five years in charge, and the quinquennium would be up in March 1999. The remaining few months of his tenure were to be unhappy ones, and although to a certain extent he must take some of the blame for allowing Wim Jansen to depart, the barracking was an astonishingly ungrateful reaction to a man who had saved the club, built arguably the best stadium in Britain and broken the stranglehold of Rangers in Scotland.

Although amends were made for the St Pat's result in the return leg in Dublin, the chickens came home to roost in a big way against Croatia Zagreb in the next qualifying round. Celtic had fought hard to gain a 1–0 lead at Celtic Park on 12 August – through a goal from substitute Darren Jackson – but by the time they travelled to Zagreb for the second leg, the team were at sixes and sevens over a dispute about bonuses, which the grateful press manipulated into a crisis. Zagreb eliminated a Celtic team which, frankly, appalled supporters watching back home on television. Some players did not seem to be putting much into it, and gave up the fight far too easily, losing 3–0.

By the end of August, Celtic, who had already lost to Aberdeen and drawn with Dundee in the league, were in big trouble. The Aberdeen game at Pittodrie on 16 August was a classic case of a team lacking confidence in itself playing against a team with a similar problem. The teams, who had contributed so much in years gone by to Scottish football, played like sides from a pub league. The end result was probably good entertainment for the television audience, but really there was a marked lack of professionalism in the Celtic team which was at one point 3–0 down, then pulled two back and also missed two penalties! Jock Brown was unfortunate enough to be caught by a press photographer with a smile on his face, and the photograph, taken out of context, was much exploited by those who saw yet another chance to get the knife in Jock.

The whole Pittodrie episode had a touch of vaudeville farce about it, but a more serious lack of professionalism came to the fore only three days later. It concerned the bonus-money dispute mentioned earlier. Not for the first time, allegations were made about verbal promises not being honoured and the whole sorry affair spiralled out of control. Fergus McCann refused to be blackmailed. Players refused to have their photographs taken, both sides (players and management) made donations of unspecified amounts to the children's hospital at Yorkhill to show what nice people they really were, McCann suggested that the players should get a reality check and the irony was that the team played so badly as a result of the dispute that any bonus money was lost anyway!

It is a sad fact of life that industrial unrest at a football club will always lead to disaster. Such is the competitive nature of modern football that the opposition will always be able to seize on such a weakness. A footballer must have his mind totally focused on defeating the opposition. What he cannot do is defeat the opposition and at the same time win a political point over his manager or board of directors. It is a particular problem in Scotland where the press are always keen to stir things up when one or other of the Old Firm is involved. Here we had the classic cocktail of disorientated players, an inexperienced coach, a bloody-minded boss, everyone behaving like spoilt brats and, crucially and fatally, the magnifying glass of the Scottish newspapers. The fans were powerless, unable to do anything other than watch the whole sad spectacle slowly unfold.

As far as the supporters were concerned, the dispute was an inevitable side-effect of the loss of Wim Jansen and the failure to get an adequate replacement quickly enough. A good coach would have detected the signs of trouble at an earlier stage and taken adequate steps to solve the problem before it got out of hand. Poor Dr Jo could hardly have been expected to deal with this serious matter at such an early stage of his career. Once more, fingers were pointed at Jock Brown.

The two permanent losses were a campaign in the European Champions' League and the League Cup. The European loss might well have happened anyway – Croatia Zagreb were seasoned campaigners at that level – but the League Cup defeat to Airdrie was a disgrace. Some players, notably Henrik Larsson, were away on international duty, but those available for selection should have easily disposed of Airdrie. The attitude was just not right, and Celtic's first ever visit to New Broomfield was a disaster. Those who shrugged their shoulders and said it was 'only' the League Cup did a great disservice to Scottish football, for the way was now clear for Rangers to take the first step to a domestic treble by defeating St Johnstone in a sadly one-sided final.

All of this was a severe blow to the bewildered supporters. Some sympathised with the players, but the majority thought they were behaving like mothers whose children had been taken away from them by the social work department. Perhaps the lion's share of the blame lay with the management of the club, who should never have allowed the situation to get out of control in the first place and then be picked over endlessly in the media. The campaign against Jock Brown gathered momentum. How could it otherwise when Celtic had gone from the dizzy heights of 9 May to the laughing stock of Scottish football by the end of August?

Celtic's football during the autumn months, in which the league now assumed greater importance thanks to the self-inflicted disasters of August, was poor. Danish defender Marc Rieper was struggling with an injury to his foot sustained in the World Cup and from which his career would never recover. Draws were the order of the day. A draw at Ibrox on 20 September was creditable and possibly even unlucky, but any respectability gained was immediately thrown away when Celtic lost to St Johnstone at home the following Wednesday night and then played out a weak draw with Hearts on the Saturday.

Celtic had signed the Norwegian Vidar Riseth from Linz for £750,000. He was a competent enough defender-cum-midfielder, although he often claimed that he was played on the wrong side of the midfield. The main transfer activity however centred on a man who had played against Celtic for Croatia Zagreb earlier in the season, a man of Croat/Australian extraction. He was called Marco Viduka, but very soon indicated that he wished to anglicise his first name to Mark. He had played exceptionally well in the games against Celtic.

His arrival was much anticipated, but the negotiations were labyrinthine. He was pursued from October onwards, gave a few promises in November then eventually signed on 2 December. But it was February 1999 before he played his first game. The problem seemed to be psychological. The man was apparently suffering from depression. This indeed was understandable, for he had been play-ing football in a land that had seen some dreadful, and to Western eyes, incomprehensible civil wars in recent years. Such things would, one imagines, have an effect on anyone. Yet Australians are reputed to be aggressive and professional. Certainly anyone who has watched and admired Australian cricket or rugby had to accept this point. One would have to imagine that a man like this would be mentally tough, tough enough quickly to throw off what he had gone through and come out fighting for his new club.

But Viduka returned to Australia 'for a rest'. At one point Celtic wanted their money back (£3 million) and the whole thing degen-erated into yet another of these fiascos that hit Celtic Park in the 1990s. The satirical programmes on Radio Scotland had a field day. Viduka's depression they said was a direct result of him meeting Fergus McCann and Jock Brown, followed by the sight of his new team-mates in action. One bright spark pointed out that if you spelt Viduka backwards, you got Akudiv.

Jock Brown was probably not to blame for all this. Yet he was identified once more with fruitless negotiations and a failure to deliver. It was clear that Jock could not last much longer in his job. The exit from the UEFA Cup on 3 November to the mediocre Swiss side Zurich – on a 5–3 aggregate – was hardly Brown's fault but it meant that Celtic had already been knocked out of three cups. The result came immediately after a 2–0 defeat at the hands of Kilmarnock, and it was now apparent that the supporters were not going to stand for such ineptitude for much longer.

Nevertheless 58,974 supporters – a highly impressive turnout in the circumstances – appeared at Celtic Park on 7 November to witness a league game against Dundee. It was clear that there was going to be a massive demonstration against the hapless Jock, but it was forestalled when Jock's resignation was announced at lunch time. Resignations are hard to get excited about, and it was difficult to get carried away by the hype surrounding this news. Jock had tried hard but had simply been unlucky. He was at least partly to blame for not getting along with key figures such as Jansen, and he had made a few misjudgements on transfers, but he was far from the anti-Christ portrayed by many people.

He was also one of the many people for whom Celtic Park is a career graveyard. One can think of many managers, players, business executives and others who enjoyed considerable success in their working lives until they came to the club. Now a general manager had spectacularly bitten the dust. The truth is that Celtic is a remarkable institution, possibly unique in world football, not least in the demands made on those who work there. It has long been the author's contention that supporting Celtic is not like supporting any other team. Those who have flirted with others – perhaps smaller Scottish clubs – in the author's case, Forfar Athletic and Raith Rovers, or an English or European outfit, will always find that they return to Celtic. The first result that they look for on a Saturday or a Sunday – no matter where they may be in the world – is that of the green-and-white brigade.

The ecstasies and the agonies are so much greater, something that is intensified by the realisation that so many others are involved. A glance round Celtic Park on any match day will confirm that one never walks alone and that is a comforting feeling. But, as the well-known scientific theory tells us, 'every action has a reaction', and there will always be those happy to rejoice in any misfortune that befalls those who wear the green. There is therefore a greater responsibility falling on those who have key roles.

Be that as it may, Saturday 7 November saw one of Celtic's finest performances for some time. Dundee were trounced by six goals to one and Larsson scored a hat trick. The team selection was also interesting. A goalkeeping crisis saw Andy McCondichie handed a starting berth, and there was also a debut for an unknown Slovakian signed by Jo Venglos and Jock Brown. It was a much-ridiculed signing for the player was well into his thirties and none-too-expensive. The press wondered if Lubo Moravcik was all Celtic could afford.

Lubo, as he was affectionately christened by the fans, was 33 years old and cost Celtic £300,000 from the obscure German side MSV Duisburg. He had fallen out with his German coach, who wanted him to play in defence, whereas his preference was to be a forward. At Celtic he was given a free role behind the front two and his subsequent success in that position is one of the lasting testimonies to Josef Venglos. Lubo soon became a hero to the supporters, thoroughly deserving of the 'we are not worthy' prostrations of the crowd. Indeed on one occasion he seemed to come close to castration, rather than prostration. The ball came to him on the left just in front of the main stand, about two feet from the ground and travelling fast. Moravcik trapped and controlled the ball brilliantly with an extremely delicate part of his anatomy!

The roller-coaster season went on. St Johnstone's hex continued in the next fixture as Celtic went down 2–1 at McDiarmid Park. This game was played in the wake of astonishing news, which had broken the previous midweek, to the effect that Kenny Dalglish and pop star Jim Kerr wanted to buy the club. The 'simple minds' of the players perhaps could not cope with this and the result was a feckless performance.

The fans reaction to the news, however, was favourable. Peter Rafferty who represented the Affiliation of Registered Celtic Supporters' Clubs was very happy: 'It is one of the most positive things I have heard about Celtic in the past five years'. Matt McGlone , a columnist in the *Celtic View* and of course the leader of 'Celts For Change' which had played its part in ousting the Kellys in 1994, was more cautious, and wanted to know more about who was behind Kerr and Dalglish.

But then on 21 November speculation was blown away in a tide of acclaim for a truly great performance on the field of play, the place with which most Celtic fans are primarily concerned. It was a display that demonstrated that perhaps the season could yet be kick-started and it was also Dr Jo's one real triumph. Rangers came to Celtic Park and were cuffed 5–1. Larsson scored twice, young Mark Burchill grabbed the last goal (and should have had another) but the man who orchestrated it all was Lubo Moravcik who chipped in with two goals and a master-class in the midfield. It was an astonishing performance and totally different from the feckless disasters that we had seen early in the season.

Celtic's debutant that day was Johan Mjallby. The tall, blond, 27-year-old Swede from AIK Stockholm cost £1.5 million and had been signed to help stem the flow of goals that were now being conceded at an alarming rate with the absence through injury of Alan Stubbs and Marc Rieper. Stubbs, as it happened, returned that day and the new-look defence was solid throughout. What Mjallby thought of his first taste of an Old Firm game can only be imagined, and similar questions should be asked of Celtic's on-loan goalkeeper Tony Warner who said afterwards that he had never experienced anything like it.

All that it really did was put a spring in the step of supporters for a limited time. A fortnight later Celtic brought everyone back down to earth by losing to Hearts at Tynecastle. The team formation that night was faulty. Larsson was the only recognised forward. We certainly could have done with the long-promised Viduka, but something should have been done to fill the gap. A striker to partner the admirable Larsson was needed. Amazingly, Burchill, one of the stars of the hammering of Rangers a fortnight earlier was brought on as a substitute only after it was too late.

This was in early December, and it was a few days earlier that the official signing of Viduka was announced. It was announced, but not yet delivered. The season of Advent was now in full swing and seasonal hymns (for those of a religious bent) contain references to 'the Saviour promised long' and 'late in time, behold him come'. There was still however no sign of Celtic's saviour. In fact, the blasphemous among us were now saying that the second coming of Christ would arrive before Viduka.

It was also too late to resurrect Celtic's title challenge. The form did settle down and after a creditable New Year 2–2 draw at Ibrox, we had to thole the nonsense of the midwinter break. This was a new idea introduced by the SPL and modelled on what happens in some European countries. It was wisely ignored by England and, until 1999, by Scotland as well. It is an attempt to avoid postponements through bad weather. The problem however is that British weather is highly unpredictable, and in any case, if one is looking for the worst weather in statistical terms, and the most postponements, February is the winner.

It was also rather odd that the SPL, most of whose clubs had undersoil heating, closed down, whereas the lower divisions continued as normal. The shutdown was by no means popular with the fans, however much the authorities argued that it gave players a well-earned rest and a chance for injuries to heal. In any case, some teams cut the ground from under their own feet by taking their players to places like Florida to play pointless friendlies. In any event, Celtic came back from the shutdown and began to play very well indeed, although they never seriously looked like catching Rangers, even when the Ibrox men gave the impression of slipping now and again under pressure from Celtic's fine form.

Celtic's league results in February and March were good, the only blot on the copybook being a 0–0 draw at Rugby Park. Hopes began to rise of a belated championship challenge after Rangers lost two games in a row at the end of March and the beginning of April, reducing the points' difference from an unbridgeable ten to a negotiable four, particularly as Rangers still had to visit Celtic Park. As an indication of what might have been, Viduka made his long delayed debut on 27 February and was soon in among the goals. The rest of the team was also functioning well, even though Moravcik had now picked up an injury.

Lubo had been an instant success with his ball control, visionary passing and goalscoring ability. The bad injury he sustained in a game against Motherwell at Fir Park – as Celtic were in the process of dishing out a 7–1 thrashing to the men in claret-and-amber – meant that he would not return until the last league game of the season. It is hard to believe that Moravcik would not have made some difference in the dire losses to St Johnstone and Rangers in the run-in.

By this time Fergus McCann had gone, leaving Allan MacDonald as chief executive. MacDonald had an impressive track record in business, and had previously been a senior executive with British Aerospace. He had plans to bring his friend Kenny Dalglish back to Celtic Park in some capacity. But the man with effective control of the club was the Irish multi-millionaire Dermot Desmond, who was now the largest single shareholder. The distinguished looking Desmond had, on McCann's invitation, invested £4 million in the club. Brian Quinn and Sir Patrick Sheehy were now on the board, and the takeover suggested by Jim Kerr and Kenny Dalglish the previous November had been rejected. Dalglish's hour was yet to come.

This was of less concern to the fans than the opportunity of lifting an honour, for the Scottish Cup was always a possibility and the title not yet totally out of the question. But the fifth last game of the campaign was at McDiarmid Park on Saturday 24 April. St Johnstone were having a good year, having already beaten Celtic twice in the dreadful autumn of that season and had beaten Rangers as well three weeks previously. The Saints would eventually finish fourth in the league and no one who saw that game against Celtic could argue against the proposition that they were a good team, and that the Perth side for all their limited resources and small support base had done very well.

For Celtic the game was a disaster and all the fine work of the past few weeks came to naught as the few chances that came Celtic's way were spurned. O'Halloran scored for St Johnstone in the second half and their well-organised defence was good enough to take everything that Celtic threw at them.

Rangers were not playing that Saturday, but the result meant that if Rangers beat Aberdeen on the Sunday, they could then win the title at Celtic Park in the Old Firm clash the following Sunday night. Sensing blood, the Ibrox men made no mistake against Aberdeen and so Rangers came to Celtic Park on Sunday 2 May 1999 knowing that a win would give them the title.

Thus the stage was set for Celtic's saddest night of the 1990s. There had been many worse footballing performances, but on this occasion some players and many fans let themselves down very badly. The referee was Hugh Dallas, widely suspected of being anti-Celtic. In fact, there is no evidence for this and indeed Dallas, although fallible on occasion and certainly giving the appearance of a man who loves to court controversy, has handled many difficult games very well at both domestic and international level.

Celtic were weakened by suspension and injury. There was no Craig Burley, Tosh McKinlay, Tom Boyd, Lubomir Moravcik, Johan Mjallby or Jackie McNamara. Yet they fought well and had cause for complaint when Rangers scored their first goal in thirteen minutes. There had quite clearly been a handball in the early part of the build-up to the goal.

But the main cause for concern centred on Celtic's temperamental French full back, Stephane Mahe. Soon after Rangers first goal, with Celtic and their supporters still nursing a sense of injustice, Mahe clashed with Rangers striker Rod Wallace. Mahe was shown a yellow card for this incident, even though it looked as if Wallace had been equally guilty and was in fact the instigator. It was not clear whether Mahe's yellow card was for the foul or for arguing against its award.

Then quarter of an hour later with Celtic slowly coming into the game and building a few promising moves, Mahe was quite clearly tripped by Neil McCann. Mahe then gestured to Dallas that McCann should be booked for the trip, but made his point rather too vehemently and, ill-advisedly for a man who had already been booked, argued with Dallas in such a way that the referee had to produce a second yellow and therefore a red card.

It is possible to argue that Mahe was unjustly awarded a red card. What cannot be disputed is that he immediately and completely lost the place and did enough to deserve several more red cards in the immediate aftermath. There could be no justification for his behaviour – he had to be encouraged and escorted off the field by his teammates – and equally there could be no doubt that there was a connection between Mahe's behaviour and what followed.

McCann was shown a yellow card for his trip on Mahe, and in the eyes of the supporters there was a bone to pick with him, for he had been brought up as a Celtic supporter and might have been described as Celtic-minded in the same way as Maurice Johnston had once been so defined! As a professional footballer, McCann had the right to play for Hearts and later Rangers, but he could hardly be surprised at cries like 'scab' that were hurled at him. Be that as it may, it was McCann's foul that was the main reason and catalyst for what happened. In the meantime Rangers were happy. They were a goal up and a man up. All they had to do was to keep the heid and the title would be theirs.

Sadly keeping the heid was not a feature of the Celtic Park stands that night. There were three field-invasions by hotheads – fortunately not en masse – which were handled by Celtic players and ground stewards, but the image that did irreparable damage to the club and to the game in Scotland was that of Hugh Dallas crouching on the ground with blood flowing from his head, caused by a missile thrown from the stand.

This was shameful and Mr Dallas might well have been justified in abandoning the game, thus earning worldwide opprobrium for Celtic Football Club. It does him credit that he did not follow that course of action, but where Celtic suffered was in the award of a soft penalty kick by Dallas shortly after he had been hit by the coin. The referee may have been traumatised, in shock or simply bloody-minded, immediately after the blow to his head. Rangers thus went in at half time 2–0 up and one man up, simply because they had indeed kept the head, when all around them were losing theirs, as Rudyard Kipling might have said.

At half time, the stands and the television commentators speculated that the game would have to be abandoned, such was the poisonous atmosphere and the threat of further violence in the second half. At half time a Celtic supporter fell from the top tier of the stadium on to the heads of the people below. There was bizarre speculation that this might have been an attempted murder of an infiltrating Rangers fan, or that it might have been a suicide attempt. In the venomous, hate-filled atmosphere, such stories were given credence, whereas the truth was that the man had simply been over-enthusiastic and had possibly had too much to drink. Fortunately, he sustained no lasting damage.

In the event, the second half passed in an anti-climactic atmosphere with Celtic clearly under instructions not to let things get further out of hand. Rangers scored again, but the Celtic fans were too subdued to do much about it. Some indeed had gone home at half time, declaring that whatever this was, it was not a football match; others simply slumped in their seats. Rangers attempted to celebrate with a mock huddle at the end, something that was, in the circumstances, inflammatory to say the least, before the police escorted them off the field.

That night, police protection for the Rangers team bus and the referee and his assistants was unparalleled even in the long and dismal history of clashes between the Old Firm. Throughout Scotland cases were reported of fights and assaults by rival fans, and some clown threw a brick through the window of Hugh Dallas's house.

This game, dreadful though it was, was a one-off. In its aftermath changes were made to kick-off times so that fans could not get so tanked-up on alcohol. The home towns of referees would no longer be mentioned in newspaper reports and enquiries seemed to go on all summer before Celtic received their deserved fine of £45,000 on 9 August 1999.

For Celtic, this was a shocker in every respect. But it is important to recognise that this game (with all its injustices) did not

cost Celtic the league. It had been lost in the infighting about Jock
Brown, the delay in appointing a new manager in the summer, the
absurd dispute about bonuses at the beginning of the season, three
lacklustre performances against St Johnstone – in particular the
one the previous Saturday – the disappointing attitude of several
established players who seemed to think that last year's success
would automatically be repeated, and the delay in the arrival
of Mark Viduka. In addition, Dr Venglos, nice man though he
was, proved himself a little short of what was required for this
mighty task.

There would be a ludicrous sequel to the Old Firm game the following season. It was piece of folly by Allan MacDonald, the Celtic
chief executive, blown out of all proportion by the press.
MacDonald saw fit to question the advisability of appointing Hugh
Dallas to be the referee for the Celtic–Rangers league match on 27
December 1999. He was foolish enough to raise this question in
public, and also made a reference to a gesture made by Dallas
involving Giovanni van Bronckhorst of Rangers. Apparently, at one
point, Dallas had patted the Dutchman on the bottom! Television
footage was now sought to analyse this gesture in greater depth,
and it was discovered that the coin thrown at Dallas came out of
the crowd immediately after the pat. The tabloid press now linked
the pat on the bottom, the coin coming from the crowd and the
advisability or otherwise of Dallas officiating and implied that
MacDonald had linked them in the first instance. This was arrant
nonsense of course, but it did provide a certain amount of light
relief in an otherwise deadly serious business.

Before the end of the 1998/99 season, another blow was to be
delivered to the supporters and the club, and this came in the
Scottish Cup. Progress to the final of this tournament had coincided
with the time when the team was playing at its best, and therefore
there were few problems encountered in the games against Airdrie,
Dunfermline, Morton and Dundee United. The semi final against
Dundee United at Ibrox on 10 April in particular was a fine Celtic
performance with good first half goals scored by Blinker (whose
form had continued to impress and exasperate supporters in equal
measure to such an extent that he was occasionally dubbed
'Stinker') and Viduka, now at last in harness and looking as if he
wanted to play for the club and score goals.

But the final was against Rangers. It was scheduled for the new Hampden Park on Saturday 29 May, almost a month after the title-decider shocker. The referee was again to be Hugh Dallas. Laudably the authorities resisted any effort to replace him. There was a campaign for such a change, not inspired by either of the two teams, but by ratings-seeking journalists and one or two aspiring politicians who were able to make pious statements about the 'danger to public order'. Fortunately this sort of emotional blackmail cut no ice with the SFA.

Both teams, Celtic in particular, were very aware of the danger to public safety and players were well and truly lectured on the need to behave. Clearly Scottish football could not afford anything vaguely like the shocker of Sunday 2 May. They needn't have worried. The behaviour of both fans and players was impeccable. Celtic's performance was less so.

The teams that fine afternoon of 29 May 1999 were;

Celtic: Gould, Boyd, Mahe, Mjallby, Stubbs, Annoni, Lambert, Wieghorst, Larsson, Moravcik, Blinker. Substitutes: O'Donnell, Johnson.

Rangers: Klos, Porrini, Amoruso, Hendry, Vidmar, McCann, McInnes, Van Bronckhorst, Wallace, Amato, Albertz. Substitutes: Kanchelskis, Wilson.

The Viduka saga, which seemed to have ended, began again. Mark Viduka was not with us for the Scottish Cup final. On 8 May in a meaningless game against Dunfermline Athletic, Viduka was seen spitting at a Dunfermline player after being fouled. This latest piece of bizarre behaviour meant that Mark was once again the subject of demands for Celtic to hire a psychiatrist. Spitting after all is something that cannot be tolerated or excused in the way that one can perhaps find a reason for a piece of violent retaliation after provocation. Jimmy Greaves, commenting on a spitting incident in a World Cup tie, rightly said, 'Spitting is sheer filth'. Grim jokes were heard along the lines of, 'Who is the Australian Olympic swimmer who plays for Celtic?' Answer: Mark Spitz!

In this very dull final, bereft of attacking play, Celtic gave every impression (not for the first time in recent history) of having been psyched-out before the start. With a weakened team, they were against a Rangers side that for all its many and sometimes glaring deficiencies had already been allowed to win the Scottish Premier League and the League Cup. In circumstances like this, an inspiring coach is required. Sadly, this was what Dr Venglos, who already knew that this would be his last game, was not.

At half time the score was still 0–0, and although the television pundits trotted out phrases like 'level pegging', 'even-Steven' and 'Dr Venglos will be as happy as Dick Advocaat', most of us, in our heart of hearts, knew that Rangers were enjoying distinctly the better of the exchanges. Yet, it was a cup final, and anything could happen.

Early in the second half Rangers scored through Rod Wallace in front of their fans at the Mount Florida end. It was no more than they deserved but, to their credit, Celtic fought to produce some sort of excitement for the fans. Near the end, a net-bound shot seemed to hit a Rangers player on the arm. The Celtic fans behind the goal immediately claimed a penalty, as did some players. Gordon Smith, commentating for the BBC and a self-confessed, although scrupulously honest, Rangers man agreed. Hugh Dallas disagreed, and replays showed that the referee was possibly correct. It was nevertheless a blow for Celtic, who could have done with a break.

Not for the first time Celtic supporters were aggrieved about a refereeing decision in a Scottish Cup final. The older supporters among us recalled the 1970 Scottish Cup final when a penalty kick was awarded to Aberdeen after a ball hit Bobby Murdoch on the chest! And then there were the dreadful decisions against Celtic in 1984, also against Aberdeen. Once again, however, the point was clear – no team can rely on breaks from the referee. The team must be so far ahead that refereeing decisions do not matter. This was not the case here.

No other clear chance came the way of the disappointing Celtic forwards, and Rangers had won a domestic treble. It had been a dreadfully heartbreaking season for the men and women in green, the bhoys and ghirls whose loyalty had stayed firm throughout this crazy and incomprehensible time. There was an air of resignation as they trooped to their buses that sunny May evening – no great hatred nor rancour, no impassioned cursing of Dr Jo, nor the Celtic establishment, simply an air of depression and the all-pervasive, recurrent feeling that, in spite of last year's successes, self-inflicted wounds meant that Celtic were second best to Rangers. It was a dreadful feeling.

It was that night that Donald Finlay QC was caught on camera singing songs of sectarian hatred at a Rangers supporters' victory function. To their credit, Rangers immediately relieved him of his position as vice chairman, but it was a clear indication that the campaigns of both clubs to rid Scotland of sectarianism perhaps had not made as much ground as they would have led the rest of Scotland to believe. In any case, it was of little comfort to Celtic fans as they licked their wounds following the dreadful season of 1998/99.

It meant of course the end of Dr Josef Venglos. *Rothman's Football Yearbook* for the following season sums him up rather well when it says that he was 'a cultivated and unpretentious gentleman who had a difficult row to hoe, but who had done it with dignity'. His great achievement was the recruitment of Lubomir Moravcik, his great failure was his inability to deal with the recurrent Viduka crises, and his greatest misfortune was quite simply to be at Celtic Park at the wrong time in history. He remains a nice and lovable man.

On the business side, Fergus McCann had now made his way home to North America. He had always said that he would stay no more than five years, once the finances of the club were in order and the new stadium built, and he was true to his word. Thus departed the insignificant-looking man who had saved Celtic five years previously. His departure was anonymous and low key, yet where would Celtic have been without him? And few could begrudge him the profit of many millions made on his Celtic shares.

There is a certain amount of justification for Fergus McCann to be considered the greatest, or at least the most significant, Celt of all time. Naturally most supporters and historians would plump for Jock Stein or Willie Maley for this accolade, not to mention the myriad of players who have worn the green with distinction. Time will tell just how much this little man from the Croy Supporters Bus has done for the club. One thing is sure however. He will never be ignored in future histories, nor relegated to a mere footnote.

That summer of 1999 saw the opening of the Scottish Parliament. Scotland as a nation was clearly moving forward. It was ironic that football, Scotland's traditional and obsessive pastime, was not moving forward simultaneously. The national team's per-

formances continued to be a disgrace, and there was still no answer
to the question that might logically have been asked throughout
the 1990s: 'Why is there not a challenge to Rangers, if Celtic continue to self destruct?' As Sheila Wellington sang Rabbie Burns's 'A
Man's A Man For A' That' at the opening of the Parliament, we
thanked God that we were spared the execrable 'Flower Of
Scotland', but might well have been justified yet again in asking
Scottish football in general and Celtic in particular, 'When will we
see your like again?'

7

1999/2000: 'The departing, the traumatised and the angry'

There was a grim determination about Celtic supporters as they approached Hampden Park for the League Cup final on 19 March 2000, the first major cup final of the new millennium. It was a fine spring day, and in normal circumstances there would have been a bounce in the step, a feeling of enthusiasm and the idea that they were going, green-and-white bedecked, to a showpiece game at the national stadium. But in the context of the early months of 2000, these were far from normal circumstances. The disgrace of the previous month had not been expunged from the memory, nor was it likely to be for some considerable time. The ridicule of opponents and rivals was too recent, as indeed was the justified anger against those who had allowed the situation to develop. It would indeed be a long time before anyone could forget, or be allowed to forget, Celtic's night of infamy.

But for a Celtic fan, the sight of someone in green-and-white hoops holding up a piece of silverware always provides a certain amount of relief. The League Cup, quite clearly a poor fourth behind Europe, SPL and Scottish Cup in importance, suddenly became a consuming passion for the Celtic Park faithful. This trophy was often contemptuously dismissed by managers, players and journalists who give the impression that it is not worth bothering about. In December 1997, in the wake of Celtic's last triumph in this competition, a radio programme had held a competition for anagrams and some bright spark had come up with the idea that C–E–L–T–I–C could stand for Celtic Elatedly Lift Totally Insignificant Cup.

In spring 2000, the League Cup was anything but insignificant. In the past, it had of course been the setting for the 7–1 victory over Rangers in 1957, and there were Jock Stein's five-in-a-row successes between 1965 and 1969. Since then, Celtic's record had been woeful as 1974/75, 1982/83 and 1997/98 had been the only years of triumph but it was now in 1999/2000 Celtic's only hope for a modicum of respectability in a desperate season. In truth, all that it could do was give supporters something to cheer about by papering over the cracks of what had been a truly devastating experience.

And what of our opponents in the final, Aberdeen? Once, fifteen years previously, when Alex Ferguson was the manager, they were the scourge of both Celtic and Rangers. The Dons won the title in 1980, 1984 and 1985, the Scottish Cup in 1982, 1983 and 1984, the League Cup in 1985, an impressive array of domestic triumphs. In addition they had delighted all Scotland with their capture of the now defunct European Cup Winners' Cup in 1983 when they beat, of all teams, Real Madrid in the final in Gothenburg.

The 1984 Scottish Cup final between Celtic sand Aberdeen with the illegal Eric Black goal, the unjustified sending off of Roy Aitken and the extra-time winner still hurt, but there was nevertheless always a feeling of mutual respect between the two sets of supporters – if we ignore the lunatic fringe on both sides – that certainly did not exist between the fans of Aberdeen and Rangers. One recalled for example the penalty shoot-out Scottish Cup final of 1990 when Aberdeen fans magnanimously proffered hands to the disconsolate green-and-white brigade and acknowledged it was a dreadful way to win and lose a cup.

The Dons were now in an even worse position than Celtic. Alex Ferguson had long since gone to Manchester United, energetic director Chris Anderson had died and they had blown their great opportunity of winning the league in 1991 when a draw against Rangers at Ibrox on the final day would have sufficed. Since winning the League Cup of 1995/96, the Dons had gone downhill rapidly, thanks to a succession of poor managers, a chairman who was certainly going to do his own thing and an over-reliance on second-rate foreign players. Aberdeen were now no strangers to the bottom of the table and indeed would only be saved the ignominy of relegation by the restructuring of the leagues and a certain amount of diplomatic and political help from their old pals, Celtic and Rangers. In similar manner to Celtic supporters, this League Cup final meant an awful lot to the Dons.

The fans of both sides managed to shrug off their frustrations and disappointments of the previous part of the season and turned up at Hampden in impressive numbers. The 50,000 crowd and the millions watching on television saw a game that was sadly in tune with previous form that season. A minor mystery surrounded the non-appearance of Celtic's Mark Burchill, one of the few genuine hopes on the horizon. He did have talent, but his absence that day was the start of a gradual disappearance from the Celtic scene. Celtic went in at half time one goal up and that scored by a mishit shot by Vidar Riseth in front of goal. Hardly a classic strike, but much celebrated by the fans.

In the second half, Tommy Johnson, that likeable, hard-working but incredibly unlucky player had his brief moment of glory when he picked up a good ball from Viduka and angled the ball across veteran goalkeeper Jim Leighton and into the net. That Celtic were on easy street was emphasised by an Aberdeen player getting himself sent off by referee Kenny Clark for two not particularly vicious tackles, and the game finished with Celtic well on top. Mark Viduka in fact was culpable of not scoring a good few more, particularly in the latter stages.

Not that it mattered. Aberdeen got a sporting and sympathetic cheer as they collected their losers' medals. It was after all analogous to wakening up in hospital after a life-threatening operation to find that not only have you survived, but so too has an old enemy of yours, who in these circumstances is hardly an enemy any more. Solidarity is established, at least for the time being.

Celtic got a rapturous reception as Tom Boyd, the gnarled veteran of many disasters in the 1990s, picked up the trophy and everybody seemed happy enough. Kenny Dalglish, the interim manager, failed to catch the mood of the occasion when he was rude to a television reporter who asked him the perfectly reasonable question about his long-term future. He delivered the terrible insult that 'You're getting as bad as Chick Young!'

That was strong, ungracious stuff from Kenny, but at least this was one Sunday night on which Celtic fans could celebrate and face Monday with a certain degree of equanimity, if not ecstasy. The teams were:

Celtic: Gould, Boyd, Riseth, Mjallby, Mahe, McNamara, Wieghorst, Petrov, Moravcik, Johnson, Viduka. Substitutes: Stubbs, Berkovic, Kerr.

Aberdeen: Leighton, Perry, McAllister, Solberg, Anderson, Dow, Bernard, Jess, Guntweit, Zerouali, Stavrum. Substitutes: Mayer, Belabed, Winters.

The League Cup win had been so necessary because, hitherto, season 1999/00 had been a shocker, possibly the worst in recent times, although that is a spectacularly ambitious claim. Two factors in particular contributed to the gloom: the first was Henrik Larsson's dreadful broken leg in Lyon in the UEFA Cup in the autumn of 1999 and the second was the Scottish Cup tie against Inverness Caledonian Thistle in those dark and dreadful events of early February 2000.

But the underlying causes ran deeper than that. The departure of Dr Jo Venglos in summer 1999 to a rather nebulous job that involved scouting for players in Europe was not unexpected and indeed was demanded by the fans following the unsuccessful season of 1998/99. He had in any case been on a one-year contract.

Now that Fergus McCann had returned to Canada as he had promised, new chief executive Allan MacDonald had brought in his friend Kenny Dalglish to be director of football, given that Kenny's own bid to buy the club had failed. Dalglish in turn appointed his friend John Barnes to be the coach, and an assortment of cronies in ill-specified jobs like social manager, as Terry McDermott was now to be called. 'What did that mean?' we asked ourselves, and no one could give us an answer. Frankly this new management team never looked anything like convincing. Even on that summer's night of 10 June 1999 when the crowds gathered outside Celtic Park to greet their new manager – more or less an annual event – a few wise heads wondered whether the new boys were going to succeed where others had failed.

Kenny Dalglish was an enigma. Although his Celtic career had contained a fair amount of disappointments, there were those who argued, with some justification, that Kenny had to be recognised as the club's greatest-ever player for the quality of his performances at Celtic Park between 1967 and 1977. Liverpool fans would say the same about him. Scotland fans are less convinced. One recalled a fine goal against Belgium in December 1982, and another against Spain at Hampden in November 1984, but there had been too many games, notably big occasions in the World Cup finals of 1978 and 1982, where the Dalglish magic, so blindingly obvious for Liverpool, had failed to materialise for Scotland.

In any case, his playing ability was not the point at issue. The two questions concerned his managerial skills and his commitment to the club. He had managed Liverpool, Blackburn Rovers and Newcastle United with declining degrees of success. Liverpool were already a successful club and it would have been difficult to imagine him not doing well in that job. Blackburn Rovers with a spendthrift chairman happened to have bucket-loads of money at the time and he had done reasonably well for them, including landing the Premiership in 1995. Newcastle United, on the other hand, that longest running tragedy of English football, was a graveyard for Kenny, as it had been for so many others.

Was Dalglish really committed to the club? Well, he had done his bit to buy-in along with assorted business associates, but did this show a love of the green and white? His early Rangers sympathies were forgiven – many players of a similar persuasion had grown to love Celtic – but supporters were likely to recall with some bitterness his departure for Liverpool in 1977, just at the time when Jock Stein could have built his third great Celtic team. Kenny would of course argue that he left because of a lack of ambition for the club at board level.

And what of John Barnes? Certainly, a great player and a winner on the field at the highest level, winning trophies for Watford and Liverpool and gaining seventy-nine caps for England, but like the tragic Liam Brady of almost ten years ago, having no managerial experience. Extrovert and media friendly, he certainly talked a good game, but could he cope with the pressure of managing this huge Glasgow club with its massive and demanding following? Frankly, many felt that the likeable John really did not understand what he was letting himself in for. Nevertheless, early indications were optimistic and he paid £5.5 million for West Ham's talented midfielder Eyal Berkovic.

Olivier Tebily joined Celtic from Sheffield United for £1.25 million. He appeared to be a good defender, but very soon exhibited a propensity to be caught out of position and to concede easy goals. He earned a certain amount of notoriety following an international match for the Ivory Coast. The game was lost, and the team were locked up in their training camp and had their mobile phones confiscated as a punishment by a management who clearly found defeat even harder to take than the average Celtic fan!

The season got off to a reasonable start. The first Sunday night of the season saw a spectacular 5–0 thrashing of Aberdeen, the start of a dreadful run for the Dons. But for Celtic, Berkovic, Larsson and Viduka were all impressive as the first nine league games brought only one defeat – to Dundee United at Tannadice, a ground that had often produced problems for the Old Firm – the competent demolition of inferior European opposition in Cwmbran Town and Hapoel Tel Aviv, and a similar advance in the League Cup against Ayr United.

Team formation however tended to raise a few eyebrows. Injuries compelled a certain amount of chopping and changing, but sometimes the formation looked a somewhat bizarre 4–2–2–2. Yet if the team kept winning, no one could complain. Certainly, given that Barnes started from a low baseline it seemed that some progress had been made.

In playing terms, of course, the previous season, 1998/99, was a disaster. No amount of rhetoric about bad luck, Hugh Dallas and how out of touch poor Dr Jo had been could hide the fact that Celtic were some considerable distance below Rangers where it really mattered – on the field. This at least seemed now to be being acknowledged and a start was being made to address the issue.

Other new players were brought in as well as Berkovic and Tebilly. Bobby Petta and Stilian Petrov arrived at the same time. Sadly neither of these players hit the headlines instantly or early enough to make an impact under Barnes. Petrov, the young Bulgarian, would become a great character, but under Martin O'Neill and not the current regime. Petta, however, although capable of some good performances, most notably against Rangers in August 2000 – once again, long after the departure of the ill-starred Barnes – remained a disappointing reserve for most of his subsequent Celtic Park career.

It was on 21 October 1999 at Lyon in the UEFA Cup that the pattern for the season was determined. Henrik Larsson sustained a broken leg in an accidental collision with a Lyon player. The damage was shockingly obvious and television pictures showed a horrified

Scottish nation the sight of Henrik's leg, broken in two places. Not a few supporters fainted, apparently, at such a hideous injury to such a fine player.

In the circumstances, Celtic probably did well to leave Lyon only one goal down, but Larsson was now out for virtually the rest of the season. His loss was felt immediately. Celtic were very lucky to beat St Johnstone at McDiarmid Park on the subsequent Sunday thanks to a last minute Morten Wieghorst counter, and then in the following midweek they went down to Motherwell at Celtic Park, even though their opponents had been reduced to ten men. Then, the following midweek in early November, Celtic exited from Europe by losing 1–0 to Lyon at Celtic Park.

By this time, the panicky management had tried to replace Henrik Larsson by buying, at a knockdown price, Ian Wright, an ageing extrovert now in his mid thirties. Wright had made his name at Arsenal even though he arrived via Nottingham Forest, for whom he was not a first-team regular. Wright scored on his debut against Kilmarnock on 30 October and was clearly an instant hit with the fans, but when the team followed its European exit by going down 4–2 to Rangers at Ibrox, then losing to Motherwell at Fir Park before November was out, it was clear that the club was in a great deal of trouble.

The 4–2 defeat at Ibrox on 7 November not only meant the loss of three points, it also lost Celtic another star player when Paul Lambert was injured. Celtic were winning 2–1 as half time approached and Eyal Berkovic, having scored two goals, was finally looking as if he was worth his transfer fee. But almost on the half-time whistle, Lambert mistimed a challenge on Jorg Albertz on the wet surface, brought him down and the far from lightweight Albertz fell on his head. Television cameras and the watching Celtic end were shocked by how still he was and the fact that his face seemed to have lost all colour.

Fortunately the paramedics and the Celtic backroom staff were able to bring him round and fears that he might have swallowed his tongue proved groundless. The diagnosis however was hardly any more cheerful, for he had broken his jaw in three places and would be out for some considerable time. Paul Lambert of course was a deserved favourite among the Celtic fans and his loss, coming so soon after Larsson's injury, meant that John Barnes was hardly enjoying the best of luck at the start of his Celtic Park career.

The immediate effect of the collision was a penalty for Rangers, which Albertz converted to bring the Ibrox man level at half time en route to winning the game in the second period. This was contentious enough, but several Rangers players and backroom staff protested that Paul Lambert should have been given a red card for his challenge. This was crass, and Dick Advocaat, the Rangers manager, was rightly castigated in the press for his asinine, provocative and insensitive comments. At New Year the satirical television programme *Only An Excuse* would show a sketch of Advocaat visiting Lambert in hospital. Lambert, scarcely able to raise his head was informed, 'You should have been sent off!'

For Celtic and Barnes this dreadful autumn was too bad to be true. Losing five games out of the last eight was unacceptable for a Celtic team, but the main cause for concern was not so much the results as the way that the team was playing. Players were seen to argue with their colleagues, passes went astray, the defending was naïve and the forward play ineffective. The fans were beginning to make it plain that they did not like what they were witnessing, and relationships between crowd and management took a decided turn for the worse when Craig Burley, always popular, cheerful and hard-working was allowed to go to Derby County on 1 December for a sum cited as £3 million.

Whatever was said about this transfer for public consumption, it seemed to be a clear example of a face not fitting with the management. This particular face was felt by the fans to be worth making an effort for, because he was respected as a wholehearted and talented player, as well as being an established Scotland internationalist. Only a couple of weeks previously, Burley had played creditably for his country against England in the home-and-away play-off matches for Euro 2000.

Given the loss of Larsson and Lambert, the stops should have been pulled out to retain Burley's services. In the triumphant season of 1997/98, no one had worked harder or done more for the cause than this likeable and determined midfielder. The point at issue was that Barnes felt that Burley should play more as a defensive midfielder rather than in the attacking role which he relished and had enjoyed hitherto. Many Celtic fans felt that a more sensitive and enlightened management would have taken Burley's ideas on board.

But those in charge had other ideas and for the first time since the dark days of 1993, there was a distinct sense of alienation between fans and officials. With Tommy Burns, Wim Jansen and Dr Venglos, there had been disagreement about some decisions and occasional bewilderment, but never the outright hostility that was now beginning to emerge.

That same Wednesday 1 December 1999 which saw the transfer of Burley was highly significant for Celtic's season, and for once it was a positive development. It was the night of the League Cup quarter finals. Celtic defeated a plucky and hard working Dundee at a half empty Celtic Park with a looping header from Morten Wieghorst in the last minute, whereas at Pittodrie in a live television transmission of another League Cup quarter final, the Aberdeen team who were currently at the bottom of the SPL and having a shocking season took Rangers to extra time and then incredibly scored a goal so late in extra time that Rangers did not have enough time to equalise.

This performance by Aberdeen was like a cry of laughter at a funeral in the context of how awful the Dons had been throughout the campaign. Celtic supporters sitting in their buses waiting for the traffic jams to evaporate cheered this goal by Andy Dow. At least there would be no treble this year for Rangers to crow about and it immediately made those of a green-and-white persuasion forget their current troubles due to the realisation that they were now clear favourites for at least one trophy.

Indeed, there was an immediate resurgence in form during the month of December as Hibs, Aberdeen and Dundee United were all comprehensively beaten. The Dundee United game in particular had seen the revival of an almost extinct quality known as character. The team were a goal down at half time, but rallied brilliantly to win 4–1. The form of Eyal Berkovic was particularly impressive in December. Celtic fans had been less than impressed by Eyal since his transfer, but there was now the hope that with Viduka also on song, and apparently showing a positive attitude at last, that the season could still be rescued.

The team's form was certainly good in December – good enough for John Barnes to win the manager-of-the-month award – but Rangers were winning too, and it was clear that Celtic needed a result in the Old Firm game at Celtic Park on 27 December. The fans witnessed an excellent game with Mark Viduka scoring for

Celtic and Billy Dodds equalising for Rangers before half time, but neither side was able to exert overwhelming superiority in the second half. Celtic supporters, however, felt that their team had the edge and that perhaps the corner had been turned, although Rangers were still seven points ahead in the league race.

But then came the winter shutdown. This idea had not taken a trick with the fans of any team and this year it certainly worked against Celtic. By the time that the campaign resumed towards the end of a mild January in which football would have been possible, Celtic had lost momentum. The winter shutdown was not entirely to blame and the coaching staff had to shoulder some of the responsibility for allowing the team to lose focus.

During the shutdown, when the newspapers were desperate for anything to fill their pages, a certain amount of humour was expended on a Brazilian with the distinctly unfortunate name of Rafael Scheidt, although Celtic for reasons that are obvious insisted that he should be referred to as just Rafael. He was signed for the not inconsiderable sum of £5.5 million, but as was inevitably the case in those days, there was a delay between his agreement, arrival and eventual debut. In fact he would end up starting only one game, and coming on as substitute in another two, before the end of the season. It was one of the many embarrassing purchases of foreign players by Celtic, and the situation was greatly exacerbated by the Brazilian's unfortunate moniker. There was no doubt that Celtic needed to supplement their defence: Alan Stubbs had been diagnosed with testicular cancer (thankfully he made a full recovery) and Olivier Tebily was simply not up to the standard that Celtic required. But Rafael was hardly the answer, and the management team were justifiably criticised for not even taking the trouble to watch him in action before making the fateful decision to complete the transfer.

Celtic went to the Algarve in Portugal during the winter break. This turned out to be a good idea in theory only. The idea was that the players could bond, develop team spirit, work out new moves and have a relaxing few days off. But Barnes failed to notice the personality clashes that were developing, or if he did, failed to do anything to stop them, or even to ask his social manager to resolve them. Viduka was resented for his attitude and some players had not forgiven him for his delayed arrival, while for his part he was unhappy about his salary. Berkovic was considered to be something of a troublemaker, and with the atmosphere in the camp had a fair amount of material to work with. Various other members of the squad were not on speaking terms. Everyone was suspicious of Barnes with his bizarre and quixotic dealings in the transfer market and his curiously laid-back approach to management. And so the scene was set for the impending disaster.

The first game after the restart was on Sunday 23 January 2000 at Kilmarnock at Rugby Park, a ground that had so often seen damage inflicted on Celtic in recent years. Significantly Paul Lambert, who had returned for a brief spell in December after his broken jaw, was again out injured. Rangers had already launched a pre-emptive strike by beating Aberdeen comprehensively the day before, and the television audience were now treated to a Celtic team at its worst. Once again, Celtic went ahead then threw away the lead before half time, and the second half – like the Old Firm game in December – was a stalemate. The difference was that the opposition was not Rangers, but Kilmarnock, and that Celtic chose to play very badly with Eyal Berkovic in particular giving the impression that he wanted to be somewhere else.

The booing that greeted the players at the end came from Celtic fans who now realised that the December form had been a false dawn. There was also frustration among the players as reports emanated that Ian Wright had been involved in a fracas in the tunnel. Supporters hoped that it was with a Kilmarnock player; cynics feared it might have been with one of his own side or a member of the management team!

The following Saturday, 29 January, should have seen the Scottish Cup tie against Inverness Caledonian Thistle. At this point fate intervened. Rain and high winds with the potential for damage to Celtic Park's high stands meant that on safety grounds the tie had to be postponed until Tuesday 8 February 2000. Had the game been played on its original date, no one knows what would have happened, but the rearrangement meant that Celtic, fatefully, played a league fixture against Hearts at Celtic Park on the intervening Saturday.

For a while all went well. Moravcik and Viduka put the home side two ahead, and although Hearts pulled one back almost immediately, Celtic still went in at half time 2–1 up. The second half saw an appalling Celtic performance with no rhythm, no fluidity and no sense of common purpose. As a wit put it, 'They played together with all the teamwork and cohesion of a starving mob at a bread riot!' As Hearts first equalised, then went ahead with a penalty, the team imploded and proceeded to snarl and shout at each other and several players appeared to have given up. 'These bastards arenae' f****** tryin' said one irate fan. Interestingly, no one in the ground disagreed.

To say there was a complete lack of effort would be harsh and erroneous. Lack of significant effort from well paid professional footballers was closer to the mark. But more telling was the feeling of disorientation, bewilderment and lack of purpose. John Barnes waved his arms from the dugout and brought on Burchill, Blinker and Johnson in a desperate effort to stem the tide, but Barnes too was overwhelmed by the comprehensive mood of despair over the performance of a team which, for all the money that had been spent on it, was manifestly not Celtic class.

Spleen was vented on Eyal Berkovic and Mark Viduka, two highly expensive imports who did not seem to be fitting the bill and for whom little excuse was possible. There was a demonstration against John Barnes by disappointed and concerned supporters outside the ground at the end of the game. The media played this up, something that was hardly calculated to pour balm on the wounded nerves of the Celtic management team and players, although Barnes himself was honest enough to say that it was all part of the game.

The title was now almost certainly outwith Celtic's grasp, and one or two supporters were heard to say that they were not even confident of a win next Tuesday night over the upstart Inverness outfit that had only been in existence since 1994. The club in question was formed after the amalgamation of Inverness Caledonian and Inverness Thistle, both of which had graced the Highland League, and through their union had gained admission to the Scottish League. This was something that all genuine fans were glad to see, as the Highlands deserved to have a side in the higher echelons of the game.

The thought, however, of Celtic losing the match was too outrageous for words. Those who expressed that view seriously could be likened to the Classical prophetess Cassandra, the daughter of Priam, King of Troy. She was fated to tell the truth, but not to be believed. She said that one day a horse made of wood would capture the city. Everyone thought she was mad, and didn't listen to her. Similarly, Celtic couldn't possibly lose to the Highland *arrivistes*. In fact, many of their fans took the view that the cup tie was exactly what was required to build up a little confidence for more difficult encounters in the SPL.

A disappointing crowd of 34,389 filtered into Celtic Park after a troubled and unsettled weekend for the game against Inverness Caledonian Thistle. The attendance included a fair amount of Invernesians, some of them clearly Celtic fans as well as having an allegiance for their local team, and they were wide-eyed in admiration at the sight of the stadium. The game kicked off in a subdued atmosphere and the fare on view initially provided little sustenance for the purist. Passes went astray and the hopeful punt upfield was very much in evidence . . . but it was early yet.

The wake-up call came when Wilson scored with a fine header for Inverness in the thirteenth minute. Now Celtic would have to take their opponents seriously. This seemed to happen when Burchill levelled accounts a few minutes later with a fine strike. But then one of life's misfortunes befell the peerless Lubomir Moravcik. A corner kick taken by Sheerin reached Bobby Mann and the luckless Lubo got in the way of the Inverness man's header and diverted it into his own net.

This need not have been fatal, for only twenty-five minutes had elapsed, but what was deeply disturbing was the lack of any constructive play in the twenty minutes before half time. The crowd's reaction went from constructive support to frustrated exasperation, then to downright abuse of their own players. Often when this happens, the crowd split into those who hurl abuse on the one hand and those who are inclined to give the team the benefit of the doubt. Sadly those who normally spoke in mitigation had little to say on this occasion, for very few players seemed to be giving maximum effort.

Berkovic, Blinker, Mahe and Viduka all seemed to be strangers to each other. Young Colin Healy battled manfully in midfield but it was obvious that he needed support and guidance from the experienced players around him. With the laudable exception of Tommy Boyd, this was not forthcoming. Players were seen to argue with each other, raising hands in elaborate gestures of 'it's not my fault' when it manifestly was. Eric Black looked like a little boy lost on the touchline and John Barnes was no doubt wishing that he was in Spain playing golf with his friend Kenny Dalglish.

When the halftime whistle blew Celtic were booed off the park. The jeers and catcalls in that half-empty bowl had an eerie echo and were not unlike a wolf pack howling for blood. The possibility was now being openly discussed in the queues for the refreshment stalls that we might be heading for a real upset. Such talk was usually dismissed as defeatist and alarmist, but there was a genuine feeling that socks would have to be pulled up . . . and quickly. BBC Radio was full of praise for the Highlanders but Murdo MacLeod and the other pundits had little doubt that Celtic would pull through in the end.

In the dressing room, Inverness's management team of Steve Paterson and Duncan Shearer had to curb their players' *joie de vivre* and point out to them that they had done well and that a steady approach to the game in the second period might just see them hit the headlines in tomorrow's papers. Celtic's management team needed to point a few fingers, do a little geeing up and flattery and wait for nature to take its course and redress the balance. After all, millions of pounds had been spent on this team.

What actually transpired within the Celtic dressing room that night, no one will ever know. Dressing rooms are quite rightly off limits to outsiders, and what happens within the hallowed walls is not for outside consumption. Nevertheless, there were leaks which appeared later in sundry tabloid newspapers but it was obvious in any case that something pretty serious had taken place, because Mark Viduka did not reappear after the interval.

Viduka, for all his flaws on the night, represented Celtic's best hope, for he was a tried and tested striker and indeed had scored in each of the two games since the New Year. Ironically, he would end the season as top goalscorer in Scotland. Other things being equal, Viduka would not have been substituted. But he was, and the Glasgow gossip-mills were not backward at coming forward with all sorts of lurid speculation: he had refused to play in the second half; he had assaulted or been assaulted by a member of the management team; he had been sent home.

A similar incident had occurred in the New Year's Day Old Firm game of 1963. The brilliant Pat Crerand had been out of sorts in the first half and Celtic were 1–0 down. He had then fallen out with a member of the management team and had only with great diffi-culty been persuaded to take the field in the second half (not that it did much good as Rangers went on to win 4–0). That was 1963 before the days of substitutes. By 2000, at least Celtic were permitted a substitute.

Anyone can put his own particular spin on the Viduka story, but the fact remained that Viduka (one recalled again that his name spelt backwards was Akudiv!) did not reappear and the charge of saving Celtic was handed to the unlikely figure of substitute Ian Wright. Wright had already earned himself a degree of opprobrium in the eyes of some of the Celtic fans that night. As the first half was coming to an end with the crowd anxious and angry, he was told to limber up behind the goal at the Jock Stein end of the ground. After a few high kicks and general showing-off, which failed to impress punters who were much more concerned at the events unfolding on the pitch, Ian then made great show of trying to get at Jonathan Gould's water bottle which was of course on the inside of the net! The angry reply from the fans indicated that this was no time to try to be funny.

To his credit, however, Wright buckled down in the second half and there was no clowning or showing off. But sadly, his best days (and a glorious career it had been with Arsenal) were some way behind him, and his impact was minimal. Everyone reflected bit-terly of course that Celtic's real man of destiny, Henrik Larsson, was still not available because of his horrific injury.

An early goal in the second half would have immediately taken the sting out of the situation and allowed Celtic to go for the winner. Sadly this never looked like a possibility. Ten minutes into the sec-ond half, the bells of hell began to ring very loudly for Celtic when Inverness were awarded a penalty thanks to a clumsy challenge by Blinker in front of a half-empty Lisbon Lions stand, and Sheerin scored. Blinker did at least have the grace to put his hands to his head after conceding such a foolish penalty . . . but the stands were unforgiving.

The fans from the Highlands were ecstatic after they pinched themselves to make sure it was not just a dream. Celtic fans slumped in their seats or collapsed over the empty seat in the row in front of them, unbelieving of what was happening in front of them. BBC Radio, which had hitherto been doing a commentary of

Aberdeen versus St Mirren with only score-flashes from Celtic Park, abruptly jumped ship from Pittodrie and concentrated exclusively on the action from Celtic Park as the nation gathered round transistor radios to listen to Celtic's demise with either despair or glee, according to one's conviction.

The remaining half hour saw some belated effort from those guilty of the sin of sloth in midfield, but more composure was evident from a fine Inverness team that now realised glory was at hand. The minutes ticked away, and still no adequate response came from Celtic. The fans, some of them too stunned to hurl bile at the men on the bench and on the field, glanced at timepieces, all of which were counting down to zero. Significantly, from about the seventieth minute onwards, the sound of seats being tipped up was much in evidence as supporters began to trickle away. Some Celtic fans are much criticised by other Celtic fans for leaving early, but they normally do so when the team is comfortably in the lead. This was totally different. The booing intensified. It was akin to a science-fiction movie in which the world is going to end with a nuclear blast at a given time, and all that can save us is a moment of courage. Sadly this quality was not in evidence at Celtic Park that night. No Superman nor James Bond nor even John Wayne with the United States cavalry appeared over the hillside.

The last five minutes as the apocalypse came closer saw Celtic fans fall in to three distinct categories – the departing, the traumatised and the angry. The departing went, noisily, blasphemously and disgustedly throwing away their colours in total contempt for those who had so betrayed the traditions of Celtic Football Club. The traumatised looked like the shattered remnants of Rommel's Afrika Korps in 1943, grey-eyed, disbelieving and broken people, some of them willing to admit some time later that they had actually sought psychiatric help the following day.

It was the angry who made the headlines, however, delivering torrents of abuse at the Celtic board and management team in a way that had not been seen since New Year's Day, 1994. The heads of Barnes, Black, McDermott and Dalglish were called for and those in charge had little choice but to do something about it in the next few days.

Full time brought joy to the Invernesians. It has to be acknowledged that they played very well, did not waste time and deserved their triumph even though their ecstasy was somewhat dimmed by the media concentration on Celtic's pain. Those who had disgraced the colours slunk off the field unable to look in the eye those who had spent their hard-earned cash on such a debacle. The press box was a hive of activity as the assorted journalists put their slant on the night's events. *The Sun*, ingenious as ever, and recalling the movie *Mary Poppins*, coined perhaps the most memorable headline in Scottish football history: 'Super Caley Go Ballistic, Celtic Are Atrocious'. If anything, atrocious understated it. Celtic had been far, far worse than that.

To his credit – some might have said with consummate gall – Barnes did not hide. He spoke to the media after the game, talked about the work he had to do and mentioned that Celtic were in the semi final of the League Cup next week, and that he was looking forward to it. He fooled no one. You cannot disgrace Celtic and their supporters to that extent and expect to survive.

The board acted quickly and creditably. A meeting was arranged the following day. By the Thursday of that week Barnes, McDermott (the social manager) and Black (the glorified trainer) were on their way after barely half a year of a three-year contract. Dalglish was summoned back post-haste from his holiday (although a half-hearted attempt was made to convince the unbelieving public that it was a business trip from which Celtic would benefit in some vague and ill-defined way) to take over the team on a temporary basis. It was a move that did not pacify the fans who had seen Kenny's social trip to Spain as akin to General Custer taking a coffee break during his last stand. It was also clear that several players would be lucky to play again for the club they had shamed.

The ghosts of Maley and Stein would have turned in their graves at all this. The traditions of Celtic had been disgraced. The players who played in this game were like the soldiers of a Roman legion that had lost its eagle standard. There was an ignominy which need not necessarily last for ever, but would take some considerable time to expunge. One was sorry for the likes of Jonathan Gould, Lubomir Moravcik and Tommy Boyd, honest Celts unfortunate enough to be caught up in this nightmare. Even more sorrow could be expressed for novices like Colin Healy and Mark Burchill, inexperienced youngsters exposed to the pain of a bitter defeat. The others however must accept the guilty verdict of history, and little sympathy is possible.

Only once in the long history of Celtic Football Club can this ignominy be paralleled and there was one factor in common. In January 1897, Celtic went down to Arthurlie in the Scottish Cup. The link was player discontent. The great Dan Doyle did not turn up for the tie, and several other players claimed they were injured. The Arthurlie game shocked Victorian Scotland and, 103 years later, Inverness Caledonian Thistle did the same to the world of Scottish football in the new millennium. The parallel continues in that, after both disasters, Celtic's directors took a tumble to themselves and appointed good managers. In the same way that Willie Maley emerged from the ruins of Arthurlie, so Martin O'Neill was to appear from the shambles of Inverness. Not, however, for the immediate or foreseeable future, and a Herculean effort was needed to restore a semblance of credibility.

Even after the gloating of Inverness and Rangers supporters died down, it was clear that supporting Celtic would never be the same again. Of course we would get over it, but in the same way that Rangers would never forget or be allowed to forget Berwick in 1967, Celtic would never entirely dismiss Inverness Caledonian Thistle from their consciousness. Interim manager Kenny Dalglish had a fight on his hands to regain for Celtic, not glory, not honour but self-respect.

Bad weather now descended, although not enough to put off Celtic's next two games. One was at Dens Park on a snowy day where Celtic won 3–0, a very respectable victory. Inverness Caledonian Thistle incidentally lost 2–0 to St Mirren that day, a result that put their defeat of Celtic into some kind of perspective. Then more crucially for Celtic, came the League Cup semi final on Wednesday 16 February. It was at Hampden against Kilmarnock on a freezing-cold night, and was live on television. Only 22,000 turned up to see a very poor game, but there was at least a happy ending as Moravcik scored with a header off the bar to give Celtic a 1–0 victory.

The team then staggered towards their League Cup final date with Aberdeen by losing in the league to Hibs and Rangers. Granted luck was not with them on either occasion, but in any case, supporters were more concerned about the League Cup. Home crowds remained at a commendably high level, but there was increasing evidence that Celtic's huge away support was more reluctant to travel.

To his credit, Dalglish did try to rally the team. On one occasion he held his Friday press conference in Baird's Bar in the Gallowgate, an establishment widely recognised as being the epicentre of the Celtic-supporting fraternity. There he sat fielding question from journalists and punters alike, earning grudging respect even from those who did not like him. Kenny was as upset, presumably, as the rest of us and as uncertain of the future. Yet no one's cause was helped by the continual ducking of the real issue about who would be the next manager. Would it be Dalglish himself or one of the many names that the press kept bringing forward?

The League Cup was won, but any possibility of other success was shattered when Celtic went to Ibrox the Sunday after the League Cup success and appalled everyone by going down 4–0. Once again, it was not the actual defeat that caused the distress so much as the apparent acceptance of it. The absence of a fightback in the second half was appalling and almost unprecedented, recalling yet again that dreadful day in August 1988 when the 5–1 trouncing by Rangers, with so many long-term consequences, had been administered.

So the close season came early for Celtic fans. 1999/2000 had been traumatic. But whatever happened, the club obstinately refused to stay out of the news. Hardly a day passed without some-one writing an exclusive about who the next manager was going to be, or what was going to happen to this or that player. Celtic sup-porters with their infinite capacity to rally and regroup noted with optimism that Tommy Burns had returned to his spiritual home as a backroom bhoy and that Henrik Larsson was back doing light training – he would be in action before the end of the season – and tried to clutch at other straws. When you have reached rock bottom, the only way is up.

On the field, the tail end of a long season was played out with nothing at stake, other than the trying out of youngsters, notably Stephen Crainey. The form of the team was actually quite good. Some people felt, and not without cause, that there was a lesson here, namely that the way ahead for Celtic might be young Scottish talent rather than spending money on foreign players with all their attendant psychiatric problems. In either case, it said very little for Scottish football that Celtic in spite of their appalling form actually finished second in the SPL! Even more disturbing was the fact that they were a massive twenty-one points behind Rangers, yet fifteen points ahead of third-placed Hearts! Small wonder that Scottish football was either sneered at by the rest of the world, or simply ignored.

Indeed the game was at a low ebb. Euro 2000 in the Low Countries was a fine television spectacle in the summer, but there was no Scotland. Scotland had exited the tournament at the play-off stage after being eliminated by England over two legs, despite winning 1–0 at Wembley. This happened during the dark days of November 1999 when Barnes's Celtic also began to lose the plot. Both of these losses were grievous.

8

2000/01:
The Right Man At Last

T he crowd that gathered outside Celtic Park on the night of Thursday 1 June 2000 no doubt had a sense of *déja vu*. They had been here twelve months before to welcome their new boss, John Barnes. Everything had seemed fine then. What was the difference with this year's new manager, incredibly the ninth in nine years if we include caretakers like Frank Connor and Kenny Dalglish? Well, for a start the weather was not as good as it normally was for what had become an annual event. It was raining this time! Was this an omen?

The fans were not necessarily impressed by Martin O'Neill's statement that he was a lifelong Celtic supporter. He was certainly Northern Irish and it had at one point been erroneously believed by the support that he came from an Orange or Protestant background. This was simply not true – he was indeed Celtic-minded as that awful cliché had it. The belief that he was Orange rather than Green presumably stemmed from the fact that he had been captain of Northern Ireland at one point in the early 1980s and very few Roman Catholics have ever received such an honour. In fact, O'Neill had been appointed captain by the excellent Billy Bingham in a deliberate attempt to unite both sections of that sad country.

But even with his Green credentials established, that was not enough. Celtic-minded people or unashamed Celtic supporters had failed before, both as players and as managers. Some indeed had deserted. It was of course the execrable Maurice Johnston who said that, 'Celtic were the only team he ever wanted to play for' only a few weeks before he signed for Rangers!

Nor were fans necessarily overjoyed by the statement that O'Neill needed only two-and-a-half seconds to make a decision. Once more, it had to be reckoned, these statements meant very little. All managers taking on new jobs will say that sort of thing. No doubt his rival for the job, Guus Hiddink, the former manager of *La Liga* outfit Real Betis, would have said exactly the same.

The appearance of Dutchman Guus Hiddink in the frame was thanks to a very deliberate leak from those within the club who did not like Allan MacDonald. MacDonald had lost a great deal of credibility after the Barnes-Dalglish fiasco, and Dermot Desmond, now the majority shareholder, seemed to wish to rid the club of the former British Aerospace man. It was thus leaked to the press that MacDonald was interested in Hiddink. In the meantime, Joe Kinnear of Wimbledon, a hardy annual in the 'Who will be Celtic's next manager?' stakes was also put forward as a stalking horse. But the real target was O'Neill, and when he was landed, MacDonald was further discredited.

What was impressive about the appointment was that Martin O'Neill was without any doubt a proven winner. As a player he had been in the squad that won two European Cups for Nottingham Forest in 1979 and 1980, even though the impression had often been given that manager Brian Clough did not like him. Indeed, Cloughie seemed to take a certain amount of sadistic pleasure in dropping O'Neill from important games. Distillery, Manchester City, Norwich City and Notts County had been O'Neill's other teams. He played sixty-four times for his country and was team captain in the very impressive campaign during the 1982 World Cup finals when Northern Ireland achieved the immensely creditable feat of beating hosts Spain in Valencia 1–0.

It was however as a manager that O'Neill came into his own. Non-league Wycombe Wanderers had benefited from his presence to the extent that they were elevated into the Football League. Following a brief and unhappy spell at Norwich, he moved to Leicester City in late 1995 to succeed former Celtic striker Mark McGhee and proceeded instantly to revitalise the club. In his first season the Foxes were promoted to the Premiership via the play-offs and then finished in the top ten of that highly competitive league four seasons in a row. Indeed at the end of season 1999/2000 they were in eighth place, a club record. Leicester also reached the

League Cup final three times in four years, and won it twice, beating Middlesbrough in 1997, Tranmere in 2000 and were very unlucky to lose to Tottenham Hotspur in 1999. For a provincial side, lacking the huge fan base of the Lancashire or London teams, this was as good as it gets and the club was clearly punching above its weight. Perhaps O'Neill took the view that he had gone as far as he could with the Midlands outfit. Perhaps it was time to move on, and when the call came from the team he had always loved, it was impossible to say no. But he is a man known for taking an inordinate length of time to make a decision on employment and contractual matters, and had previously vacillated over joining Everton and Leeds before electing to stay at Filbert Street. Despite the reputed two-and-a-half seconds he said it took him to decide to join Celtic it was clear that the decision was not that straightforward. At the eleventh hour it was reported that he was in talks with Leicester chairman John Elsom and other board members at a secret location as they tried to persuade him to stay. But it was not to be and the emotional pull of Celtic was too strong. Elsom, perhaps understandably bitter, later announced that O'Neill had decided to pursue his Roman Catholic heritage by signing on at Celtic Park.

Despite his occasional indecisiveness O'Neill was clearly a man who knew how to win and success was craved by all those connected with Celtic. The sight of a figure clad in green and white lifting a trophy, albeit the League Cup after a poor final against an even poorer Aberdeen team, was something that we had last seen in March 2000, and which we needed an awful lot more of, if the clouds of depression which had been circling over Celtic Park for most of the 1990s were not to become a permanent feature.

Yet O'Neill was a curiously unimposing man as he faced his first press conferences. He lacked the build and gravitas of Maley and Stein, the two other great Celtic managers of the past, and with his glasses and short hair, looked more like a scholar than a sportsman. Born on 1 March 1952, Martin was the sixth child in a family of nine. His father Leo O'Neill – a Gaelic footballer and unashamed lover of Celtic – was a barber in the staunchly pro-Celtic town of Kilrea some forty miles from Belfast. Rare among football people, Martin O'Neill had a boarding-school education, having won a scholarship to St Columba's Christian Brothers School in Derry. Other former pupils of that school include such luminaries as the politician John Hume, poet Seamus Heaney and Bishop Edward Daly. At school he passed A Levels in Ancient History, English Literature and Latin (with very high grades), and demonstrated all-round sporting ability, notably in cricket, Gaelic football and, of course, soccer. He was reading law at Queen's University, Belfast when he was invited to join Nottingham Forest as a professional footballer. He accepted without much hesitation, and from then on football was his passion.

His lovely Irish accent and soft voice gave him a persona that impressed by its sincerity, but not necessarily its forcefulness. But we recalled the Beatitudes in the New Testament which point out, 'Blessed are the meek' and students of British history argue that Britain's best twentieth century leader was not the bullish Thatcher or Churchill, nor the conniving, scheming Wilson or Lloyd George, but the mild-mannered Clement Attlee, prime minister from 1945–1951, a man whom you would have passed on the street, but who nevertheless changed British society beyond recognition.

An interesting facet of his character came to light several years later when it emerged that he was a keen student of murder cases. In this he is most unusual in the brotherhood of football managers. His illustrious predecessors at Celtic Park, Maley and Stein, both had interests away from the game: Maley in athletics and cycling and Stein in horse racing, gambling and the occasional game of bowls. Apparently, O'Neill has visited the scenes of the Hanratty murder of 1962, the Lord Lucan disappearance of 1974 and once when in America, went to Dallas to see where John F. Kennedy met his death and where Lee Harvey Oswald was shot by Jack Ruby.

Clearly an interesting character was Martin O'Neill. But attention in summer 2000 focused on his football-management abilities. Very soon he would appoint capable assistants in John Robertson, formerly of Nottingham Forest and Scotland and a comparative unknown, Steve Walford. Robertson of course was a Scottish hero, having played twenty-eight times for his country between 1978 and 1984. He had never let Scotland down and was adept at sinking penalty kicks, most notably the one he scored against England at Wembley in 1981. He had always been close to O'Neill in their days as teammates at Forest, and being a Scotsman from Uddingston, he had a thorough knowledge of the Scottish scene. Curiously, whether or not Robertson was Celtic-minded was never an issue with either the media or the support.

There would be other appointments as well to what was

undoubtedly a strong backroom team. Traditionalists among the supporters were delighted to see John Clark retain his post as kit man. Clark was a Lisbon Lion and his words of wisdom would be invaluable. The changes however meant that there would be no place for Kenny Dalglish in the new set-up and he departed at the end of June in a somewhat petulant manner that did his already tarnished reputation no good.

Would Martin O'Neill (or MON as he soon became in fanzine speak) take Celtic back to their rightful place at the top of Scottish and even European football? Those of us who still relished 1967 were becoming fed up of having to talk about it time and time again, simply because there was precious little else of more recent vintage to get excited about. Twenty long, painful years had passed without Celtic supporters being able to wish each other a Happy New Year with the team still in Europe. Clearly, such were the demands of modern European football that it would be a long time before 1967 could be emulated. A few victories in Scotland would however be a start.

The events of Euro 2000 in Holland and Belgium were a temporary distraction as France emphatically added the European trophy to their world crown, but O'Neill, although doing a little commentating and studio analysis for television, had not been idle. The Scottish transfer record was broken when he paid £6 million for Chris Sutton from Chelsea on 11 July. Sutton was an aggressive centre forward with impressive aerial power, but whose face did not fit at Gianluca Vialli's Chelsea. He had not been included in the FA Cup final win over Aston Villa, although he had played in the semi final and sporadically throughout the league campaign. He clearly felt that a change in career direction might be no bad thing.

Going the other way was Mark Viduka. Leeds United paid £6 million for him, and Celtic inserted a clause into the agreement with the Yorkshire club that would entitle them – depending on which newspaper you believed – to between 10 and 20 per cent of any future transfer fee. His departure was not particularly regretted by the fans. He was certainly an excellent goalscorer and by the end of the 2000 season had proven as much, but he could not be forgiven for his part in the disgraceful events of last February and Celtic's departure from the Scottish Cup. Annoyingly, we read several times in newspapers about how much he loved Celtic. Such affection had not always been too obvious over the last eighteen months.

Joos Valgaeren also joined the club, from Roda JC Kerkrade, for £3.8 million at the end of July. He was a tall, slim, energetic centre half. He would be a great asset, for the defence had been leaking goals in a way that was fatal to any attempt on the SPL title, let alone in a European context. More signings would be made in the early part of the season but for the moment, the good news was that Henrik Larsson, having come on as a substitute in the last game of the 1999/2000 season, was now back to full fitness. Whatever one says about the inadequacies of the Barnes and Dalglish regimes, their one misfortune was the leg break of Larsson at Lyon the previous autumn. Had Serge Blanc of Lyon failed to make contact with him, the season would have been totally different. It is difficult to imagine, for example, a fully fit Larsson unable to conjure up a piece of magic against Inverness Caledonian Thistle.

In the domestic game, there was a major change to contend with: an increase in the number of teams in the SPL from ten to twelve. While this in itself was hardly controversial the arrangements made to accommodate the new set-up attracted scorn from many quarters. In order to ensure the optimum number of games, the twelve teams in the SPL would play three rounds of fixtures against each other, making a total of thirty-three matches. After these three rounds the SPL would split into two mini-leagues of six, with teams playing each other once, giving a total for the season of thirty-eight matches. Obvious anomalies were thrown up; for example it was perfectly possible that teams finishing in the bottom six could end the season with a higher number of points than those in the top six.

However, it was hardly likely that Celtic, or Rangers, would finish anywhere apart from in the top two and as the new season dawned players' minds were focused on the task in hand. The domestic campaign started on the ridiculously early date of 29 July 2000. Celtic had to wait another day for their debut, which was played on Sunday 30 July with a 6-05 p.m. kick off to satisfy the demands of satellite television. The game was against Dundee United at Tannadice Park and the meagre attendance of 5,896 showed how unimpressed fans were with this outrageous kick-off time and indeed the unwarranted incursion of the football season into summer pastimes.

It is not often that Celtic fans are in raptures about the demise of a team wearing green. Dundee United chose to wear their new all-green strip. It was in fact their original strip, for they wore green and had been called Dundee Hibernian from their foundation in 1909 until 1923. In those days they were an unashamedly Irish team like Hibernian of Edinburgh and indeed Celtic of Glasgow, but changed the name to United in an attempt, presumably, to win over the non-Irish population of the city. While there were good historical reasons for the strip, the fact that they chose to launch it on this particular day looked like a ham-fisted way of upstaging their distinguished Glasgow visitors.

Not that it mattered a great deal, for Celtic played very well in their yellow change-strip and won a traditionally difficult fixture 2–1. To the delight of the Celtic faithful, both Larsson and Sutton scored and showed every sign of being able to work well together. The next week saw a less pleasing game, but one in which the points were nevertheless satisfactorily secured. This was when Motherwell came to Celtic Park, and an over-fussy referee spoiled the game by not allowing the action to flow. He even sent off Chris Sutton for an offence that might have deserved a yellow card, but hardly the ultimate penalty.

Eyal Berkovic in fact scored the only goal of the game. It was not a bad goal, but would turn out to be Eyal's swansong in a singularly disappointing Celtic Park career. He might have hoped to resurrect things under O'Neill, for he had grievously failed Barnes and Dalglish, both of whom had faith in him. But Berkovic was substituted, and played in only a handful of games after that, invariably as a substitute. He blamed O'Neill for his predicament, complaining that the manager hardly ever spoke to him before his eventual, low-key departure to Blackburn Rovers on loan in February 2001 and then on a permanent basis to Manchester City in August 2001 for £1.5 million. Once O'Neill had built up his own team, he could hardly be expected to change it just for the sake of giving Berkovic a game. Eyal enjoyed little sympathy from the support, who were keen to erase forever from their psyche the memories of Inverness Caledonian Thistle and all who were associated with that debacle. Eyal will have to join the 'Tony Cascarino club' of those who performed successfully for other clubs, but could not cope with the pressures of playing for Celtic.

The next week after a European jaunt to dispose of Jeunesse Esch of Luxemburg in the preliminary round of the UEFA Cup, Kilmarnock came to town. It was a Sunday game and Killie scored first through a fine drive by Andy McLaren. But this Celtic team was not without character, and patrons noticed with approval their impressive work ethic. 'You have to be prepared to die for us' remarked a discerning north stand punter that day. It was indeed hard work rather than any brilliance which won the day. Larsson equalised and the ever popular Tommy Johnson got the winner.

Four league wins in a row were now registered. The following week a vibrant Celtic went to Tynecastle and defeated a weak Hearts team. The Edinburgh men were 3–0 down at half time. Although they pulled back a couple of goals, Lubomir Moravcik scored another and Hearts never looked like taking a point. This Celtic team were simply getting better and better, but the big test was to come the following week against Rangers.

The first Old Firm game usually sets the scene for the season. One recalled the game twelve years previously in 1988 when Celtic, league and Scottish Cup winners, went to Ibrox and unaccountably crashed 5–1. They never recovered from that one for the rest of the season. In fact, some people would say that they did not fully recover until Martin O'Neill arrived. Therefore Sunday 27 August 2000, with its lunch time kick-off, would be a very important fixture indeed. It would, one felt, be axiomatic for the future of Martin O'Neill.

In fact it was the defining moment in O'Neill's short Celtic career. It was the start of the modern Celtic, symbolic of it all being the rebirth of Bobby Petta. Petta had not impressed anyone under the Barnes-Dalglish regime and questions were being asked about how long he would stay at the club. The luckless Dutchman looked as if he would join the long list of those who, however well they had played for other clubs, simply lacked the ability or the temperament to do well at Celtic Park.

But in this game Petta excelled, ripping the luckless Fernando Ricksen to shreds and compelling his fellow countryman's early substitution. After only fifteen minutes, Celtic, incredibly, were three goals to the good. The first came after Sutton latched onto a Larsson shot that seemed to be going wide, the second when Petrov headed home a Moravcik cross and the third when Paul Lambert rammed home an unstoppable drive. Then, completely out of character, Henrik Larsson missed two half-chances and Rangers pulled a goal back. Celtic fans were quite disappointed that they were going in at half time only 3–1 up when it could have been 5–0.

But further joy was forthcoming. Larsson atoned for his first half failures by scoring a truly remarkable goal. Sutton chested a ball down to him just inside the Rangers half. Henrik then charged towards the goal evading the challenge of Tugay and then slipped the ball between the legs of Konterman before delicately chipping the ball over the head of the Rangers goalkeeper to release bedlam behind the goal. Larsson scored again with a header from a Petta free kick to make it five after Rangers had pulled one back through a penalty, and then after Barry Ferguson was given his marching orders for a second bookable offence, Sutton scored from a Mahe cross to make it 6–2 and complete a remarkable Sunday lunchtime of football. Ferguson, a jersey player in the mould of Peter Grant on the other side of the Old Firm divide, was clearly still smarting at the crushing defeat and reportedly got involved in a brawl with Celtic fans later that night.

The upbeat, rampant Celtic supporters celebrated noisily and raucously, and with good cause, for they had witnessed a great performance and one that hinted at greater things to come. The green-and-white brigade had a great time of it for months after, wearing T-shirts with a 6–2 logo and the ascription 'and the cry was No Defenders', a deliberate mockery of the sectarian Rangers song, 'No Surrender'. And much to the chagrin of Rangers manager Dick Advocaat, Celtic's commercial department immediately produced a video of the match.

From then on, the odd stumble apart, Celtic seldom looked back and some of the football played particularly around the turn of the year was stunning. A key game in the winter months was an encounter with Dunfermline on 2 December. The previous Saturday, Celtic had played poorly to lose 5–1 at Ibrox, allowing Rangers a little revenge for 27 August. Then on the Wednesday night, there had been a disappointing 0–0 draw at Easter Road. Celtic now teetered on the brink. The slippery slope beckoned and Celtic looked a hairsbreadth away from disappearing down it, in the way that they had done all so predictably, under weaker management, in previous seasons.

The hard-working Fifers came to Celtic Park that early December day and scored in the first minute through Jason Dair. This young man was the nephew of Jim Baxter and those with long memories recalled that in his Raith Rovers days, he had been the man whose shot Gordon Marshall could not hold in that dreadful League Cup final. The atmosphere was now distinctly edgy. Celtic had to come back, or all the good work was wasted and the mindset of 'not being allowed to beat Rangers and therefore dropping further points the week after' that had bedevilled Celtic so often in the past would return. Fortunately Moravcik, Larsson and Johnson inspired the fightback and Celtic ran out 3–1 winners. It was by no means one of the most impressive victories that season, but it was possibly the most vital.

That luck was with Celtic seemed to be proved the following week at Dens Park. The balance of the play was even, both teams missed chances and a draw would probably have been a fair result. Then in a goalmouth scramble following a corner kick, Didier Agathe chested in a last-minute winner. It had actually been a fine game with a spirited performance from Dundee, but Celtic's character and determination, rather than their skill, won the day. Celtic's opponents would say that it was undeserved, but that is football. There are times when teams create their own luck.

Didier Agathe had joined Celtic a few weeks previously from Hibs. The Easter Road club had foolishly and parsimoniously failed to give him a season's contract after picking him up for a song from near-bankrupt Raith Rovers. Under freedom of contract, Agathe had few qualms about joining Celtic for about £50,000, and he would have a very impressive season. Hibs would have cause to rue their reluctance to spend money on him. Alan Thompson, Rab Douglas, Neil Lennon and Ramon Vega had also joined the club from Aston Villa, Dundee, Leicester City and Tottenham Hotspur respectively, and the squad now looked very strong.

Of these, the most expensive was Neil Lennon for whom O'Neill paid £5.75 million in December 2000 to prise away from his former associates at Leicester City, after a bid of £4 million was rejected a month earlier. Lennon fitted in very well from the start, and it was perhaps an indication of how good he was that the barracking from Rangers fans started almost immediately. In a more sinister turn of events, it became a lot worse when he played for Northern Ireland, a phenomenon that spoke volumes about the state of that tragic part of the world.

The baying of Lennon and the placards that read 'Neil Lennon RIP' would still have been deplorable but would have had some logic behind them if they had been directed at an opponent. But this was the Windsor Park crowd directing their hate against one of their own players. In recent years, Anton Rogan was subjected to similar abuse in Belfast because he played for Celtic and in more distant times Charlie Tully and Bertie Peacock had also suffered, although neither had made any big issue of it. It is possibly true in any case that in the 1950s people in that unfortunate province were more interested in football, and the abuse had been limited to the real bigots.

Thompson was also an interesting signing. He had been struggling to hold down a place in John Gregory's Aston Villa side and O'Neill snapped him up for a fee of £2.7 million. Clearly the Irishman saw something in the 26-year-old Geordie, whose career had perhaps gone sideways at Villa Park after spells at Bolton Wanderers and Newcastle United. An aggressive left-sided midfielder, Thompson was proficient with the dead ball and would add much to Celtic's set-pieces.

Rab Douglas was signed to replace Jonathan Gould, who had failed to convince O'Neill that he was up to the standard required by Celtic. Tall, heavily built and courageous Douglas was prone, on occasion, to make unforced errors in big games although he would turn in many fine performances for the club. But many supporters were sorry to see the eclipse of Gould. Son of the one-time Wales international manager, Bobby Gould, he was a likeable character who had immersed himself in the history and traditions of the club and was keen to live up to the standards set by illustrious predecessors like Charlie Shaw, John Thomson, Ronnie Simpson and Pat Bonner. In truth he was a little short of that calibre but one incident at East End Park epitomises the relationship he enjoyed with the fans. Finding himself without a cap, and facing strong sunlight, he immediately turned to the Celtic supporters and asked one for the loan of his cap. So he faced the Dunfermline attack dressed in the headgear of a supporter, which of course he was.

Dundee had scored a goal that night of Agathe's chest-in at Dens Park, and the next goal to be scored against Celtic in the league was at the end of February at Easter Road. In between Celtic played eight games on both sides of the winter shutdown, won them all and did not concede a goal. Some of the victories were very impressive indeed: Aberdeen and Kilmarnock were both hammered 6–0 for example, and hitherto traditionally tricky away venues like Tannadice and Tynecastle were more than competently dealt with.

The game at Tynecastle in particular proved, if there ever had been the slightest doubt, that Celtic had a world-class finisher in Henrik Larsson. This game, the first in the SPL game after the winter shutdown, was played in a snowstorm on Sunday 4 February, and Larsson's hat trick was outstanding. The last goal will remain in the memory for a long time. He picked up a cross from the right, was surrounded by four Hearts defenders, yet succeeded in doing the needful.

A casualty of this fine run however was Celtic's campaign in Europe. Once again, the team failed to step up a gear and last beyond Christmas in the UEFA Cup. Such European exits, however customary and habitual they may be, are painful, but it was generally recognised that this new Celtic team was not yet of the necessary calibre. HJK Helsinki, hardly European giants, took Celtic to extra time in the return leg in Finland after Celtic had won 2–0 at home. It took a Chris Sutton goal to send Celtic through to the next round. Extra time was also necessary in the second leg against Bordeaux at Celtic Park, but on this occasion it was Laslandes who got the winner for the French side. Celtic had done well to hold Bordeaux to 1–1 in France, and in the return were winning 1–0, thanks to a fine Moravcik strike, until late in the game. By no means disgraced, it was nevertheless apparent that Celtic were a shade below the French team. Success in Europe was still some way off.

More progress was being made in the League Cup. Raith Rovers, by now a mere shadow of their former selves, were beaten 4–0 at Celtic Park in early September, and then television viewers saw a great game when Celtic went to Tynecastle on 1 November. This game was played on the Wednesday between the two Bordeaux games, and O'Neill raised a few eyebrows by playing what looked like a weakened squad with Stephen Crainey, Jamie Smith and Colin Healy all given a start, and several of the regulars, notably Henrik Larsson, missing.

This might well have backfired, but in fact it created a level playing field, and it was only in extra time that Celtic took charge. The youngsters acquitted themselves well and all three of them got on the score sheet in a fine 5–2 victory, marred as far as Hearts were concerned by a nasty clash of heads which caused them to lose the services of Flogel and Locke. For O'Neill any flak that might have come his way for not fielding his strongest side was easily answered by the fact that Celtic won.

Supporters of the Scottish game should really have been happy about this, because one of the side-effects of Celtic's success was that it was becoming increasingly difficult for young Scottish players to break into the team. A knock-on effect was the paucity of talent available to the Scotland international team, for most of the SPL teams were now bringing in foreign players, and not always exercising sound judgement with some of their recruits. Quite a few of us deplored this development, reminding everyone *ad nauseam* that the Lisbon Lions were all Scottish and that it was not all that long ago that the best players in the English leagues were invariably Scottish.

Yet the counter argument to that must surely be that we should look to Celtic's record in Europe when they did employ mainly and often exclusively Scots. In a word, it was awful. It was clear that an all-Scottish policy would be doomed to failure. Yet this did not mean that talented youngsters like Crainey, for example, needed to be excluded from the first team. If they were good enough, they would be selected. In any case, there were now many opportunities for youngsters to shine. If Celtic were involved in four tournaments per year, including European competitions with mini-league formats, then clearly there would have to be a strong squad of around twenty players who would be rotated as the manager thought fit.

The next League Cup tie was against Rangers in the semi final in early February 2001. It was in fact the first of two Old Firm games in four days, because the pair were due to meet at Celtic Park on league business on the following Sunday. It was acknowledged that the SPL was the more important competition, and so there was a degree of speculation about whether the managers might field weakened teams in the semi final. Both sets of supporters took the view that a victory in the League Cup would be all very well, but what was really important was the race for the title.

Neither manager took the option of sending out a weakened side and Celtic won a curious game 3–1. Two up in the first quarter of an hour with goals from Vega and Larsson, Celtic looked well on top. Then the refereeing of that amiable eccentric Willie Young became silly with the award of two soft penalties, one for each side. Both were converted, by Larsson and Albertz. The game ended with a free-for-all in which Moravcik of Celtic and Mols and Reyna of Rangers, none of them among the most physical of players, received their marching orders, and several others in both sides might have followed. Celtic however had been the better team throughout, and as well as earning a place in the final against

Kilmarnock, who beat St Mirren in the other semi, a marker had been laid down for Sunday's league match.

Once again on the Sunday marching orders were issued, this time to Fernando Ricksen, and it was our old friend Hugh Dallas who did the needful, shaking his head at the folly of professional footballers as he did so, for Fernando had given every impression of trying to get sent off. Substituted in one game at Celtic Park, sent off in the next, Fernando was clearly having problems seeing out ninety minutes in the East End of Glasgow! Celtic were more on top in this game than the one–nil scoreline suggests. The goal had come from the ever dependable Alan Thompson, a man who was becoming a favourite for his endeavour and commitment.

It was at this point that Celtic fans realised that, unless something out of the ordinary occurred, their team were going to win the championship. It was hard to spot a weakness in the side. Idol number one was of course the inimitable Henrik Larsson whose ability was now freely compared with the great goalscorers of the past like Jimmy McGrory and Jimmy Quinn. But in addition to that, there was his excellent leading of the line, distribution and a level-headed approach to the game that made him an ideal role model for youngsters. It has to be stated yet again that if Larsson had not broken his leg in France, there would have been no Inverness Caledonian Thistle disaster.

The defence looked stronger than it had done for some time with Mjallby, Valgaeren and Vega the three centre-backs in O'Neill's favoured 3–5–2 formation. And with Rab Douglas now playing well in goal after a hesitant start, very few goals were conceded. Midfield contained Lambert and Lennon, whom many had said could not play with each other, the fast improving Stilian Petrov and that veteran genius Lubomir Moravcik, now vindicating the judgement of the good Dr Jo.

Lubo, now a hero and causing us to regret that he had not joined Celtic at an earlier stage of his career, was at his best when used sparingly and he frequently excelled as a second half substitute. O'Neill realised this and was able to exploit it. An excellent case in point was a game, postponed because of snow the week between Christmas and New Year and played eventually on Wednesday 21 February, against Motherwell at Celtic Park. Motherwell with Andy Goram in goal, frustrated Celtic time and again with their depressingly effective defensive play and time-wasting tactics. Seven minutes remained when a free kick was awarded on the edge of the box. Lubo took it . . . and the game was won.

Progress had also been made in the Scottish Cup. The first game after the pointless winter shutdown had seen Celtic at the unlikely venue of Stair Park, Stranraer at the end of January. A hard pitch on a frosty night was something of a leveller, and the television audience witnessed a good game of football, although Celtic surprised no one by running out 4–1 winners. The next round sent Celtic to Dunfermline. It was a game in the tradition of fine Scottish Cup encounters between these two. It finished 2–2 with three goals in the last ten minutes, and Dunfermline's equaliser was scored well into injury time. Not that it did the Pars any lasting good, other than a share in a big gate, as Celtic comfortably won the replay 4–1.

Sunday 11 March was a good day for Celtic. In the afternoon Celtic beat Hearts 1–0 in the quarter final of the Scottish Cup. In fact the scoreline was deceptive, for once Larsson scored just before half time, Celtic remained well on top throughout the second half and should have scored a lot more. That evening, Dundee United surprised the world of Scottish football and delighted bhoys everywhere by defeating Rangers at Tannadice. Their goal came from erstwhile Celtic player, David Hannah, who had returned to United whence he came in the first place. Hannah had been a hard working, if not particularly outstanding, player for Celtic, and it did seem that the less intense atmosphere of Tannadice was his natural habitat. He was certainly the toast of both Dundee United and Celtic that evening, as Celtic fans again recalled that he was a palindrome.

This defeat effectively marked the end of the season for Rangers. Out of both domestic cup competitions and 'needing snookers' to have any hope at all in the SPL, they had disappointed their fans who were already tightening the noose round the neck of manager Dick Advocaat. Celtic fans sang songs advising Dick to cheer up, but also telling him that he was corpulent and going to get the sack. Another particularly pathetic ditty went along the lines of:

Oh the poor Teddy Berrs,
They've got no silverwerr!

The season was now approaching its climax for Celtic, but a bad blow came their way on 14 March. It was the Wednesday night before the League Cup final against Kilmarnock. The game against St Johnstone at McDiarmid Park was rearranged for this date after it had been called off because of fog – at virtually the last minute – on 31 January. This game ended up in a hard fought 2–1 win, but the tragedy for Celtic was that Stilian Petrov was carried off after an accidental clash with a St Johnstone player. It was a broken ankle, effectively curtailing Stan's season and casting a shadow over the future of this talented Bulgar who had not immediately impressed but had improved so rapidly under O'Neill.

The League Cup final was played on Sunday 18 March. In normal circumstances, Kilmarnock would have had no hope against Celtic, who had trounced them 6–0 in the SPL on 2 January. But Celtic had major problems. The loss of Petrov had to be added to other injuries to Sutton and Petta, the suspensions of McNamara and Thompson and the ineligibility of Douglas and Agathe who were cup-tied, having already played in the League Cup for Dundee and Hibs respectively this season.

Martin O'Neill was thus in a quandary for his first cup final in charge of Celtic. But he had faith in his youngsters whom he had blooded in that quarter final against Hearts the previous November. Colin Healy was given a start and Jamie Smith and Stephen Crainey were on the bench, and in the event Sutton and Petta, although neither was totally fit, did start the game.

In Petta's case 'start the game' was almost the sum total of his contribution to proceedings, for twice in the first few minutes he was cynically fouled by two Kilmarnock men who knew exactly what they were doing. It reflected badly on the well-respected Kilmarnock manager, Bobby Williamson, as it gave every indication of being a deliberate plan. The tragedy was that it worked, because Petta had to go off after ten minutes and was replaced by Stephen Crainey.

This hardly weakened the Celtic team for Crainey turned in a solid performance, but the first half was disappointing with neither team taking a grip on the game and although Celtic were marginally ahead on chances, the trophy was still up for grabs. But a feature of Celtic in that great season of 2000/01 was they way in which they could step up a gear immediately after half time, while the well-organised defence simply snuffed out any possibility of a counter attack.

This was what happened here. Celtic started the second half playing towards the King's Park goal with a great deal more purpose and urgency than had hitherto been the case. A corner kick soon after the break found Larsson who swivelled in mid air and scored. Celtic, with youngsters Healy and Crainey now on song, took command of the game and even the loss of Chris Sutton, harshly sent off by referee Hugh Dallas for a high but hardly dangerous challenge on Gary Holt, did not lessen Celtic's supremacy. Larsson scored again, this time via a deflection after a lovely pass from Moravcik, but the pick of the Swede's hat trick was the last one where he ran the length of the Kilmarnock half, shrugging off fouls by the Kilmarnock defence, before rounding Gordon Marshall. As the commentators would say, 'Was this class or was this class?'

It was a fine day, spoiled to a certain extent by the fact that Celtic were not wearing their traditional jerseys. The reason given by the authorities was that the green-and-white hoops would clash with Kilmarnock's blue-and-white stripes! The cynics thought it had more to do with the marketing of the reserve strip, while the traditionalists, and those who simply love the sight of green-and-white jerseys deplored it all. Whatever, the reason, it ultimately didn't matter and the performance and result confirmed that Celtic were there to stay at the top of Scottish football. The teams were:

Celtic: Gould, Mjallby, Vega, Valgaeren, Petta, Moravcik, Lennon, Lambert, Healy, Sutton, Larsson. Substitutes: Crainey, Smith, Kharine, Boyd, Johnson.

Kilmarnock: Marshall, MacPherson, Innes, Dindeleux, McGowne, Hay, Holt, Durrant, Mahood, Cocard, Dargo. Substitutes: Canero, Reilly, McLaren, McCoist, Meldrum.

Celtic fans might have been disappointed that their old adversary Ally McCoist sat on the substitutes' bench and was not given a game by Killie. Ally was symbolic of Rangers' nine-in-a-row and Celtic fans would have loved to put one over him, but perhaps even Bobby Williamson realised that Ally's best days were behind him. On the football field, that is. He was still up to his old tricks in the television studio and, according to the tabloids, the bedroom.

But the hero of it all was that unassuming and taciturn Swede Henrik Larsson. Historically Celtic have always needed and loved a personality goal scorer. Sandy McMahon, Jimmy Quinn, Jimmy McGrory, Joe McBride, Dixie Deans and many others have fitted the bill. Indeed a striking and telling feature of the terrible days of the early 1990s was the lack of such a player. But now, at long last, a hero had been found and it was no coincidence that the Messianic qualities of Larsson were stressed in an adaptation of the evangelic hymn that went:

Henrik Larsson, Henrik Larsson
Henrik Larsson is the King of Kings!
Henrik Larsson, Henrik Larsson
Is the King.

Significantly, no one complained about blasphemy in the same way as no one apparently had complained about insensitivity to religious matters seventy years previously when the supporters had adapted a Victorian revivalist hymn:

Tell me the old old story
A hat–trick for McGrory

The parallels were striking however. Both generations of Celtic supporters had their idols and both are attributed with almost divine status. The fact that Larsson beat McGrory's goalscoring record for a season indicated how special he was.

One small, almost insignificant incident perhaps showed how much he valued his fans. After the League Cup victory over Kilmarnock, he was hardly surprisingly given the man-of-the-match award. It was a silver salver. As the team walked round the park showing the League Cup off to their delighted supporters, Larsson made as if to throw the silver salver, Frisbee-style, into the crowd as if to indicate that it was they who deserved it.

Celtic tails were now well and truly up, and following a week's break for World Cup qualifiers, Celtic then won the league in the space of seven days. The defeat of Rangers by Dundee United (once again the Tannadice men doing us proud) on Saturday 31 March meant that the championship would be secured if Celtic won their next three games. They proceeded to do just that.

The first game was away to Aberdeen on the Sunday evening of 1

April. The Dons had of course drawn with Celtic in October at Pittodrie, bringing a temporary halt to the Celtic juggernaut. For a long time it looked as if they were going to do the same here. The second half was well advanced before Didier Agathe scored and Celtic were then professional enough to hold out and seal the three points.

There followed a truly great game at Celtic Park on the Wednesday night against Dundee, a charismatic and quixotic outfit in these days with several talented but volatile Latins and a few decent but uninspired Scots. Dundee fought very hard, pulling back to equalise Tommy Johnson's strike and, if anything, with the score at 1–1, looking the team more likely to score the winner. But there are times when destiny must be obeyed and with time running out, Johan Mjallby was able to hook the ball home in a goalmouth scramble. To use the cliché 'Celtic Park erupted' at that point is somewhat understating the welter of excitement, relief and gratitude that deliverance was now at hand.

Somewhat prematurely, plans were put in motion for street parties on the Saturday. Three points were still required. The game against St Mirren, a team struggling against relegation, was due to kick off at 1-00 p.m. and was on pay-per-view television. In the circumstances, it was hardly surprising that the standard of football was not high, but the only goal of the game was scored by Tommy Johnson who needed two bites of the cherry before eventually putting the ball away. The goal came towards the end of an undistinguished first half, and the second half was even less memorable, with neither goal particularly threatened. It did not matter however when the referee blew for full time. The SPL title had been won in the first year of Martin O'Neill's stewardship and the emotions generated in the Celtic Park stands were terrifying in their intensity.

Two trophies were now safely on the sideboard, and the following Sunday saw the Scottish Cup semi final against Dundee United. By the time that game was played, Celtic knew that the other finalists would be Hibs, for the Easter Road men had defeated Livingston in a poor semi final the previous day. One of the effects of this game was to leave the Hampden pitch in a disgraceful state for the Celtic–Dundee United tie, and there were quite clearly bare patches that caused the ball to go astray.

The decent side of Celtic supporters was also shown to the world in their total respect for Jim Baxter who had died the previous night. Baxter had of course played most of his career for Rangers and had starred in the Rangers team of the early 1960s who had frequently proved themselves the masters of Celtic. The one minute's silence was impeccably observed and a (green!) banner described Jim Baxter as 'Simply The Best'. Celtic supporters have a deserved reputation for loving good footballers, even if he is not one of our own. This was an excellent example.

In this match itself, Dundee United fought hard, but never recovered from a first half Larsson header that bulleted into the net and which would have done credit to the great McGrory. Celtic then controlled the game but it was not until the last quarter of an hour that they secured their place in the final when Larsson again, then the ever-dependable Jackie McNamara, wrapped up the win. United then scored a fine but irrelevant consolation goal through Alan Lilley, but it was Celtic who would face Hibs in the 2001 Scottish Cup final.

Even the hardest hearted of Celtic fans could not deny that Hibs were due a Scottish Cup success. Their last win in a Scottish Cup final was against Celtic and at Celtic Park at that. But it was in 1902, some ninety-nine years before. Cruel Hearts fans, in an attempt presumably to divert attention from their own inadequate performances, would sing songs to the Hibees about 'ninety-nine years in a row'. But now managed by Alex McLeish, the Easter Road men had a few good players and a commendable team spirit. Nobody would ever have written them off, but their confidence must have been dented when Celtic brushed them aside 5–2 in an inconsequential league game at Easter Road three weeks before the final.

In fact, there had been six weeks between the semi and the final, and a certain amount of football politics entered the fray to fill up pages due to the lack of any real action on the field. In the first place, the SFA and Queen's Park were eventually shamed into digging up the Hampden pitch and relaying it. This had come about because the pitch which had been problematic, to put it mildly, at the semi final stage had deteriorated badly thanks to American football being played on it. Queen's Park's last home game was against Forfar – a vital relegation encounter in the second division of the Scottish Football League – and they lost it, due partly to the poor condition of the pitch which had 'Claymores' written on it and lines for American football as well. Thank heaven the authorities gave in to justified pressure and prevented the Scottish Cup final becoming the laughing stock of the world game. The result was a fine surface, conducive to good football.

In another move inimical to those who love the traditions of the Scottish game, Celtic were denied the opportunity (as in the League Cup final) of wearing their green-and-white hoops. So too were Hibs prevented from wearing their traditional green jersey with white sleeves. This nonsense apparently emanated from the refereeing fraternity who claimed that there would be too much green, for the grass was also green and most of the supporters would be wearing green! It would therefore be difficult, they argued, to adjudge tricky issues like offside. Media commentators ridiculed this assertion, as previous referees had no such problems. But once officialdom makes up its mind, it stays made up. Both teams gave a huge sop to their supporters by saying that if they won the Scottish Cup, they would change into their traditional strip to receive the trophy.

Celtic fans had another gripe. Hibs were allocated the same amount of tickets as Celtic. While the SFA has to make every effort to be even handed, it did seem odd that a team whose average home gate was only a little short of 60,000 were allocated 25,000 briefs whereas a team who seldom played in front of more than 10,000 got the same amount. In the event, quite a few Celtic inter-lopers managed to insinuate themselves among the other supporters in green, and the Mount Florida end was not entirely without its Celtic sympathies.

In the run-up to the final, Celtic beat Rangers in the league at Ibrox 3–0, the goals coming from Moravcik (2) and Larsson. This was a rampant Celtic team and the silence coming from the Rangers stands from half time onwards bore eloquent testimony to the superiority of the men in green and white. Almost as an after-thought, 17-year-old Shaun Maloney was brought on as a substitute and impressed everyone in his first-team debut. Celtic actually finished the league fifteen points ahead of Rangers, whose high spending – in particular on Tore Andre Flo, for whom they paid Chelsea £12 million – had proved totally ineffective.

Celtic also did something very strange that season by losing two games to Dundee and Kilmarnock. In both games, they fielded weakened teams, in the Kilmarnock game particularly so, earning the scorn of Hearts who needed Celtic to beat Kilmarnock so that they could gain a UEFA Cup place. Celtic's argument was that youngsters like Mark Fotheringham and Shaun Maloney need to be blooded in first-team football at some point and that the fans needed a chance to see men like Stephan Mahe, Olivier Tebily and, in particular, the brave Alan Stubbs who had fought and won a battle against testicular cancer in a very dignified way. In any case, Hearts themselves were surely to blame for not winning more games and for needing Celtic to beat Killie.

Tragic events overshadowed all this, however. On 15 May 2001, one of Celtic's great heroes Bobby Murdoch passed away at the age of 56. Bobby was of course one of the Lisbon Lions and had been in ill health for some time. At a testimonial game for Tom Boyd against Manchester United, a moving minute's silence was observed by the crowd of 57,286, for anyone who had seen Bobby Murdoch in his prime could claim to have seen a real master of Scottish football. A humble and loveable man, he could justifiably claim a place in an all-time Celtic eleven. The contrast between the eras of Murdoch and Boyd was highlighted by the £1 million Tom Boyd was estimated to have earned from the testimonial, an unimaginable sum for players from the sixties, even if they were Celtic legends.

As his old rival and friend Jim Baxter, late of Rangers, Sunderland and Nottingham Forest had also died a few weeks previously, it was a sad time for those who loved the game in Scotland and had watched it in the 1960s. A placard among the floral tributes read 'Baxter RIP, Murdoch RIP – God has some halfback line now!' It was a tribute that at once combined football with religion, and drove another stake into the hearts of the bigots who thought that God was the monopoly of one denomination or another.

The Scottish Cup final was almost an anti-climax to the season, and the second half in particular was distinctly one sided. Hibs started off brightly, and Celtic seemed to suffer a severe blow when Lubo Moravcik had to go off injured. It was his replacement, the ever-reliable Jackie McNamara who got the first goal. Henrik Larsson scored a fine goal early in the second half, and rounded things off with a penalty near the end. Celtic finished the game well on top, and the only minor regret was that it would have been nice to see Larsson notch a Scottish Cup final hat-trick to emulate the feats of Jimmy Quinn in 1904 and Dixie Deans in 1972, but it was not to be.

Thus it was men in green-and-white hooped jerseys, hurriedly put on for the presentation, who collected the trophy for the thirty-first time. It was nice to see Paul Lambert and Tom Boyd lift the trophy together. Boyd was of course club captain, but was now struggling to get a first-team berth, and Lambert was captain of the team. Four of these thirty-one victories had been against Hibs in the final and there had to be some sympathy for the men from Easter Road. It would now be a hundred years since they had won the Scottish Cup, and in these one hundred years, folks had gone to Glasgow four times from the grim Leith tenements for a final against the other men in green. It had been their lot to see Patsy Gallacher in 1914, Joe Cassidy in 1923, Dixie Deans in 1972 and now Henrik Larsson in 2001 dash their hopes.

The teams were:

Celtic: Douglas, Mjallby, Valgaeren, Vega, Thompson, Agathe, Lennon, Lambert, Moravcik, Larsson, Sutton. Substitutes: Johnson, Boyd, McNamara.

Hibernian: Colgan, Fenwick, Smith, Sauzee, Jack, Laursen, Murray, Brebner, O'Neill, Paatelainen, Libbra. Substitutes: Arpinon, Lovell, Zitelli.

For Celtic, this was a wonderful day and a wonderful end to a wonderful season. The treble had been won for the first time in thirty-two years, a feat unthinkable just twelve months before. There is little doubt that the main reason was Martin O'Neill, who had done so much to rejuvenate this sleeping giant. Little wonder that his name was glorified in that paean of praise to him, the words of which were not difficult to learn, going as they did along the lines of 'Martin O'Neill, Martin O'Neill, Martin O'Neill' *ad infinitum.* He was of course ably served by the men under his command. While the entire first-team squad must be given credit, pride of place has to go to Henrik Larsson who, apart from scoring fifty times in the season, was voted player of the year not only by his fellow professionals but also by the Scottish football writers. And to round off a clean sweep of the awards Martin O' Neill was named manager of the year and Stilian Petrov collected the young player's award. Celtic's cup did indeed runneth over.

9

2001/02: Another Title . . . and the Champions' League

R arely have Celtic supporters had such a good summer as in 2001. For the first time since 1969, there was a domestic treble to savour. Everything had been faithfully recorded and whenever the weather turned rainy and prevented traditional summer pursuits, the video recorder was there to play back the mighty feats of Henrik Larsson and his merry men. We were even in the luxurious position of being able to quibble about things and to be angry that both cup finals were won by the team wearing yellow rather than the traditional green and white. It detracted from the occasion somewhat even though in the case of the Scottish Cup final, Celtic did the decent thing and put on the hoops for the trophy presentation.

A concomitant to this was the total lack of controversy emanating from Celtic Park. For the first summer since 1996, there was neither a change of manager, nor speculation about who the new man was going to be. Martin O'Neill was there, in essence for as long as he wanted. The press would persist in their very annoying attempts to get him to Old Trafford to relieve Alex Ferguson – implying on at least one occasion that a deal had been struck – taking Henrik Larsson with him. These were themes that would recur several times throughout the season, but although it was perhaps taken seriously at first, it was quickly dismissed by the supporters.

In fact, we were almost sorry for the press who had nothing to stir up at Celtic Park and had to look elsewhere for scandal. The older supporters recalled that Jock Stein had done exactly the same thing in the 1960s. He dried up most of the mischievous gossip and replaced it by positive news. All that the papers could do was, yes, try to persuade Stein to go to Old Trafford!

One minor disappointment was the decision of Ramon Vega to leave. The tall Swiss defender had been a great success, although there had been a few statements that hinted he was unhappy. It was a mystery as well why anyone who had played so well for Celtic and impressed everyone for six months, winning all three Scottish medals, should forsake the chance of playing in the Champions' League in favour of . . . Watford. It was particularly hard to comprehend when he had been in a winning Celtic team, and had on three occasions seen Celtic fans feting their players with green-and-white scarves uplifted:

Dull would he be of soul who could pass by
A sight so touching in its majesty.

As William Wordsworth might have said. It would have brought a tear to a glass eye but Vega, nevertheless, decided to go.

Vega's departure was by no means high profile and in any case his absence was soon compensated for by the arrival of Dianbobo Balde, who was signed from French club Toulouse for £900,000. Balde was born in Marseilles but qualified to play for Guinea because that was the country of his parents. A tall, muscular and rugged defender, Bobo, as he was immediately christened by the Celtic fans, would make a huge impact in Scottish football. Other new arrivals included John Hartson from Coventry City, Momo Sylla from St Johnstone and Steve Guppy from Leicester City. The last three arrived on the same day – 2 August, just in time to beat the European deadline – and cost the club a total of £7.5 million.

Of these three, the most interesting was the Wales internationalist John Hartson. He arrived via Luton Town, Arsenal, West Ham, Wimbledon and Coventry, but had never quite reached the superstar status that his early years had indicated. He was already a fixture in the Wales team, but cynics said that it was none too difficult to be selected. He had also failed a medical for Rangers in August 2000, after a fee of £4.5 million had been agreed with Wimbledon. The highlight of his hitherto disappointing career had been scoring the only goal in a losing cause for Arsenal in the 2–1 defeat in the European Cup Winners' Cup Final against Real

Zaragoza in Paris in 1995. He did look, at first sight, a little over-
weight. 'As sharp as a wooden spoon', the unkind would say.

The big question that Celtic fans asked however was whether
the side was good enough to move up a gear for the forthcoming
campaign in Europe. It certainly seemed that one day the Old Firm
were going to leave Scotland and play elsewhere. Could Celtic in
the meantime make any impact on the Champions League? There
was no doubt that the club's record over the past two decades had
been shocking. 1980 was the last year that they had been in Europe
after the New Year, and although it was true that Celtic were by no
means unique in the list of European Cup winners who disappeared out of sight after their glory years – one thinks of Steaua
Bucharest, Nottingham Forest, Hamburg and Aston Villa, for
example – a little more was expected of Celtic, especially by those
of us who remembered the really great days, and urgently awaited
their reappearance.

Celtic's poor record in Europe was shared by Rangers. The Ibrox
men's much vaunted nine in a row had produced little return in
Europe – with the possible exception of 1993 when they did well
enough to reach the equivalent of the semi-final stage – and the
result was the Scottish teams now had to play in qualifying rounds.
Celtic found themselves drawn against the great Ajax of Holland,
another team that had fallen from favour recently. They had won
the European Cup as recently as 1995, but had been unable to sus-
tain their momentum. They were still however an excellent side
with a tremendous pedigree and many young players with great
potential. The games against Ajax would be an early test of how
good Celtic really were.

And what about the rest of Scotland? It was a sad feature of the
times that teams other than Celtic and Rangers were not now really
considered as contenders for the SPL championship. The gulf
between the Old Firm and the rest of Scotland in the old days had
always been a large one, but it was not unbridgeable. One thinks
wistfully of Aberdeen, for example in the 1980s or Dundee United
at the same time. These sides were real tests to the Old Firm.
Aberdeen won four Scottish Cups in 1982, 1983, 1984 and 1986
and championships in 1984 and 1985. The Dons also did well in
Europe, and lifted the European Cup Winners' Cup in 1983 when
they beat Real Madrid in the final. Even further back, in the 1950s,

teams like Hearts, Hibs and Aberdeen won the title, and Dundee did likewise in 1962 with an excellent football side that the veteran football historian Bob Crampsey describes as one of the best he had ever seen.

But at the turn of the century, such was the concentration of wealth in the hands of the big two that the gulf, which used to be as large as the river Clyde, was now the width of the Atlantic Ocean. It was always possible that other teams would have an occasional good day and beat an Old Firm side. A smaller team might even think they could win a cup competition – but the now thirty-eight game SPL campaign was frankly beyond them – and tacitly, or even openly, admitted as such.

This was all very regrettable, and it was difficult to avoid the contention that something was going to have to change. Joining the Premiership in England, an Atlantic League, a European League were all discussed endlessly in pubs, clubs, factories and on the media usually in the context of television income, but the status quo seemed to be here for the foreseeable future.

How did Rangers and their fans spend the summer of 2001? Frankly, they were shell shocked. They had never really recovered from the 6–2 trouncing in August 2000. Although they did have their moment of glory in November when they beat Celtic 5–1 at Ibrox, Celtic had quickly turned that round. They beat Rangers three times after the turn of the year and Rangers compounded the felony in the eyes of their own supporters by going down to Dundee United in the Scottish Cup. The head of Dick Advocaat was now openly called for, and it was clear that things were far from happy down Ibrox way.

The sheer power of Celtic in games where Rangers were not directly involved frightened and intimidated them. This was because of the way the fixtures were now arranged. Usually, both teams played at different times and it was always possible to watch the enemy on television or at least listen to them on the excellent Radio Scotland. It was thus possible to compare the two teams. Rangers fans and even their players watched Celtic and were mightily impressed. Celtic fans doing likewise were less so with what they saw from the men in blue.

But more important than that was the way in which Martin O'Neill had instilled the belief into Celtic that they were entitled to win and that Rangers could be beaten. No longer did we have the attitude that just because Andy Goram got his big toe in the way of a shot, destiny had decreed that Rangers had to win. This was the attitude Tommy Burns fought hard against but had not overcome. It was now Rangers who had the major psychological problem and some inferiority complexes among their players.

Celtic's season opened quietly enough at the end of July with a competent win over St Johnstone at Celtic Park and a narrower win at Rugby Park over Kilmarnock, a team who as usual were to give a great deal of bother to the Old Firm. The first big game of the season however was the qualifying round for the Champions League against Ajax in Amsterdam. Celtic were confident, having already beaten Manchester United in a testimonial for Ryan Giggs at Old Trafford on 1 August thanks to goals from Chris Sutton, Paul Lambert, Neil Lennon and Lubo Moravcik. The snag was that the Manchester United game was just that – a friendly, not a real, competitive game (despite the running feuds between the two sets of players throughout the game) but it did give the team a massive psychological boost.

The night of Wednesday 8 August 2001 saw Celtic return to Europe in the real sense of the word. A huge travelling support was delighted when Petta, Agathe and Sutton scored great goals to give Celtic a 3–1 victory. More importantly, the game was shown live on the BBC and the world was mightily impressed. Martin O'Neill was euphoric in his press conference and used words like 'extraordinary' and 'immense'. His choice of vocabulary was justified and the Champions' League now beckoned for the first time.

By the time that Ajax came to Celtic Park, Celtic had beaten an unambitious Hearts side at Celtic Park and dropped a couple of points at Livingston when Henrik Larsson proved his fallibility – this had been in some dispute – by missing a penalty. Livingston were newcomers to the SPL, and an excellent example of how it is possible for a new team to join the league and progress all the way to the top flight. They were a likeable bunch, and had the advantage – to our eyes – of being staffed to a considerable extent from directors to players by people who were in some cases blatant, in other cases more discreet, Celtic sympathisers!

It was a more determined Ajax who came to Celtic Park for the return leg on 22 August 2001, for a game that was always going to be a tense affair, especially after the thirtieth minute when the

Brazilian Wamberto put the Dutch side ahead on the night. But Celtic were still effectively two goals to the good because of their three away strikes and managed to hold out. It was a comparatively new experience for the Celtic Park stands to see their team having to defend. They were grateful for the likes of Chris Sutton who showed the world that he is as accomplished in defence as he is in attack.

Scotland's other representatives in the competition, Rangers, failed to qualify for the Champions' League group stage. This was bad news for Scotland because it meant that for the next season, 2002/03, Scotland would in all probability have only one representative. Narrow minded Celtic fans did not see it that way, of course. Such an event merely added cream to the already rich dessert. Celtic celebrated their success over Ajax by going to Easter Road and whipping a poor Hibs team in a grossly one-sided game to finish the month of August on a high note.

The Champions' League experience was tantalising. Some fine football was played, but the end result was disappointing. There were clear indications, particularly in the games against Juventus, that the team could on occasion play well enough to be up there among the best of them, but the sad fact was that on a couple of other occasions away from home, the team could not play well enough either in defence or attack, and were found wanting. The Champions' League contains the top sides in Europe; poor teams do not come into the equation. Therefore, concentration must be 100 per cent. Sadly, this was not always true of Celtic.

One key factor at work was that Scotland is no great training ground for Europe. Everyone at Celtic Park was aware of that, of course. Celtic simply had not been put to the test often enough in domestic competition. Scottish teams would come to Celtic Park often expecting to be swept aside. Sadly this was a case of the self-fulfilling prophecy. Weaknesses in the Celtic line-up were not exposed in the way that they should have been. In 1967 when European success was achieved, in a very real sense it was a triumph for Scotland, simply because the other Scottish teams had always given Celtic a very hard time. Celtic had had to fight in Scotland every bit as much as they had to in Europe.

Rangers, for example, reached the final of the Cup Winners' Cup in 1967, no mean achievement, however much it has been over-shadowed by Celtic's winning of the European Cup and their own failure at Berwick. That same season, Dundee United beat Barcelona – and would do so again in 1987 – and Dunfermline, Kilmarnock and Dundee were teams respected on the Continent. This status was a thing of the past in 2001/02.

Celtic's Champions' League campaign ought to have begun on Wednesday 12 September, against Rosenborg in Glasgow, but unfortunately the terrorist outrages in the USA on the previous day forced the cancellation of such fixtures. It was a decision that did not meet with unanimous approval as many saw it as caving-in to terrorists. Celtic's first game was thus against Juventus in Turin the following week. It was a game in which Celtic had precious little luck and when this was allied to some dubious refereeing – in particular a shocking penalty decision late in the game – the outcome was a 3–2 win for the Italian giants. It was clear however that the Italians were made to work harder than they had expected to, and that the names of Celtic and Scotland were now to be treated with respect.

Two 1–0 home wins followed over the impressive Porto and a Rosenborg side that included our old friend Harald Brattbakk. In both games, Celtic had had to defend and a packed, atmospheric Celtic Park was glad to hear the final whistle. But the defending had been competent enough, and there was no reason to be unhappy at the halfway stage in the group matches, which saw Celtic at the top of the table with six points.

It was on 17 October in Portugal when things began to go wrong. Playing away from home is always a much tougher challenge, but nevertheless there was something about Celtic's play in Oporto that was baffling to the large travelling support and the millions watching at home. The loss of an early goal was a bad blow, and the Portuguese side stayed on top, adding another goal just before half time. Sutton was not playing, Larsson was well policed, Celtic's midfield never really got their teeth into the game to take command, and when another goal went in on the hour mark, Celtic were a well-beaten side. The best that one could say about it was that it was a learning experience.

If the lack of fight in that game was disappointing, an even greater heartbreak came our way when we went to Norway the following week. This time it was Harald Brattbakk who did the damage. Harald, who looked more like an accountant or a librarian than a professional footballer, had been a disappointment in his time with Celtic. He had enjoyed some fine moments, most notably the crucial goal against St Johnstone in 1998 that guaranteed the league championship, but he had also been prodigal of many chances – on one notorious occasion at Dunfermline, actually stopping the ball from crossing the line! Yet he retained his popularity among the fans, who respected his endeavour and honesty. Indeed when he was substituted by Rosenborg in the Celtic Park game, he was given a standing ovation of an affectionate, albeit slightly patronising nature.

On this occasion in Norway, he scored the two goals that rendered Celtic's qualification very difficult. Both were well taken, and the sad fact was that if he had done these things while in a Celtic jersey, he would still have been with us, rivalling even Larsson in popularity. In the second half, Celtic tried hard to get back into the game, but were clearly a good way short of pulling back two goals even against Rosenborg, the side destined to finish bottom of the group.

In fact, Celtic could still qualify for the second phase if they could beat Juventus at home on 31 October and Rosenborg could beat Porto. In spite of the cosmopolitan, multi-national nature of Celtic in these days, there was something intrinsically, perhaps even quintessentially, Scottish in all this. How often, for example, had Scotland gone to a World Cup, blown it through sheer incompetence at an early stage against a team like Iran or Costa Rica, then played brilliantly in the last game but failed to qualify by the narrowest of margins.

The parallels with Scotland were clear when Celtic played what some supporters thought was their best game for many years to beat Juventus by four goals to three. But sadly, Porto beat Rosenborg. This was in spite of the many statements from Harald Brattbakk that he would do a turn for his old mates. Not for the first time, it seemed that Harald was unable to perform when Celtic needed him to, and Celtic were out of the Champions' League.

This must not detract in any way from that fine performance against Juventus, a game that had the 57,717 crowd in a state of perpetual fervour. There was not a bad player on the field, and the Celtic crowd, which has always appreciated good football even when it comes from the opposition, were not slow to applaud players like Trezeguet and Tacchinardi off the park, as well as their own Sutton and Larsson. This game rivalled the Paris St Germain tussle of a few years earlier for sheer excitement and quality of football, and showed, if nothing else, the capacity of the Celtic ground and the Celtic crowd for absorbing this kind of entertainment.

Third place in the group was a disappointment, but the lesson was that you must be able to win, or at least get something, away from home in Europe. But there was some compensation in the shape of the UEFA Cup, to which teams that had finished third in their Champions' League group were admitted. It was far from an easy option, because Celtic drew the Spanish giants Valencia, European Cup finalists in 2000 and 2001.

These were two more big games for the club with maximum television exposure, but they finished disappointingly. Both legs were won 1–0 by the respective home team, Celtic's goal at home coming from the ever-productive Larsson. Extra time at Celtic Park failed to produce a winner, and we moved to a penalty shoot-out. Penalty shoot-outs and Celtic generally mix like oil and water. The pessimists among us recalled with horror the Scottish Cup final of 1990 against Aberdeen and, even worse, the League Cup final of 1994 against Raith Rovers. On the European scene there had also been the infamous semi final of the European Cup in 1972 when the luckless Dixie Deans took the first penalty and skied it high over the crossbar to deprive us of another European Cup final.

This penalty shoot-out rivalled them all in heartbreak, and once again Celtic fans had to endure the sight of opponents celebrating a penalty shoot-out victory. Once again we had to commiserate with the luckless Celts who missed their penalties, namely Larsson, Petrov and Valgaeren (who also missed a retaken kick), having been psyched out by the Spanish goalkeeper Canizares. Once again, we had the long bus journey home to reflect on the disproportionate miseries involved with supporting Celtic, not helped by the news that Rangers had won their penalty shoot-out in the same round of the same competition at about the same time!

But if Europe continued its melancholy tale for Celtic, there was little wrong with what was happening in Scotland. Celtic reached midwinter's day of 21 December having dropped only two points and that was in the goalless draw at Livingston on 18 August. Most of the victories had been convincing, and they had beaten Rangers at both Ibrox and Celtic Park. Indeed Rangers had dropped quite a few other points in draws to teams like Dundee, Hibs and Motherwell and their Old Firm rivals had a commanding and possibly even impregnable lead in the SPL. Indeed at one point when Celtic were thirteen points ahead of Rangers, Ibrox was likened to the North Pole where it was also thirteen below!

Not that Celtic hadn't enjoyed a slice of luck from time to time. On three occasions, they had needed late winners to lift the points. Perhaps significantly, all of these games were on the Saturday after an outing in the Champions' League. A late Henrik Larsson penalty kick, for example, was required to beat a spirited Motherwell side at Fir Park on 13 October, and on 27 October, Joos Valgaeren somehow managed to squeeze a late winner past Kilmarnock at Celtic Park in the five minutes allotted for added-on time.

The following week, 3 November, threw up a hard game at St Johnstone. The Perth men had often been a tough nut to crack, particularly at McDiarmid Park, and this time was no exception. St Johnstone's left back, Darren Dods, had in the first half achieved the rare but by no means unprecedented feat of scoring at both ends, first an own goal for Celtic and then a good one for his own team. The second half was fast and furious, but there were a few signs that Celtic, after their midweek efforts against Juventus, were tired.

The exertions against Juventus had of course been in a losing cause in the context of qualification for the next stage of the Champions' League, and this in itself brought its own share of fatigue to both players and fans. Those of little faith had departed the Perth scene. Time was almost up when Celtic were awarded a free kick on the edge of the box. Henrik Larsson took it and scored in spectacular fashion. One had to feel sorry for St Johnstone. They were destined to be relegated at the end of the season, yet they were probably the team that put up the most resistance to Celtic in 2001/02.

22 December at Pittodrie saw Celtic's first domestic defeat of the season. The conditions were bad, although the pitch was just playable. Travelling to the game however was by no means easy, because north of Stonehaven, the snow became hazardous and within the Granite City itself the roads were treacherous. The Aberdeen fans did not endear themselves to anyone by throwing snowballs at Celtic players – worse was to happen when Rangers visited Aberdeen a few weeks after the New Year – but the Dons did have one of their rare triumphs against Celtic in a 2–0 victory.

In fact Celtic underperformed in this match with the midfield of Petrov and Lennon nothing like as influential on the slippery pitch as they normally were. Aberdeen went ahead early in the second half with a penalty scored by the appropriately named Robbie Winters. Then after Celtic almost equalised in the last minute, Aberdeen scored again. It was a fluke goal as Mackie was on hand to take advantage of a fluffed Rab Douglas kick upfield. This win over Celtic remains as one of the very few high points of Ebbe Skovdahl's unfortunate tenure of the managerial post at Pittodrie.

At this point, Celtic could have stumbled or even fallen apart. Such things had happened too often in the recent past for the supporters to be anything other than apprehensive as they approached the Boxing Day fixture against Livingston at Celtic Park. On a cold day, and in a game characterised by poor refereeing, the visitors twice equalised, and it looked as if Livingston's first ever trip to Celtic Park was to earn them a draw until Henrik Larsson yet again turned up trumps with a last-minute winner.

From this moment on, Celtic never really looked back in the title race. Apart from a draw with Hibs at Easter Road, and another draw at Ibrox – which in the context of the league was effectively a victory as Rangers needed to take all three points – Celtic won all their games until the next visit of Livingston on 6 April. On a fine spring day with an early kick off, a 5–1 victory sealed the championship, exactly a year after Celtic had clinched it in the previous season. Larsson scored a hat trick and Hartson notched another two and the crowd was in such party mood that day that even Barry Wilson's consolation goal for Livingston earned itself a cheer.

It was a great day to be present at Celtic Park for the second title party inside twelve months. The release of green-and-white ticker tape and green-and-white balloons was a fine piece of theatre. The SPL trophy, apparently a very heavy one, was presented to Paul Lambert by a lady from the Scotland curling team that had recently won a gold medal in the Winter Olympics. What passed virtually unnoticed in the mayhem was that Henrik Larsson's hat-trick was his eleventh and that he had now completed a century of goals in league football in Scotland. The goals themselves were tremendous and well worthy of the occasion.

During the second half of the season, some of the wins were first class. There was a 5–0 demolition of Dunfermline at Celtic Park on 9 February, a 2–0 win at Kilmarnock in January – always a hard ground to go to – and a 4–0 win over Motherwell almost on the eve of the championship clincher, which showed Celtic to the television audience at their very best. The hardest game was probably at Livingston's excellent Almondvale Stadium, where Celtic recovered from an early setback to win 3–1.

Some of the wins on the other hand were less impressive. St Johnstone for example came to Celtic Park on 19 January and had the temerity to score first before succumbing 2–1. Aberdeen and Dundee United – shades of more forthright teams in the past – both came to Celtic Park to play stuffily and concede only the one goal. Such occasions do however prove the point that championships are not given to any team on a silver platter and that results often have to be ground out of a stubborn opposition.

After the league was won on 6 April, four meaningless fixtures still had to be played. One was when Rangers came to Celtic Park. In an otherwise anodyne game, Mjallby and Hartson of Celtic and Ricksen of Rangers all saw red cards in a gross overreaction by the referee, following a certain amount of pushing and shoving on the Rangers goal line. There was a touch of farce about this, and mercifully no strong action was taken by the authorities, although the cliché 'handbags at thirty paces' was distinctly overused in the discussion of the incident. Hartson claimed with some justification that he was only trying to keep the peace.

There was a touch of humour about the game at Tynecastle. Celtic's reserve team, more or less, took on Hearts and were beating them 4–1, a brace of goals coming from both Shaun Maloney and Simon Lynch, two young players who deserved a lot more than simply to be described as promising. Celtic were awarded a penalty kick near the end, and there was the most undignified scramble as both young men claimed the right to take it and give them the chance of a hat trick. Even the radio commentators found this amusing but, in the event, the kick was missed by Maloney. Celtic's league season came to a quiet end at Pittodrie when a Shaun Maloney goal was enough to defeat his hometown team and so avenge the one league defeat of the season.

But there were disappointments in the two national cup competitions. Celtic's defence of the League Cup began on 6 November with an 8–0 thrashing of Stirling Albion at Celtic Park. Fringe players scored the goals that night, and it is to be hoped that the Stirling players enjoyed their trip to Glasgow. It was nice to see Stirling

Albion again. Older supporters remembered Celtic's dreadful season of 1962 when one Johnnie Lawlor earned his only real moment of glory as Stirling Albion beat Celtic. Even more incredibly Albion also won in 1966 and drew in 1967 with Jock Stein in charge and en route to Lisbon; in summer 1980 they had been a matter of minutes away from putting a feckless Celtic side out of the League Cup. On this occasion in 2001 the 8–0 scoreline flattered the part-timers who were now in the Third Division, having fallen on distinctly hard times.

A touch of comic opera was inflicted on the Scottish public for the next tie in the League Cup. It was 28 November at Livingston. The players were there, the crowd were there, STV's cameras were there – but the electricity wasn't and the game could not go ahead. The commentators wondered what was to happen to the pies and then a television announcer informed the disappointed nation that there would be a real treat in the shape of the *Royal Variety Performance*! The game was eventually rescheduled for 19 December and O'Neill again adopted the somewhat dangerous strategy of relying on fringe players and resting men like Larsson and Lambert, while keeping Lennon on the bench.

It made for a good game of football, and Celtic won 2–0 with goals from Balde and Hartson. A feature of the game was the accurate crossing of another fringe player Steve Guppy, and all in all, it was a very satisfying affair. There was a moment of controversy when Sutton scored what appeared to be a valid third goal, but sadly it came from an indirect free kick that had not been adequately signalled by the referee.

The semi finalists were Celtic, Rangers, Hibs and Ayr United. Luck had it that the Old Firm were drawn together for the second year in succession at this stage, thereby further confounding the conspiracy theorists and their received wisdom that the big two are kept apart for the final. Tuesday 5 February was the date for this Hampden showdown but, this time, Rangers, under the management of Alex McLeish, won by a whisker. The first half had seen Celtic on top with Didier Agathe in top form. Several good crosses were sent across and several other chances went a-begging, Hartson and Larsson being the sinners. But then just on half time, Celtic conceded a free kick on the edge of the box. The kick was charged down but the ball broke to Lovenkrands who scored at a bad psychological time for Celtic.

Nevertheless, Celtic fought back strongly and Bobo Balde scrambled an equaliser half way through the second half. Both teams now came close as the game went to extra time, but it was Rangers who got the winner with a Bert Konterman strike in the fourteenth minute of extra time. It was one of those hit-and-hope shots that usually end up in Row Z of the stand but this time the amiable Bert's luck was in and the ball thundered into the Celtic net. He had not always been so fortunate, and was frequently the object of worry for Rangers fans and ridicule by their Celtic counterparts. Hard though Celtic tried, they could not get an equaliser and Rangers went on to beat Ayr United in the final.

The Scottish Cup began with a trip to Brockville, not to play Falkirk, but Alloa Athletic. Recreation Park, Alloa, one of Scottish football's most idiosyncratic and charming stadiums, was considered too small for the visit of Celtic. Point taken, but the world was more than a little amazed at the decision to play the game at Brockville. Dunfermline and Livingston were available and even one of the Edinburgh grounds would not have been too far away, but Brockville – commonly known as Brokendownville by unkind fans – was the reason why the luckless Bairns were denied promotion to the SPL in 1999 and 2003. It was deemed unsuitable for big crowds, and those Celtic fans who were there for that cup tie saw enough to come to the conclusion that the SPL were correct. So why on earth then did the SFA decide to play this game there?

Whatever the reason the game was played there on Tuesday 8 January, inclement weather causing a postponement the previous Saturday. More mature supporters in the 5,763 crowd might well have turned nostalgic about Brockville of long ago, recalling that the great Charlie Tully scored direct from a corner kick but was then told to retake it as the ball had been outside the arc. The bold Charlie carefully replaced the ball inside the arc, took the corner again and scored! There were other less pleasant memories, for example the recent departure of Celtic from the Scottish Cup in 1993. Falkirk had often been a graveyard for Celtic in the 1950s and 1960s as well as occasionally the scene of some unpleasant hooliganism. But in 2002, it was obvious that the grand old lady was well past her sell-by date with inadequate toilets and catering facilities. Indeed, in an extremely rare move, a few games previously at Celtic Park, the public-address announcer had warned lady supporters that female toilets at Brockville were virtually non-existent, implying that it might be an idea to give the game a miss.

Amazingly Celtic, who gave a game to Morten Wieghorst, now mercifully recovered from his brain disease, took nineteen minutes to find the net. Tebily, Sylla and Maloney were given deserved outings and the latter two found the net in a 5–0 win over the men from Clackmannanshire who somehow contrived to lose money on the deal because of the rent they had to pay to Falkirk. That same night, incidentally, hopes were being raised that history might repeat itself, for Berwick Rangers were holding the other Rangers in a goalless encounter . . . and rumours were spreading round Brockville to the effect that they were actually winning. These were untrue and the product of wishful thinking, and the big Rangers won the replay.

Celtic's next port of call was Kilmarnock. This game was played on a Saturday night and was delayed by an electrical failure, which was at least the third such occurrence that season. There had been the Livingston fiasco, and the league game at Celtic Park against Dundee in December had seen a temporary failure of lights as well. Conspiracy theorists were beginning to enjoy themselves once more. Who was to say that Osama Bin Laden or Al Qaeda were not behind this? Not to mention the Scotsmen who travel back and forward to Northern Ireland with the flutes and the funny handshakes? Among other things, the power failure at Rugby Park prevented the effective functioning of the turnstiles, but when the game did get going, Celtic took advantage of an own goal and ran out 2–0 winners, Larsson scoring the other goal.

A potential banana skin was clearly visible when Celtic travelled to Pittodrie for the quarter final on Monday 25 February. This was of course the only ground in Scotland at which Celtic had lost this season, and Aberdeen, although inconsistent and clearly a good deal short of the Aberdeen of old, were playing with some spirit. Laudably, they were also bringing on Scottish talent. The Dons, more than most clubs, had had their fingers burned badly in recent years by importing foreign players who were some way short of top class. Such a policy had led the club to near ruin, and had alienated a great deal of their fans, but now youngsters like McGuire, McAllister, Derek and Darren Young and Mackie were playing alongside experienced campaigners like ex-Celt Derek Whyte and

Robbie Winters and a smattering of foreigners. The neutrals, we were told by the press, wanted Aberdeen to win.

Certainly it had to be said that Celtic's nurturing of young Scottish talent was slow and fitful, to put it mildly. Crainey, Smith, Maloney and one or two others looked good but were not getting a run in the team, even in Crainey's case when he was capped for Scotland. Yet, before one condemns O'Neill for such a policy, it is wise perhaps to recall the days of the late 1950s and early 1960s when young Scottish talent was brought on in huge quantities but the team got nowhere. Eventually of course in 1967 the European Cup was won, by and large, with Celtic's home-grown talent to the fore, but for every Murdoch, Clark, Johnstone or McNeill that came through, many were left by the wayside, reminding one of the Biblical tag that 'many are called, but few are chosen'.

This particular game saw Aberdeen make a good fist of it, but when Celtic scored early in each half through Hartson and Petrov, they retained control in a mature and professional way with Paul Lambert absolutely inspirational at the back, and only the somewhat harsh dismissal of Hartson near the end spoiling the occasion. It was ample revenge for the league defeat.

Critics of the Scottish Premier League had ample ammunition when they saw the semi finalists in the Scottish Cup. Once the dust of the replays settled, the four lucky teams were Celtic, Rangers . . . and Ayr United and Partick Thistle, two hard-working and plucky teams from the First Division. The SPL had not been able to produce a semi finalist other than the big two, and indeed, the League Cup final lacked Celtic only because Rangers had put them out, and the same Ayr United were playing Rangers in that final. The Honest Men had played Hibs in the other League Cup semi final the night after the Old Firm and in a grim, but riveting, match had edged out the Edinburgh men with an extra-time penalty kick scored by Eddie Annand. This game, broadcast on STV, more than any other, caused the Scottish public to despair of the top flight.

It became therefore increasingly difficult to argue against the contention that the SPL was a failure and that fundamental change was required. The Old Firm, frustrated by their repeated failures in Europe – one of the reasons for which was the lack of top-class opposition in Scotland – and impoverished by the absence of lucrative television revenue available to leading teams in England, Italy,

Spain and Germany were clearly exploring ways of leaving Scotland. But where were they to go? The English Premiership did not want them, simply because they were a threat to clubs like Southampton, Fulham and Birmingham City who were in danger of losing their place in the top flight to the Old Firm clubs. In addition, the Premiership did not need them as it generated substantial revenues from television rights and other sponsors and there was no need to import the raucous Scotsmen who sang so much about Ireland. In addition, some had the distinct impression that teams at the other end of the spectrum in England like Arsenal, Manchester United and Liverpool feared a strong Scottish challenge for places in the lucrative Champions' League, a feeling that would gain ground a year later when Celtic removed Blackburn Rovers and then Liverpool from the UEFA Cup, winning in England in both cases.

The Nationwide Football League was suggested and apparently this idea was pursued by those who did not see the absurdity of fixtures like Celtic–Grimsby and Gillingham–Rangers. A more credible alternative came in the shape of an Atlantic League involving teams from Holland and Portugal, but this idea had been around since season 1999/00 without anything coming of it. The sense of disharmony on the domestic scene also added fuel to the fire. A decision to reject Sky Television's offer for broadcasting rights to replace the four-year deal that was due to expire at the end of the season had major ramifications. A plan hatched by Roger Mitchell, chief executive of the SPL, to launch a television channel owned by the twelve clubs themselves was eventually scuppered by the Old Firm and open warfare broke out between what became known as the rebel ten clubs and Celtic and Rangers. Disputes raged on any number of issues including the voting structure within the SPL and how television and other revenues were to be divided up.

The apparent irony of all this was that Celtic and Rangers, however much their supporters claimed to hate one another, were now linked indissolubly. There was nothing surprising in this and indeed it had always been so. Their propensity jointly to profit from their intense rivalry together was the reason why, even before the First World War, they were known as the Old Firm. In 1952 when Hibs – of all teams – and the authorities had tried to prevent the flying of the Irish tricolour at Celtic Park, Celtic had been loyally supported by Rangers, and for all the deserved contempt poured on the Ibrox club's failure knowingly to sign Catholics no overt criticism on this issue ever emanated from Celtic Park.

The truth was that Celtic and Rangers have a symbiotic relationship in which one cannot survive without the other. One supporter, in a letter to a fanzine, summed it up very well when he pointed out that: 'It is only when you sing 'The Sash My Father Wore', then 'Sean South of Garryowen' and realise that the words can be sung to the tune of the other, (that) you realise that you are being taken to the cleaners!'

Be that as it may, the Scottish Cup semi finals of 2002 included Celtic, Rangers and two minnows. Celtic played Ayr United on the night of Saturday 23 March. Ayr had played valiantly the previous Sunday against Rangers in the League Cup final and lasted almost to half time before Rangers scored. This time it took Celtic until the second half before they got the opener, scored by Henrik Larsson, and it was inside the last ten minutes before they clinched the tie with two further goals by Alan Thompson. The Somerset Park men had a few chances of their own early in the game and the loud applause that they were given by the Celtic fans at the end was tinged with a little relief, one felt. Ayr United had given Celtic a harder game than many teams in the SPL.

Rangers against Partick Thistle the following day was more or less a carbon copy, setting up an Old Firm final on 4 May. Celtic had comfortably won the title at that stage, and perhaps a little complacency was creeping in. The recent form produced by Rangers had been none too impressive either, but this could not disguise a distinct improvement under the management of Alex McLeish. The man known as 'Big Eck' had engendered a strong team spirit in the Light Blues, which had been conspicuous by its absence under the stewardship of Dick Advocaat. In addition Celtic had injury worries. Valgaeren was out, Balde was just back from a lay off and Lambert, Lennon and Sutton were all doubtful.

It was probably a mistake to select all of these players. As it turned out, Lambert was taken off and replaced by substitute McNamara – Lambert would later admit that it was a mistake to play – and Lennon and Sutton were clearly below par. Larsson had a bad game, frequently losing out to Amoruso and apparently upset by the barracking from the Rangers fans who accused him of diving. Stilian Petrov, who had had a good season considering his horrific injury the previous year, found this was one game too many for him.

In addition, O'Neill made a big mistake – arguably his first tactical misjudgement in two years – in not bringing on Lubomir Moravcik after Rangers equalised for the second time. It would have been about Lubo's optimum time (the seventieth minute) and it was hard to believe that he would not have made a difference. Perhaps the manager was influenced by the fact that it would have been Lubo's last big game for the club and that the emotional argument was therefore very much for his inclusion. Perhaps O'Neill did not want everyone to think that his heart had ruled his head. In fact, it would have been a wonderful romantic moment if it had come off, and very much in the Celtic tradition, but it was not to be. This was sad, for Lubo was a proven match winner.

Having said all this, and making allowances for Rangers's undeniable midfield superiority on the day, the manner of the defeat was heartbreaking. Twice in the lead through Hartson and Balde, Celtic twice allowed their opponents back in and, as the second half went on, it was obvious that it was Rangers who had their tails up. Yet extra time beckoned, which would have allowed Celtic to regroup, allowed Martin O'Neill a chance to gee the players up, allowed the Rangers offensive to fizzle out, allowed the ebb and flow of the game to run back in Celtic's favour and – crucially – created irresistible pressure for O'Neill to bring on Moravcik. But it was not to be, as Rangers scored in the final minute of regulation time.

The silence and the almost instantaneous breaking of ranks told its own tale of a support that, yet again, had to bear the heartbreak associated with supporting this mighty club. Yet was it heartbreak? Yes, it was on the day, and defeats in a cup final are always difficult to take. But league championships are won over a season, and the SPL title had been won a month previously and was undoubtedly the most important trophy in the domestic game. One recalled the desperate years of only ten years previously and thought how much the support would have cherished a league title even if it were accompanied by the odd moment of sadness like this.

The teams in the 2002 Cup Final were:

Celtic: Douglas, Mjallby, Sutton, Balde, Thompson, Petrov, Lennon, Lambert, Agathe, Larsson, Hartson. Substitutes: Gould, McNamara, Boyd, Moravcik, Guppy.

Rangers: Klos, Ricksen, Amoruso, Moore, Numan, Ross, Ferguson, Lovenkrands, de Boer, Caniggia, McCann. Substitutes: McGregor, Vidmar, Nerlinger, Flo, Arveladze.

Referee: Hugh Dallas.

So taking everything into account the future seemed rosy. The team had a place in the Champions' League yet again, and with O'Neill still in charge, Celtic would be battling for their third championship in a row. Before season 2001/02 ended Celtic played a series of friendly and testimonial games against English opposition, most notably Leeds United and Arsenal, and performed well. The players were of a high calibre, the reserve strength was apparently adequate, the finances of the club were sound, the stadium was generally recognised as one of the best in Europe, attendances were excellent, the supporters were as devoted to the cause as they had ever been. What was the problem? Hindsight is of course a great thing, but was there not a straw in the wind that sunny day at Hampden that the squad needed to be strengthened? The season ended with the numbing realisation that, in the Scottish Cup final at least, Rangers had been the better team. But the euphoria of being champions helped Celtic supporters to enjoy the World Cup in Japan and Korea.

10

2002/03: The Road to Seville

Following the ritual of pre-season games against English opposition, the season opened on 3 August 2002. It was a low-key affair with Celtic beating Dunfermline 2–1 at Celtic Park, the goals scored by Henrik Larsson and the impression was given that normal service was being resumed. Next week saw an impressive 4–0 demolition of Aberdeen at Pittodrie, although even the hardest hearted of bigots had to express a certain sadness that Aberdeen were so comprehensively outclassed. Dundee United were then defeated 5–0, and Partick Thistle more luckily 1–0 thanks to the chest of Henrik Larsson.

But before August was out, Celtic had suffered a severe blow in their elimination from the European Champions League by Basel. In a good game of football at Celtic Park, the damage was done early on when Basel scored before most of the 58,000 had taken their seats. Celtic however fought back to win 3–1 on the night, Larsson scoring a penalty then missing another. Sutton also scored but the highlight was a great volley from Momo Sylla.

The return leg was shown on the rather amateurish Setanta television, and it was a huge disappointment for the watching fans. Celtic suffered two hammer blows early on when first Mjallby was caught out of position, then the defence in general failed to clear a corner kick. This was enough to give the Swiss the advantage thanks to the goal they had scored in Glasgow, and that was how the game finished even though Celtic had one or two half chances near the end. It was not to be, however, and Celtic were out of the Champions League before the competition proper had even started. It would certainly cost the club a great deal of money with sums like £10 million mentioned, but from a football perspective, the UEFA Cup was perhaps a more realistic target, a point made by the shrewder pundits.

The transfer window was now closing as well and O'Neill had not spent a great deal over the summer with only David Fernandez and Ulli Laursen joining the club from Livingston and Hibs respectively for relatively modest fees. They would be joined by goalkeeper Magnus Hedman, bought from Coventry City for £1.5 million. But the players that they had in 2001/02 really should have been good enough to defend the SPL title. The difference this year was that Rangers, under Alex McLeish, were not going meekly to fold in the title race as they had in the past two seasons. The Ibrox men were still on a psychological high after last season's Scottish Cup final.

Sunday 1 September saw a good win against Livingston at home, a feature of the game being a pinpoint cross from Steve Guppy to find the head of Henrik Larsson. But then after a break for international matches, Celtic went to Motherwell on a Tuesday night, and their surprise defeat in Lanarkshire allowed Rangers to top the table for the first time in over two years. Larsson had an off day, and a youngster called James McFadden had a dream game against the team he had always loved as Motherwell won 2–1. This came on top of bad news that Johan Mjallby was to be out of the game for several months.

Serious concern about Henrik Larsson was expressed when Celtic struggled to beat Hibs 1–0 on the following Saturday. The goal came from John Hartson, and, as the Swede had now gone a full two games without scoring, some wild speculation began. Had he taken too much out of himself playing for Sweden in the World Cup finals in Japan and Korea? Was he secretly injured? Did he want to leave Celtic? Even when he scored a hat trick against admittedly weak opposition in Suduva at Celtic Park the following Thursday in the first round of the UEFA Cup, the speculation still did not subside.

The pessimism received a grievous knock when Larsson notched a lovely goal to win a tight encounter at Dens Park. The game was on the BBC and so the nation was able to see a class act. It was Larsson who started the move in the centre of the field when he fed Guppy. Guppy returned the ball to Larsson on the edge of the box, and he leaned back to score with immense style. It turned out to be the only goal, but in fact the game was won far more comfortably than the 1–0 scoreline suggests.

That the decline and fall of Henrik Larsson had been ludicrously overblown was proved by the next game when Celtic turned on the style to beat Kilmarnock 5–0 at Celtic Park with Larsson scoring an outstanding hat trick and leading the line with aplomb. In fact, many take the view that the best part of Larsson's game – although it is understandably overshadowed by his goalscoring exploits – is the way that he uses his acute football brain to bring colleagues such as Sutton and Hartson into the game.

On 3 October, when a virtual reserve team was guaranteeing Celtic's progress into the next round of the UEFA Cup against Suduva in Lithuania, significant events were unfolding at Ibrox as Rangers crashed out of Europe in extra time to an unknown Czech team. This caused no little merriment in Celtic circles, but it did have one unfortunate side effect and that was that Rangers could now concentrate all their energies on the domestic scene.

Rangers did in fact have an immediate chance to redeem themselves in the eyes of their supporters when they came to Celtic Park for the first Old Firm clash of the season the Sunday after their exit from Europe. The huge television audience, including fans in England who were now being shown Old Firm games live on the BBC for the first time, witnessed a tremendous match. There was an added point to the English dimension, for the draw for the next round of the UEFA Cup had been made and Celtic had been paired with Blackburn Rovers, managed by one Graeme Souness. We held our breath and waited for the 'Battle of Britain' clichés in the media. We would not be disappointed.

Celtic were clearly the better team in the Old Firm clash but two uncharacteristic mistakes by the normally reliable Rab Douglas gave Rangers a point and allowed them to retain their points differential at the top of the table. Henrik Larsson's first goal was a gem, and then at one point Celtic were 2–1 up before trailing 3–2 and being rescued by Chris Sutton. It was breathtaking stuff, but Celtic had cause to feel aggrieved at not taking all three points.

After a break for internationals, Celtic's next game was against Hearts. A trip to Tynecastle was seldom a happy experience in the early 1990s, but since then Hearts had sagged dreadfully. Now even their pitch was in poor condition, and when Celtic scored twice in the opening ten minutes, the game was as good as over. Larsson got two, Sutton and Petrov one each in the 4–1 victory, but it was a poor advert for the game in Scotland as Celtic were so much on top of a Hearts side that gave up early in the proceedings. Their disgruntled supporters then had nothing better to do than hurl sectarian abuse at Celtic and to continue their obtuse tirades against 'Weegies' – Glaswegians – who were described as scum and as people who scoured dustbins for something to eat. It is to be hoped that the many foreign players on the pitch did not understand the nature of, or reasons for, this bile. Sadly, however, BBC viewers heard it all.

On the following Wednesday, 23 October, it was the turn of the League Cup to be fitted in. Celtic – and Rangers – often gave the impression that they were doing everyone a huge favour simply by taking part. In many ways they were, because without the big two's financial clout, this competition would have collapsed. It is however a disappointing attitude.

Inverness Caledonian Thistle made their first appearance at Celtic Park since the game that caused the downfall of John Barnes two and a half years previously. In view of that tragic episode in Celtic's history, it was with a certain apprehension that supporters heard the weakened team that O'Neill sent out. Larsson, Valgaeren, Sutton, Lambert, Lennon and Petrov were all rested. It was nice to see veteran Tom Boyd getting a game, however, and youngsters like Kennedy, Miller and Wallace were on the bench. Celtic won the game 4–2, but it was closer than supporters would have liked. Celtic got off with this extreme form of squad rotation against Inverness – this time. There was a lesson here, but it would not be learned, the hard way, until the spring. A disappointing crowd of 34,592 left the ground with a very high opinion of Inverness Caledonian Thistle. They had seen a good, evenly balanced game with John Hartson scoring two goals.

Hartson had let it be known that he was less than happy with life at Celtic Park, for he tended to be used only as a substitute as the first-choice striking partnership of Sutton and Larsson were performing so well that they could not be dropped. Things would change in the latter part of the season – although disappointingly injury ruled Hartson out at the very end of the season when his presence might have made all the difference – and this Inverness game was his way of showing his worth. He certainly now had the respect and admiration of the fans.

By this time the atmosphere was reaching hysterical proportions in view of the imminent arrival of Blackburn Rovers on 31 October 2002. Much of it centred on former Rangers manager Graeme Souness who may have been embarrassed by the talk of revenge. Four days before the Blackburn game, Celtic went to Dunfermline and won 4–1. It was not quite as easy as the final score indicates, because at one point the Pars pulled it back to 2–1 and began to look good, but the performance was highly professional with goals coming from Larsson, Thompson, Petrov and Sutton. Annoyingly, Rangers also kept winning and stayed one point ahead of Celtic.

Hallowe'en saw the nation in a frenzy as the media continued to play up the visit of Blackburn Rovers, a team placed sixth in the Premiership at the time of the draw. Indeed they had won the championship as recently as 1995. To believe the press, the Lancashire side consisted of Celtic supporters all determined to do down their favourite team for not signing them and forcing them to work for that anti-Christ Graeme Souness instead! Souness actually upstaged the BBC cameras by waiting until after the game had kicked off before taking his place in the dugout, claiming that he had been paying a visit to the toilet, although he put it more crudely than that.

It was a curious game, but showed the sheer professionalism of Celtic in a European context. For long periods of the game, Blackburn outplayed Celtic, passing the ball quickly and accurately, running at the Celtic defence and giving the impression that they could score at will. They didn't of course, for O'Neill had his men defending well and it was in fact Celtic that scored the only goal. Hartson had just replaced the tiring Paul Lambert late in the game and got his head to a corner. Larsson was there to tuck away the rebound. When the away-goals' rule is taken into account 1–0 is an excellent result for a home tie in Europe.

Naturally there were concerns about how Celtic had been outplayed during certain parts of the game, and the English media reassured the Blackburn supporters that Celtic would not be a problem at Ewood Park. Phrases like 'men against boys' emanated provocatively from the Blackburn Rovers dressing room and Chris Waddle, who had been no mean player for Newcastle United and England in his day but whose footballing ability had not been matched by good judgement, made a few asinine comments in newspapers. The ramming of words down a few throats seemed to be called for.

Celtic won two league matches between the two Blackburn ties.

Aberdeen were hammered 7–0 in an embarrassingly one-sided affair in which Hartson scored four, and then the following Sunday Celtic went to Tannadice Park for a low-key encounter that needed Sutton's late strike to seal a 2–0 victory.

There had also been a League Cup game against Partick Thistle at Celtic Park in which an under-strength team had proved the point yet again to 26,333 people that Celtic's squad was not necessarily strong enough for them to rely on fringe players. The game ended 1–1 after extra time and eventually finished 5–4 on penalties for Celtic, although Thistle on three occasions had only to sink a penalty in order to win! A feature of the crowd had been the warm and affectionate reception they gave to Thistle manager John Lambie. By no means a Celtic sympathiser, John was nevertheless much loved throughout Scottish football for his honest and somewhat uncultured approach to the game, and the Celtic Park crowd showed their affection for him and even some sympathy that Partick Thistle had to lose.

All this raised questions about the League Cup and its value to Celtic. The argument was put forward that the Old Firm clubs should withdraw from this tournament so that other teams would have a chance of winning a trophy. There was some merit in that argument, and it was certainly true that Celtic did not take the competition as seriously as the league or Europe. On the other hand, it was an opportunity for the manager to assess the calibre of those on the fringes of the first team. The games against Inverness and Partick had certainly raised doubts about some of the players in this category.

To put the issue in perspective it was noted that when Partick Thistle came to Celtic Park on 17 November for an SPL match, they were faced with the strongest available side and despatched 4–0. By this time however, Celtic were on a high for two reasons. The first was that they had defeated Blackburn Rovers at Ewood Park to progress to the next round of the UEFA Cup. Blackburn on 14 November 2002 was a great night for the club as goals from Larsson and Sutton, and an excellent all-round performance, saw Celtic home, much to the chagrin of those English scribes who had written them off so churlishly after the first leg. Henrik Larsson put it very succinctly in a television interview in which he stated that some people should learn to 'keep their mouths shut' and do their talking on the pitch.

A further cause of joy was the fact that Aberdeen had drawn

with Rangers at Pittodrie on Saturday 16 November. The win over Thistle therefore sent Celtic to the top of the league. November continued to be a good month when a 2–0 win was registered at Livingston on the twenty-fourth. Larsson scored both goals, one a penalty which should have been a goal anyway for Lambert netted after the referee had given the penalty for a bad foul on Petrov.

Then on the European front came a first-leg tie against Celta Vigo of Spain. It was an unsatisfactory game that Celtic won 1–0 after Larsson forced a header over the line. The refereeing was distinctly questionable and Martin O'Neill obviously thought so, for he was sent to the stand for disputing a number of decisions. But once again Celtic got a good result, even though we were threatened that Celta Vigo would be a different team at home. Some Spanish journalists felt that Celtic had the assistance of a twelfth man – the huge and vociferous home crowd. Indeed one wrote that Celta Vigo had left 'the hell of Celtic Park' with a highly creditable result.

By the time that Celtic went to Spain on 12 December, the team had experienced a major blow to their title hopes in a 3–2 reverse at Ibrox. It was generally agreed that Celtic were the better team, and indeed they scored in the first minute, but it was Rangers that got the goals at the key points in the game. This had followed two hard fought victories, 3–1 over Motherwell at Celtic Park, then a 1–0 win at Easter Road. The Motherwell game had seen a rare and impressive outing for David Fernandez, but had been characterised by a missed penalty by Henrik Larsson early in the proceedings.

The game away to Celta Vigo established O'Neill's Celtic on the European stage and allowed us to celebrate Christmas for the first time since 1979 with Celtic still in Europe. It was a tight affair with the four added minutes after the ninety taking forever to pass. Celtic were 2–1 down on the night and would have been eliminated if the home side had scored again. As it was, John Hartson's marvellous away goal was enough to see Celtic through, and to trigger major rejoicing in front of television screens back home. The game was partially obscured by a mass of printers' ink about a plane carrying Celtic supporters home that had to be diverted to Cardiff. The cause was put down to hooliganism, smoking in the toilet or over-reaction by the cabin crew, but it was a toothsome morsel for the scribes who would soon have another and even better scandal to report on.

Following a disappointing 1–1 draw at Kilmarnock, which

meant that further ground was lost to Rangers in the league race, Celtic organised a Christmas party for their players in Newcastle. The *Daily Record* got wind of this and followed them there uninvited under the spurious guise of public interest. This fooled nobody and it certainly cut no ice with Johan Mjallby, Joos Valgaeren and Bobby Petta who seemed to take issue with the *Record* photographer and found themselves arrested for theft and the destruction of a camera.

This was publicity that the club could have done without, but the general feeling of the support was one of sympathy for the players and a boycott was organised of the *Daily Record*, which had been nicknamed the *Daily Ranger* by many of a green-and-white persuasion on account of its perceived bias towards the Ibrox side. Yet these were criminal acts – even though charges were later dropped – and it did seem an overreaction by the players to what was admittedly a gross invasion of privacy. All in all, it was something that should never have happened.

The Christmas fixtures went well for Celtic with three good home victories over Dundee, Hearts and Dunfermline. The Dundee game saw a penalty saved by Rab Douglas and an excellent overhead kick by John Hartson to score the first goal in a 2–0 win. The following day Rangers scraped through against Partick Thistle to maintain a four point lead, but they were less lucky on Boxing Day when they went down 1–0 to Motherwell as Celtic beat Hearts 4–2. Hartson maintained his impressive form by scoring a hat-trick, and one of his goals was a magnificent first-time strike from the edge of the box.

29 December saw a spirited fight from Dunfermline but a grinding-out of a result for Celtic with a goal from Larsson. Larsson also got on the score-sheet at Pittodrie on 2 January but in so doing, injured himself and had to be taken off. Thus Celtic were deprived of their star goalscorer and could not quite force a win after Aberdeen equalised following poor defending of a corner kick. Rangers won that day against Dundee, so the result was that Celtic went into the winter shutdown three points behind their greatest rivals.

The midwinter break is unpopular with many, and it is rarely good news for Celtic. Following the adverse press coverage of the Newcastle arrests and the diversion of the flight to Cardiff, the *Daily Record* now focused entirely on Martin O'Neill, convincing itself and the Scottish public that as his contract was coming to an end in the summer, he was about to leave for pastures new, probably Manchester United or Liverpool. A far more damning story surfaced later that O'Neill had agreed to become the manager of Leeds United the previous summer, but as the season was now in full swing, the story was not allowed to grow legs. The truth of the matter as the winter break came around was that O'Neill was playing golf with Dermot Desmond in Barbados while the players were in Florida.

Did this mean anything at all? No, other than that newspapers must be sold, and if there is no football being played, the press have to manufacture their own news. The unanimous opinion of Celtic supporters was that O'Neill was very much the man for the job. Even the Lisbon Lions, on the eve of their testimonial game against Feyenoord on 23 January 2003, all said that O'Neill should stay. In fact a couple of hours before this low-key friendly, it was announced that O'Neill had now agreed a one-year rolling contract. All this meant was that either party to the contract had to give the other a year's notice before the agreement could be terminated. It was indeed much ado about nothing, and the newspaper speculation about O'Neill's future vanished as quickly as snow off a dyke and we settled down for the resumption of the football season. But if there was something that concerned many Celtic supporters more than O'Neill's contact situation it was that Celtic had failed to make any signings during the transfer window.

By the time that the press were able to dig up the story that O'Neill hadn't actually signed the new deal. and that the rolling contract was merely a gentleman's agreement, no one was really interested because the season was reaching a breathtaking climax, and in any case O'Neill did sign shortly thereafter.

Burns Day, 25 January, saw one major shock in the Scottish Cup as Hearts, who were actually third in the table, went down 4–0 to Falkirk. As far as Celtic were concerned, the draw brought St Mirren to Celtic Park for the first time in a season and a half. The Buddies were competently dispatched 3–0 after holding out well for forty-five minutes. The team was not at its strongest but Jamie Smith did well enough on the left wing to be retained for the league game against Dundee United on the following Wednesday. Once again he put in a good shift, sending over a fine cross for Hartson's goal as Celtic won 2–0 in a poor game on a very cold night. After the game, Dundee United maintained their reputation for eccentricity by sacking manager Paul Hegarty who had served the club for all of fourteen games in his eighty-six days at the helm.

There followed two competent victories: 2–0 over Partick Thistle in a snowstorm at Firhill on 2 February in the SPL, and a 3–0 win over Dundee United at Hampden in the semi final of the League Cup. Sutton scored twice against Thistle and goals came from Balde (twice) and Larsson in the semi final. Hartson was substituted in this game by Fernandez, and was seen by Channel 5's television cameras to be mouthing what looked like obscenities at his manager. Significantly, he did not play the following Sunday against Livingston.

That game on 9 February against Livingston became very important in the context of the season when Henrik Larsson broke his jaw before half time. At one point it looked as if he might miss the rest of the season, and it certainly appeared as if Celtic were about to lose to Livingston that day as well. A shocking mix-up between Valgaeren and goalkeeper Hedman gave Livi the lead, but Celtic then showed great character by storming back to take the three points. Goals came late, and both were rebounds scored by Sylla and Sutton from free kicks taken by Shaun Maloney who had replaced the injured Larsson. Valgaeren made up for his earlier lapse with a brilliant tackle in the last minute when a Livingston forward was clean through and about to score.

15 February saw a rare event when the game against Motherwell at Fir Park was postponed as the pitch was ice bound. Eyebrows were raised at this for it was felt that teams in the SPL should have adequate pitch-protection systems, but the good thing about it from Celtic's point of view was that it gave the Larsson jaw time to heal and also allowed some extra time to prepare for the coming games against Stuttgart in the last sixteen of the UEFA Cup.

The games against Stuttgart showed Celtic at their professional best, even although they lived dangerously from time to time. On Thursday 20 February at Celtic Park, Celtic, without Larsson, Hartson, Mjallby and Hedman (according to *The Scotsman* 'as pre-pared as the American Navy before Pearl Harbour') beat the Germans 3–1 in spite of losing the first goal. Stuttgart had had a man sent off before either team had got on the score-sheet, and Celtic eventually made the numerical advantage count by scoring three excellent goals through Lambert, Maloney and Petrov. It was a fine performance, and in the second leg Celtic went for the jugular and scored two excellent first-half goals: a low header from Thompson off a cross by Agathe that Hartson touched on, and then Didier Agathe was instrumental in the second goal when he had a good run and cross for Sutton.

This seemed to put Celtic on easy street with a 5–1 aggregate lead, but the Germans were not finished. They scored when the influential Thompson was receiving attention from the physio, and then in the second half Celtic made the potentially fatal mistake of sitting back and lost two more goals, fortunately too late in the game to make any real impact. Celtic thus won 5–4 and were into the last eight where they had been drawn to meet Liverpool.

In between times, Celtic beat St Johnstone 3–0 in a low-key Scottish Cup encounter at Celtic Park in front of only 26,000 spectators. Ironically in view of later developments in the season, O'Neill fielded more or less a reserve team with little resemblance to the team that started the Stuttgart game. He got off with it again. Equally ironically in view of what was to happen in three weeks time in the League Cup final, John Hartson converted two penalties. What was impressive about this game was the form of young Jamie Smith who looked a real star in the making.

Thus Celtic finished February 2003 still in the running for four trophies. March was however to be a different matter as the forthcoming fixtures read Hibs, Rangers, Liverpool, Rangers, Liverpool, Inverness. It would be a pivotal month in an already dramatic season. A lesson should have been learned from the first game. This was Hibs at Celtic Park. Celtic quickly went two ahead through John Hartson who scored with good headers from set pieces, one a free kick from Alan Thompson and the other a corner from Shaun Maloney. Then Celtic proceeded to get casual and a truly awful clearance from Javier Sanchez Broto gifted Hibs a goal before young Tom McManus scored a fine equaliser from outside the box. For a while it looked as if a draw was all that Celtic were going to get, but inside the last minute a corner from Alan Thompson found the head of Johan Mjallby and Celtic Park exploded with joy. This was fine stuff, but it concealed a number of deficiencies in the team and allowed a side in the lower half of the division, and frequently criticised by manager Bobby Williamson, back into a game in which they should have been buried.

But this edgy performance was followed by a convincing Old Firm victory at Celtic Park by 1–0. In fact it should have been a great deal more. John Hartson got the winner with a magnificent volley from a Sutton knockdown, but he should have scored on several other occasions, for Rangers were seldom in the game as an attacking force apart from a late free kick that needed a fine Douglas save to deny Amoruso. This game brought a temporary halt to Celtic's participation in the SPL, for the next game would be played a month later, thanks to a combination of cup ties and international matches. The position in the race for the title was that Celtic were three points behind Rangers with a game in hand. Other competitions now came to the fore.

The first leg of the Celtic–Liverpool game was on Thursday 13 March at Celtic Park – indeed all of Celtic's games in the UEFA Cup were played at home first – and it failed to live up to all the pre-match hype. Henrik Larsson returned from his broken jaw of 9 February – a touch prematurely one felt – and, true to form, he scored in the early minutes of the match. But without Agathe who had pulled a hamstring on Saturday, Sutton struggling and Alan Thompson having to go off injured, Celtic toiled and it was no surprise when Heskey equalised for Liverpool before half time. Chances might have been taken by both teams, but the game finished 1–1, the occasion being spoiled by a Liverpool man who spat into the Celtic crowd, something for which he was rightly punished by his embarrassed club. It was felt that Celtic should have done better, but although the odds were slightly against them, no one dared to write off a side that Martin O'Neill had imbued with a ferocious will to win.

The League Cup final was of course scheduled between the two Liverpool games. It was hardly surprising that Celtic went into it a little under-prepared and even a little under-committed, albeit that the opponents were Rangers. Rangers have always done better in the League Cup than Celtic and so it proved on this occasion, but the circumstances were bizarre and unusual. The first half saw Celtic more or less outplayed by Rangers who were good money for their two-goal lead. Celtic however came back in the second half, Larsson scored and then so did Hartson apparently, until he was flagged for offside. Television replays later showed that this was a clear mistake by the standside linesman, and there seems to be little doubt that if that goal had been given, Celtic would have gone on to win, for they were well on top at that time.

That this was not meant to be Celtic's day was proved when

Chris Sutton, who had worked very well all season, was taken off with a broken wrist and destined to be out of the game for some considerable time. Then in the last minute of regulation time, Hartson, always destined to be in the centre of things, missed a penalty. Lennon then was sent off for a second bookable offence and Rangers finished the winners. Celtic, frankly, deserved better and on another day would have won the trophy. As it was, it was in the tradition of heartbreak Celtic League Cup finals, but on this occasion we had no time for self pity for Anfield beckoned. Less than an hour after the full time whistle, Alan Thompson said to the press 'It's over. We've forgotten it.'

The teams at Hampden that day were:

Celtic: Douglas, Valgaeren, Balde, Mjallby, Lennon, Lambert, Thompson, Smith, Sutton, Larsson, Hartson. Substitutes: Petrov, Maloney, Sylla

Rangers: Klos, Ricksen, Moore, Amoruso, Bonnissel, Arteta, Ferguson, De Boer, Caniggia, Mols, Lovenkrands. Substitutes: Ross, Konterman, Arveladze

20 March 2003 saw momentous things happening in the world. It was the day of the start of the second Gulf War as United States and British forces unleashed their military might on Iraq. For Celtic fans, however, even that had to take second place to Celtic's triumph at Anfield, gaining ample revenge for 1966 and 1997 when Celtic were eliminated, unluckily on both occasions, by Liverpool. This time, it was the ever-diligent Alan Thompson who led the way with a free kick just before half time. It was not a great strike, but the players in the Liverpool wall, for reasons best known to themselves, decided to jump over the ball.

The second half was long and dour but Celtic retained the upper hand and fully deserved their second goal only seven minutes from time when, after a fine one-two with Henrik Larsson, John Hartson hammered home from the edge of the box to give Celtic a clear and undisputed victory that even the pundits in the south had to recognise as fully merited. The rejoicings were long, loud and totally deserved. Not only were Celtic in Europe after Christmas, they were now to be in Europe after Easter, drawn against a Portuguese side, Boavista, that they had easily beaten in season 1975/76, and who lacked any real European pedigree.

It was as well for Martin O'Neill that he was considered to be the hero of the hour after the Liverpool triumph, for he then proceeded to do something that shamed the club, insulted Scottish football and got its just desserts in terms of the result. On Sunday 23 March, Celtic were drawn to play Inverness Caledonian Thistle away in the quarter final of the Scottish Cup. Ah, Inverness! As this was such a momentous name in the recent history of the club surely significant measures would be put in place to ensure there was no repeat performance. O'Neill must have known what happened on 8 February 2000. He might even have taken a hint from the fine performance put up by the Highlanders in the League Cup in October.

Yet the team selected included only three of the men who had started at Liverpool. Stanislav Varga was given his debut, following a free transfer from Sunderland, (then bottom of the Premiership) and Fernandez, Maloney, Guppy, Laursen and Broto were dragged in, for no other reason than they had not had a game for a while. Henrik Larsson, who actually could have done with a rest, the better to facilitate the mending of his broken jaw, was made captain, and John Hartson, the hero of Liverpool was only brought on after the damage was done.

Jonathan Coates in *The Scotsman* put it rather well when he said that, 'His (O'Neill's) selection in the Caledonian Stadium could not be described as a reserve team, as that would imply that the players were used to working together. It was a team of reserves, each superior in their own right to their opposite number, but not vaguely imbued with the kind of cohesion for which Celtic's first XI is famed.'

There was a surreal atmosphere at the game played in that pleasant stadium near the A9 with a Sunday evening 6.15 p.m. kick off, a definite harking-back to the bizarre kick-off times to keep Sky Television happy. Celtic's lack of cohesion was immediately apparent in a lacklustre first period, and they were rewarded for their lack of impetus when the excellent Wyness scored in injury time after a fine move down the left. Thus the Invernesians scored at the psychologically correct time, and Celtic fans were justifiably concerned.

The second half saw Celtic expending a little more effort but, as one would have expected of their manager John Robertson who had played so well for Hearts and Livingston, the Inverness side were clearly up for it. They had prepared for this game in a way that Celtic had not. One recalled the dictum of Alex Ferguson that 'those who fail to prepare must prepare to fail', and although a little luck might have brought an equaliser, it was Inverness Caledonian Thistle who once again put Celtic out of the Scottish Cup.

The finger must unwaveringly be pointed at Martin O'Neill over this one. He had committed the cardinal sin of underestimating opponents. There is of course value in squad rotation, but it is surely asking for trouble if it is done on such a massive scale, and especially when the players concerned were not even gelling as a unit. They had seldom played together. In addition there was the precedent of what happened in the autumn. Twice Celtic had come close to elimination from the League Cup: to the same Inverness Caledonian Thistle and also to their namesakes from Partick. Each time had seen a weakened Celtic team struggle against opposition that would normally have been trounced. The message should have been clear, that no matter how well the team plays against Liverpool, the humble Scottish teams will always raise their game because they are desperate to beat Celtic.

Some people speculated there may have been a political factor at work. O'Neill had repeatedly stated that he needed money to strengthen his squad. The press, naturally, played this up. And they may well have been correct as it was obvious to all who observed Celtic closely that the squad was simply not strong enough to compete effectively in four competitions. Was this not perhaps O'Neill's way of demonstrating that the current squad, particularly its fringe members, was not good enough?

Either way, it was a sad night for the traditions of Celtic, the Scottish Cup and Scottish football in general, which had been on a deserved high since the previous Thursday. It meant that Rangers now had every chance of winning a treble and of equalling Celtic's record of Scottish Cup wins. This they did in the most heart-rending of circumstances in the summer. It seemed a pity that success in Europe – and glorious success it was – had to be paid for by the loss on two dreadful successive Sundays of trophies that still meant an awful lot to the fans. Those beyond a certain age would remark that in Jock Stein's day, any success in Europe was certainly not accompanied by a failure in Scotland.

The following weekend was taken up with international fixtures, but the Sunday after that, 6 April, saw another heartache as Celtic disappointingly dropped two points to Dundee. As Rangers had won luckily the previous day, it meant that the initiative in the league was also slipping away. This did seem to be a terrible price to pay for success on foreign soil.

The game at Dens Park itself was a poor show on a bumpy pitch. Celtic had gone ahead through a Thompson header in the first half but then a few minutes later, ex-Celt Mark Burchill, who left the club in 2000 and had never really settled down anywhere else, equalised. He and his family were still Celtic fans, but it was Dundee who paid the wages, and it was Mark's goal that put Rangers ahead of Celtic in the championship race. Rangers would still be two points ahead even if Celtic won their games in hand.

As Boavista hove into sight for the UEFA Cup semi final at Celtic Park, a major row developed between Celtic and the Scottish Premier League. It concerned the timing of the Old Firm encounter at Ibrox, which the SPL with the support of the Strathclyde Police wished to play on Sunday 27 April, only three days after Celtic's return from the UEFA Cup semi final in Portugal.

The argument was that, following the dreadful scenes at Celtic Park in 1999 when serious disorder and hooliganism had attended Rangers winning the league, it would not be a good idea to have the fixture later in the season when the title could be clinched. On the other hand Celtic felt, and with some justification, that playing Rangers so soon after the return from Portugal was hardly fair to a team that had, after all, brought tremendous credit to Scotland with their European run. While respecting the wishes of the forces of law and order that it would not have been a good idea to play the game on the last available weekend, it would surely have been a simple matter to play the game on, say, Sunday 4 May.

The real villain of the piece was the Scottish Premier League with its absurd idea – almost unparalleled in world football – of a split in the league, which meant that fixtures had to be arranged at short notice. The battle raged on for a few days but in the end Celtic had to withdraw and accept the word of the authorities that 27 April was the best day for the Old Firm fixture. Quite a few intemperate words were expressed by Martin O'Neill and not least by Celtic chief executive Ian McLeod, whose resignation the following week was surely not unconnected with this humiliating climb-down. It was probably true to say that most genuine football fans would have sided with Celtic, although the extremity of the views emanating from Celtic Park – 'it would have been different if it were Rangers' for example – alienated many.

A certain amount of true colours being hoisted by other SPL sides was evident when only Kilmarnock and Livingston apparently backed Celtic's position. It was clear that there was still a certain amount of strife inside the SPL – no doubt related to the disputes over television money and voting rights – and many commentators now began to question the validity of this organization with its bizarre structure, the likely exclusion of Falkirk because of concerns over their stadium, the winter shutdown and the league split.

The semi-final jousts with Boavista probably saw Celtic playing their worst football of the European campaign to date against one of the poorest sides they had faced. Yet they won through to achieve one of the club's most notable triumphs since 1967. The first leg was hardly fit for the last four of a European competition. Boavista went ahead through a Joos Valgaeren own goal. Larsson equalised with a fine strike following good work from Petrov, then saw his penalty kick saved by the goalkeeper. Several other penalty claims were denied, several good chances might have been taken and the more gullible readers of the following day's tabloids were convinced that Celtic had blown it with a 1–1 scoreline and were as good as out.

But this Celtic side had built up a reputation of being able to score away from home and to win through against all the odds. For the return in Portugal, it was an anxious night to watch television screens as Celtic, after a reasonably bright start, faded and it looked as if the game would peter out into a goalless draw, a result that would have put Celtic out on the away-goals rule. Lambert was injured and had to be replaced by Sutton who was making his return after breaking a wrist in the League Cup final and did not look anywhere close to match fitness. Boavista grew in confidence and appeared favourites to win through to the final. That is, until one Henrik Larsson struck. He tried a one-two with John Hartson, but when the ball inadvertently rebounded from a defender Larsson calmly transferred it to his left foot and scored. It was an untidy-looking goal, which the goalkeeper got his hand to, but it was a goal nevertheless.

Twelve minutes remained and the Scottish champions defended

desperately but successfully with the heading power of Bobo Balde a key factor in a siege of the Celtic goal that the BBC commentators likened to the Alamo. Four extra minutes were played, but the full-time whistle came to release scenes of joy among the small Celtic support in Portugal. The vast television audience at home, who had watched and prayed anxiously, celebrated in a way that not been seen for a generation. Celtic were en route for the final in Seville! Their opponents would be Porto, the Portuguese champions-elect, who had comprehensively beaten Italian giants Lazio in the other semi.

The days that followed saw travel agents in Scotland besieged by Celtic fans desperate to be in Seville. From an early stage it became obvious that there would be nowhere near enough tickets to go round for Celtic's massive following. It was also clear that a geography lesson might not have gone amiss, as beach balls and towels became popular. Even the *Celtic View* gave its readers a free green-and-white beach ball, clearly unaware that Seville was a considerable distance from the sea!

Spanish textbooks used by generations of pupils would predictably contain the line '*quien no ha visto Sevilla, no ha visto maravilla*' – 'he who has not seen Seville has not seen a marvel'. Indeed Seville is a beautiful city, an inland port standing on the wide river Quadalquivir, a centre of Moorish civilization and base for much of the Spanish colonisation of South America in bygone times. Beautiful buildings include the cathedral with its famous Giralda tower and a Moorish palace called the Alcazar, described in textbooks as the '*joya de la arquitectura morisca*' – 'the jewel of Moorish architecture'.

It did seem however that success in Europe came at a price for Celtic's position at the top of the SPL had been seriously weakened. Rangers kept winning, and although Celtic beat Kilmarnock (in a routine win at Celtic Park with goals from Larsson and Petrov and with Alan Thompson outstanding, as he had been so often that season), they lost to Hearts at Tynecastle on 19 April (the Saturday before the trip to Boavista) in the most agonising of fashions.

Perhaps slightly unnerved by news of Rangers's lucky win over Motherwell in the Scottish Cup semi final with a lunchtime kick off, Celtic played competently against Hearts but with little panache or flair. Hearts were more than due a victory over Celtic and they too had watched the Motherwell versus Rangers semi final. The young Motherwell side had almost beaten Rangers by having a go at them, and Craig Levein told his men to do just that against Celtic. Honours were even for most of the game, but Celtic knew that a 1–1 draw would not be enough. Men were pushed forward in the closing stages and this allowed Austin McCann – a self-confessed Celtic supporter – to score a fine late winner for Hearts.

This did not quite put the league out of Celtic's reach but it did mean they were now eight points behind and with only one game in hand. Celtic therefore needed to beat Rangers on the controversial date of 27 April, win all the rest of their games while keeping one eye on the UEFA Cup final and hope that one of the other teams in the top six – Hearts, Dundee, Dunfermline or Kilmarnock – could beat Rangers. It was not exactly a forlorn hope, but it did look rather unlikely.

Yet Celtic's star was definitely back in the ascendancy on 27 April in the controversial fixture at Ibrox. It was a tough encounter but Celtic edged it 2–1. A penalty was awarded when Amoruso bundled Hartson and this time it was the excellent Alan Thompson who took it and scored. This was after about half an hour's play, and just before half time Hartson put Celtic two up when Larsson nudged on a fine Agathe cross. Thereafter it was backs to the wall, for what the late Jock Stein used to describe as a 'boiler-suit job'. Although Rangers pulled one back, Celtic were just competent enough to hold out.

The atmosphere in this game was remarkable, as Celtic fans appeared with sombreros, beach balls, towels and singing songs with lines like 'Today we're off to sunny Spain'. It was all the more marked for being spontaneous and showed that the sense of humour of Celtic supporters knows few bounds. The media picked this up, and it became a very important factor in the build-up to the UEFA Cup final that the Scottish press, television and radio were very much onside as far as Celtic were concerned, with BBC Scotland – who had television rights for the game – leading the way.

Alarm was expressed however about a serious injury to Rab Douglas who had to go off in the early stages of the game at Ibrox, and he was still out for the visit to Dunfermline the following Saturday. Fortunately Javier Sanchez Broto had a superb game as Celtic romped to a fairly effortless 4–1 victory which saw two great goals by Petrov, one from Larsson and a penalty kick expertly slotted home by Alan Thompson. The value of this win was seen the following day when Rangers went up to Dens Park, and in front of a huge, anxious television audience dropped two points. Three penalties were awarded to them – all justified – but they could only convert one and thus Dundee carried out the same feat that they had done against Celtic by earning a draw in front of television cameras. Two questions must be asked of Dundee – why don't you do better in matches that do not involve the Old Firm, and why can't you play better in Glasgow?

Celtic went ahead in the title race on the wet night of 7 May at Fir Park in conditions as far from Seville as one could imagine. The 4–0 scoreline – two from Petrov, two from Lambert – put Celtic one goal ahead on goal difference. Motherwell's play bordered on the disgraceful, and more than one player could have been red-carded. The pitch was in very poor condition, and those who watched the game from behind the goal were reminded again of the appalling cross-field slope. But Celtic fans were less worried about Motherwell's suitability for the SPL than the realisation that Celtic were now top of the league.

The weekend of May 10/11 saw both teams at home. Celtic beat Hearts thanks to an Alan Thompson penalty in a tight encounter. A 1–0 win gave us three points but there was the feeling that there should have been more goals. This feeling intensified the following day when Rangers put four past a Kilmarnock side whose lack of commitment was disappointing, to put it mildly. Rangers were now level on points but two goals to the good.

Yet on Wednesday 14 May, the pendulum swung back. Dundee, very sportingly, had agreed to bring this game at Celtic Park forward from the Saturday in order to give Celtic more time to prepare for Seville, and so Celtic once again had the opportunity to go ahead in the title race. In a thrilling game of football, with a left-wing combination of Alan Thompson and Shaun Maloney outstanding, Celtic beat Dundee 6–2 with both Thompson and Maloney scoring twice and Larsson and Mjallby once. This put Celtic three points and two goals ahead, although the huge crowd and the television audience wondered whether the late goal conceded through lack of concentration might turn out to be fatal.

The attention now shifted to Tynecastle for the visit of Rangers on Sunday 18 May, although by that time many Celtic fans were already airborne or even in Seville. Never in the history of Scottish football had so much hysteria been engendered over a single game, even Lisbon in 1967, Milan in 1970 or Argentina in 1978. Everyone seemed to be going to the final and Celtic fans would sing lustily about 'You'll be watching The Bill when we're in Seville' or 'You'll be watching East Enders, when we're on our benders' or even less plausibly 'You'll be cashing your Giros, when we're on our lilos'. The atmosphere throughout Scotland was electric both about the Seville game and about the thrilling end to the league season, which seemed certain to 'go to the wire' as that hoary old football cliché went.

The cynics among the Celtic support were convinced that Hearts, now secure in next year's UEFA Cup, would play reserves and generally lie down against Rangers. There would have been a certain amount of revenge in that, for in 2001, Celtic played a weakened team and lost to Kilmarnock thereby depriving Hearts of a UEFA Cup spot. In addition there was the traditional Tynecastle hatred of all things Celtic, something that had existed long before 1986 when Celtic pipped Hearts for the league championship, but which had been whetted by the events of that year.

But to Craig Levein's credit, Hearts put out a strong team and pulled out all the stops. Indeed they were the better team for much of the game, being eventually ground down by Rangers and losing 2–0. This meant that Celtic and Rangers were level on points and goal difference, but Rangers had scored one more goal. In addition they were at home to Dunfermline on the last Sunday while Celtic had to travel to Kilmarnock.

The Celtic party were already in Spain when they heard the news from Tynecastle. It was however pushed to the back of their mind as they prepared for that mammoth game against Porto. There was no doubt about the calibre of the team they would face in Seville. Porto had won the Portuguese league in a canter, completely eclipsing the two giants from their country, Benfica and Sporting Lisbon. In the first leg of their semi final against Lazio they gave the Italian club – most people's favourites for the competition – a footballing lesson and ran out comfortable winners by four goals to one. Their manager, Jose Mourinho, was intelligent, articulate and knowledgeable and had a tremendous pedigree; he had spent four years on the coaching staff at Barcelona, earning the admiration of the man who was his mentor, Sir Bobby Robson. Almost overnight, Mourinho had completely transformed Porto's fortunes and brought back the glory days the club had experienced in the 1990s when the title was won eight times in ten seasons. It was a wholly different side than the one that faced Celtic the season before in the Champions League, both in terms of playing personnel and attitude.

The star was undoubtedly Anderson Luis de Souza, nicknamed Deco, who although born in Brazil, had taken out Portuguese citizenship and had recently scored the winner for his adopted country against the country of his birth in a friendly international.

The teams for a match that will earn its own place in immortality, albeit a slightly flawed one, were:

Celtic: Douglas, Valgaeren, Balde, Mjallby, Lambert, Lennon, Thompson, Petrov, Agathe, Sutton, Larsson. Substitutes: Hedman, Laursen, McNamara, Maloney, Sylla, Fernandez, Smith.

Porto: Baia, Paulo Ferreira, Jorge Costa, Carvalho, Valente, Costinha, Alenichev, Deco, Maniche, Capucho, Derlei. Substitutes used: Ricardo Costa, Emanuel, Marco Ferreira

Referee L. Michel, Slovakia.

The facts of the game are painful. In temperatures approaching ninety degrees Fahrenheit, Porto started off the better team and although Celtic rallied in the middle of the half, it was the Portuguese who scored in injury time just before the interval. A misplaced clearance by Valgaeren hit Balde and Deco capitalised on the mistake to send over a brilliant cross for Porto's Russian midfielder, Alenichev. Although Rab Douglas made an excellent save from Alenichev's shot, the ball arrived at the feet of Derlei, who slotted the ball home at the back post. It was a bitter blow after Celtic had fought manfully to get back into the game. Not long after play restarted, Derlei enraged the Celtic players and coaching staff by needlessly blasting the ball into Agathe's midriff. When the halftime whistle blew shortly thereafter the animosity caused by Derlei's bad sportsmanship caused a mass brawl to break out as the players made their way up the tunnel. Thanks to the peacekeeping efforts of Martin O'Neill and other cool heads it came to very little.

There was a surreal incident at the start of the second period when a man dressed as a referee ran onto the playing surface and 'red-carded' the referee; he then proceeded to strip off his uniform and streaked, completely naked, across the field until he was caught by security staff. This did nothing to affect Celtic's determination to claw their way back into the game and the team's true character was shown within two minutes of the restart when

Larsson outjumped the Porto defence to score with a wonderful header off the post from an Agathe cross. This was, of course, his two-hundredth goal for Celtic, and it could hardly have come at a more appropriate time or in a more vital game. As Rob McLean said in his commentary for BBC television, 'It had to be Henrik'.

Then both teams scored again. In the fifty-fourth minute that man Deco left the Celtic defence floundering after some clever play and laid the ball on a plate for Alenichev, who fired his shot under the emerging Douglas and into the net. Martin O'Neill was furious about the length of time taken by the Porto players to celebrate the goal and made his feelings known in no uncertain terms to the fourth official. But Larsson, inevitably, replied only three minutes later when, from a Thompson corner, he powered in a header and although Baia got a hand to the ball he could not keep it out if the net.

Thus thirty minutes were left for the UEFA Cup to be won. It would not be true to say that both teams went at it hammer and tongs because the intense heat meant that the pace was slower than Celtic were used to. As players tired tackles became increasingly desperate and Lennon and Balde were booked for Celtic and Nuno Valente for Porto. O'Neill introduced two substitutes – Laursen for Valgaeren and McNamara for Lambert – but ninety minutes came and went with the teams still level. If anything, Celtic were the better team towards the end of regulation time but were unable to make their advantage count.

The agony of the Celtic fans in the crowd and the millions watching back home in Scotland and throughout the world continued and intensified in extra time (which was played under UEFA's so-called 'silver goal' rule, meaning that if a team scored in the first period, and their opponents did not equalise in that first period, they would take the trophy and there would be no second period of extra time). Five minutes of extra time had elapsed when the turning point of the final arrived. Balde lunged into a tackle on Derlei. As he had already been booked – for a tackle on Deco – the red card was shown to the distraught African. In truth the referee, Lubos Michel of Slovakia, had little option but to send Balde off, a fact acknowledged by nearly all of the Scottish journalists at the match, and by the commentators on television. Although the Celtic fans sang, 'There's only one Bobo Balde' as he trooped off the truth is that the tackle was made in the midfield area and need not have been attempted.

Although Celtic were the stronger team before the dismissal, the departure of the giant stopper tipped the odds very much in favour of Porto, for Balde, although prone to the occasional error, had been outstanding in central defence. It now appeared that the Portuguese, who in any case were now just a little sharper to the ball, might well wear down the heroic Celtic. Yet Celtic held them until just five minutes from time. The winning goal came as the result of another defensive blunder: Rab Douglas failed to hold onto a pass delivered from the Porto midfield and the ball ran to Derlei. Although Douglas managed to get a glove on the Brazilian striker's shot, and Mjallby made a despairing lunge on the line, it ended up in the net. It was a goal that Rab Douglas was honest enough to accept responsibility for, but significantly, the Celtic crowd and his teammates, even in that most desperate of times, did not turn on him. Celtic, fans and players, were in this together, and the full-time whistle came to bring agony, certainly, but an agony much less intense for being shared by so many.

Larsson's two goals were not enough, sadly, but they were good ones, and it was such a shame that Celtic did not finish Porto off in the ninety minutes. Whenever the game went to extra time in that heat, the team with the fewer north Europeans in it is likely to win, and when Bobo Balde was despatched, Celtic's only hope was a penalty shoot-out. The killer blow was a tired goal . . . but although a few errors could be pointed to, no Celtic player had any cause to blame himself. Their pain was every bit as intense as that of the supporters, as Henrik Larsson's post-match television interview manifestly revealed.

Possibly, Porto were marginally the better team in that there was just a little more creativity in front of goal, whereas Celtic lacked a powerful midfield man who could take a grip on the game as Bobby Murdoch of a previous generation would have. Celtic also missed the injured John Hartson but this was balanced by the absence of Porto's star striker Helder Postiga, who was subsequently transferred to Tottenham Hotspur for a fee in excess of £8 million. The antics of the Portuguese team in feigning injury were shameful – one particular piece of somersaulting by goalkeeper Baia was spectacularly worthy of a yellow card – and there is little doubt that Balde's second tragic challenge had a little to do with the refusal of a free kick after a foul on Henrik Larsson seconds previously. Had the inexperienced referee called that one differently, things would have been totally altered.

There were recriminations from Celtic players and coaching staff, and from the supporters who roundly booed the Porto players as they went to receive their winners' medals. Martin O'Neill was particularly incensed by the attitude of the Porto players. He said, 'I wasn't pleased with them at all. They are talented footballers. But you saw the reception they got from our supporters when they went up for the cup.' He was also critical of the referee who, he argued, at the age of 35, was young to be refereeing a major final.

But such speculation is pointless. The team came back unbowed and with the consolation that they had done themselves and their country proud. No less a person than the prime minister, Tony Blair, who once apparently had confessed to a weakness for Celtic in his days at Fettes, said that 'Celtic did the country proud. To come back twice and lose was the cruellest disappointment' and his Scottish equivalent Jack McConnell, who would find it more difficult to express publicly any love for the green and white, said 'The whole team showed, passion, bravery and ability. They, their supporters and all of Scotland can be proud of their performance.'

The fans indeed deserve nothing but praise. The acceptable side of Scotland was shown to the world that night, not least in the sheer amount of green-and-white jerseys seen in Seville that night. It was estimated by some observers that 80,000 bhoys and ghirls were there, although the official figure given by UEFA and the Spanish authorities was 58,000, still an astonishing number. Apparently, 1 per cent of the world's air traffic that day consisted of Celtic fans travelling to Seville. Indeed UEFA later confirmed that Celtic had taken the biggest-ever travelling army with them in the history of football. The love of the club by the fans continues to amaze, and one really has to be part of it to understand the sheer intensity.

The European campaign gave a huge lift to the club and to Scottish football. No one who watched the match could fail to be impressed by the backing that the club had that night. Particularly impressive was the vocal support that continued to be given to the team in the immediate aftermath of an agonising night. Stuart Bathgate, the chief sports writer of *The Scotsman*, put it very well when he said: 'If this was disappointment and dejection, it was the sort that most clubs would die for'. A more detached view came from the football correspondent of the Spanish daily *El Pais* who talked about the '*aficion extraordinaria*' of the Scots for their team and made the point that no other team in Europe possessed such a following.

But not everyone in Scotland was disappointed at the outcome. *The Herald* reported that regulars at the Grapes Bar in Glasgow's Paisley Road West greeted Porto's triumph with a mass conga in the street and chants of 'Let's all laugh at Celtic'. The pub had been specially decked out in Portugal flags and balloons in the colours of Porto were hung from the ceiling. Someone had even thought to produce double-sided Rangers/Porto scarves. This was despite Alex McLeish's plea to Rangers fans to back Celtic in the final – and many to their great credit did – and Lorenzo Amoruso's comment that any Rangers fans who supported Porto were 'silly'. It was clear that the admirable efforts by both halves of the Old Firm to stamp out sectarianism in campaigns such as Bhoys against Bigotry had had only limited success. They had certainly failed to register with one regular at the Grapes, a woman from Kinning Park nicknamed 'Mrs Caniggia'. With great succinctness she summed up the feelings of bluenoses in the bar, 'It's a dream come true.'

There remained the Scottish Premier League. The situation at kick-off time on Sunday 25 May (the thirty-sixth anniversary of the Lisbon Lions game) was that both teams were level on points, goal difference, but Rangers had a marginal advantage in that they had scored one more goal. All sorts of permutations were possible, but as Rangers were at home to Dunfermline whereas Celtic had to travel to Kilmarnock, the odds were on the Ibrox team, even before any allowances were made for the exhausting and traumatic experiences that Celtic had been through over the past week.

The atmosphere at Rugby Park that day was bizarre. It was a bright sunny day and the support was there in strength, noisy, upbeat and proud of their team, determined to follow them 'through and through'. Yet there was the feeling not dissimilar to that of a Greek tragedy where the inevitable is to happen, but only after it has been played out at painful length. Little faith was expressed in Dunfermline with their management team of unashamed Rangers sympathies.

Rangers went ahead in the first minute, and Celtic lost the industrious Shaun Maloney after a nasty tackle. Thereafter things were on a knife-edge but only for the briefest of spells in the second half were

Celtic ahead. The hinge of fate turned decisively against Celtic when, at the same precise moment, Henrik Larsson hit the post and Ronald de Boer scored for Rangers. Rangers stayed ahead after that finishing 6–1 over Dunfermline as distinct from Celtic's 4–0 over Kilmarnock. Alan Thompson scored one penalty and missed another, but his miss cannot be held responsible for the loss of the title.

The key factor in all this was quite simply luck. Anyone who does not accept the existence of luck, or even fate, as a decisive factor has never been at a football match. Celtic quite simply did not get the luck when they needed it, neither at Kilmarnock, nor Ibrox, nor Seville and that is why they finished the season empty-handed. They will play worse and win silverware. Indeed on many occasions they have done just that.

Chris Sutton earned himself a certain amount of notoriety by claiming that Dunfermline had lain down to Rangers. These remarks were made in the heat of the moment, the immediate aftermath of the loss of the championship and were apologised for the following day, but Chris was by no means alone in his views. Indeed quite a few Dunfermline Athletic supporters were mystified by their side's disappointing performance after they had equalised through Jason Dair. But whatever the circumstances, the truth remained that the league had been lost by the narrowest of margins . . . but the battle had been won.

In fact season 2002/03 did belong to Celtic. In European terms, they had kept faith with the past – albeit the distant past – and handed on a tradition to the future. Martin O'Neill and his players enjoyed the total affection and love of his fans and the respect of the world. Even in defeat, the feeling was expressed that this team was one of the best teams in Scotland's recent history. Surely next season would be much better.

An unhappy fan put it rather well when he said that defeats in the UEFA Cup final and the championship would have been much easier to take if Celtic had had a bad team. Then there could have been the gut reaction of sacking a manager or transferring players and bringing in others. As it was, the question of 'What is wrong with Celtic?' could be easily answered by 'Nothing . . . other than the lack of luck at key points during the season'. Inverness was a disgrace, but one from which lessons could be learned. Other than that, it was difficult to be angry about anything connected with Celtic.

Results 1993/94 – 2002/03

Scottish League Premier Division   1993-4

Motherwell	A	8/7/93	2-2	Slater, McAvennie	13569
Hibernian	H	8/14/93	1-1	Nicholas	27690
Rangers	H	8/21/93	0-0		47942
Partick Thistle	A	8/28/83	1-0	McNally	14013
Aberdeen	H	9/4/93	0-1		34311
Raith Rovers	A	9/11/93	4-1	Nicholas 2, Payton 2	8114
Dundee United	H	9/18/93	1-1	Creaney	26377
Hearts	A	9/25/93	0-1		14761
Kilmarnock	H	10/2/93	0-0		23396
St. Johnstone	A	10/6/93	1-2	Creaney	7386
Dundee	H	10/9/93	2-1	Creaney, McGinlay	15980
Hibernian	A	10/16/93	1-1	Creaney	14991
Rangers	A	10/30/93	2-1	Collins, O'Neil	47522
Partick Thistle	H	11/6/93	3-0	McGinlay 2, Nicholas	21642
Aberdeen	A	11/9/93	1-1	O'Neil	19474
Kilmarnock	A	11/13/93	2-2	Nicholas, McGinlay	16649
Hearts	H	11/20/93	0-0		25990
Motherwell	H	11/24/93	2-0	McGinlay 2	16654
Raith Rovers	H	11/27/93	2-0	Collins 2	17453
Dundee United	A	11/30/93	0-1		10220
St. Johnstone	H	12/4/93	1-0	McGinlay	15941
Dundee	A	12/11/93	1-1	Creaney	8730
Hibernian	H	12/18/93	1-0	McStay	16808
Rangers	H	1/1/94	2-4	Collins, Nicholas	48506
Partick Thistle	A	1/8/94	0-1		12887
Motherwell	A	1/11/94	1-2	McNally	13159
Aberdeen	H	1/19/94	2-2	Byrne, McStay	19083
Dundee United	H	1/22/94	0-0		17235
Raith Rovers	A	2/5/94	0-0		7678
Hearts	A	2/12/94	2-0	Nicholas 2	14049
Kilmarnock	H	3/1/94	1-0	Collins	9887
St.Johnstone	A	3/5/94	1-0	Byrne	8622
Hibernian	A	3/19/94	0-0		14639
Motherwell	H	3/26/94	0-1		36199
Raith Rovers	H	3/30/94	2-1	Donnelly 2	14140
Dundee United	A	4/2/94	3-1	Falconer, Collins, Mowbray	9790
Dundee	H	4/6/94	1-1	Donnelly	16585
Hearts	H	4/9/94	2-2	Vata, Collins	18761
Kilmarnock	A	4/16/94	0-2		11499
Dundee	A	4/23/94	2-0	McGinlay 2	5795
St.Johnstone	H	4/27/94	1-1	Donnelly	10602
Rangers	A	4/30/94	1-1	Collins	47018
Partick Thistle	H	5/7/94	1-1	McGinlay	16827
Aberdeen	A	5/14/94	1-1	Donnelly	16417

Average home attendance   21784

Scottish League Cup

Stirling Albion	A	8/10/93	2-0	McGinlay, McAvennie	8533
Arbroath	A	8/25/93	9-1	McAvennie 3, Payton 3	5364
				Nicholas, McGinlay, McNally	
Airdrieonians	H	8/31/93	1-0	McAvennie	25738
Rangers	A	9/22/93	0-1		47420

Scottish Cup

Motherwell	A	1/29/94	0-1		14061

UEFA Cup

Young Boys	A	9/14/93	0-0		7300
Young Boys	H	9/29/93	1-0	own goal	21500
Sporting Lisbon	H	10/20/93	1-0	Creaney	31321
Sporting Lisbon	A	11/3/93	0-2		60000

Scottish League Premier Division   1994-95

Falkirk	A	8/13/94	1-1	Walker	12635
Dundee United	H	8/20/94	2-1	Walker, Mowbray	25817
Rangers	A	8/27/94	2-0	Collins, McStay	44607
Partick Thistle	A	9/10/94	2-1	O'Donnell 2	14439
Kilmarnock	H	9/17/94	1-1	McGinlay	28457
Hibernian	H	9/24/94	2-0	O'Donnell, Collins	28170
Motherwell	A	10/1/94	1-1	Walker	10869
Aberdeen	H	10/8/94	0-0		29454
Hearts	A	10/15/94	0-1		12086
Falkirk	H	10/22/94	0-2		23688
Rangers	H	10/30/94	1-3	Byrne	32171
Dundee United	A	11/5/94	2-2	Collins 2	10496
Partick Thistle	H	11/9/94	0-0		21462
Kilmarnock	A	11/19/94	0-0		13932
Hibernian	A	11/30/94	1-1	Collins	12295
Motherwell	H	12/3/94	2-2	Falconer, o.g	21465
Aberdeen	A	12/26/94	0-0		19206
Falkirk	H	12/31/94	2-0	Grant, Walker	21294
Rangers	A	1/4/95	1-1	Byrne	45794
Dundee United	H	1/7/95	1-1	Collins	21436
Hearts	H	1/11/95	1-1	van Hooijdonk	26491
Kilmarnock	H	1/14/95	2-1	Collins, Falconer	25342
Partick Thistle	A	1/21/95	0-0		11904
Motherwell	A	2/4/95	0-1		10771
Hibernian	H	2/11/95	2-2	Collins, Falconer	24284
Hearts	A	2/25/95	1-1	O'Donnell	11185
Aberdeen	H	3/5/95	2-0	van Hooijdonk 2	20621
Kilmarnock	A	3/21/95	1-0	Walker	10112
Motherwell	H	4/1/95	1-1	Walker	24047
Aberdeen	A	4/15/95	0-2		16668
Hearts	H	4/19/95	0-1		18638
Falkirk	A	4/29/95	2-1	O'Donell, Boyd	9714

Partick Thistle	H	5/2/95	1-3	Grant	18963
Rangers	H	5/7/95	3-0	van Hooijdonk, Vata, o.g.	31025
Hibernian	A	5/9/95	1-1	Falconer	6019
Dundee United	A	5/13/95	1-0	O'Donnell	10993
				Average home attendance (Hampden)	**24606**

Scottish League Cup

Ayr United	A	8/16/94	1-0	Grant	8182
Dundee	A	8/31/94	2-1	Collins, Walker	11431
Dundee United	H	9/21/94	1-0	Collins	28859
Aberdeen	Ibrox	10/26/94	1-0	O'Neil	44000
Raith Rovers	Ibrox	11/27/94	2-2 aet	Walker, Nicholas lost 5-6 penalties	45384

Scottish Cup

St.Mirren	H	1/28/95	2-0	Falconer, van Hooijdonk	28449
Meadowbank	H	2/18/95	3-0	Falconer, van Hooijdonk 2	23710
Kilmarnock	H	3/10/95	1-0	Collins	30881
Hibernian	Ibrox	4/7/95	0-0		40950
Hibernian	Ibrox	4/11/95	3-1	Falconer, Collins, O'Donnell	32410
Airdrie	Hampden	5/27/95	1-0	van Hooijdink	36915

Scottish League Premier Division 1995-96

Raith Rovers	A	8/26/95	1-0	van Hooijdonk	9300
Aberdeen	A	9/10/95	3-2	Collins 2, Thom	16489
Motherwell	H	9/16/95	1-1	O'Donnell	31365
Hearts	A	9/23/95	4-0	McLaughlin 2, Walker 2	13696
Rangers	H	9/30/95	0-2		33296
Falkirk	A	10/4/95	1-0	Hughes	9053
Partick Thistle	H	10/7/95	2-1	van Hooijdonk, Collins	29950
Hibernian	H	10/14/95	2-2	van Hooijdonk, Collins	31738
Kilmarnock	A	10/21/95	0-0		14011
Aberdeen	H	10/28/95	2-0	McLaughlin, van Hooijdonk	32275
Motherwell	A	11/4/95	2-0	Donnelly,Collins	12077
Raith Rovers	H	11/8/95	0-0		28832
Partick Thistle	A	11/11/95	2-1	van Hooijdonk 2	12223
Rangers	A	11/19/95	3-3	Thom, Collins, van Hooijdonk	46640
Hearts	H	11/25/95	3-1	Collins 3	34032
Kilmarnock	H	12/2/95	4-2	Thom, Grant, van Hooijdonk 2	33660
Hibernian	A	12/9/95	4-0	McNamara, Donnelly, O'Donnell, van Hooijdonk	13626
Falkirk	H	12/16/95	1-0	van Hooijdonk	34466
Rangers	H	1/3/96	0-0		36719
Motherwell	H	1/6/96	1-0	van Hooijdonk	34629
Raith Rovers	A	1/9/96	3-1	O'Donnell, Collins, van Hooijdonk	9300
Aberdeen	A	1/14/96	2-1	Collins, van Hooijdonk	16760
Hearts	A	1/17/96	2-1	van Hooijdonk, Walker	15871
Kilmarnock	A	1/20/96	0-0		16024

Hibernian	H	2/3/96	2-1	van Hooijdonk, McStay	36976
Falkirk	A	2/10/96	0-0		10366
Partick Thistle	H	2/24/96	4-0	Grant, van Hooijdonk 2, Wieghorst	36421
Hearts	H	3/2/96	4-0	McStay, van Hooijdonk, McLaughlin, Donnelly	37034
Rangers	A	3/17/96	1-1	Hughes	47312
Motherwell	A	3/23/96	0-0		12394
Aberdeen	H	4/1/96	5-0	Donnelly 2, van Hooijdonk 2, Cadete	35284
Kilmarnock	H	4/10/96	1-1	van Hooijdonk	36476
Hibernian	A	4/14/96	2-1	van Hooijdonk 2	10742
Falkirk	H	4/20/96	4-0	Thom 2, Cadete, Donnelly	35692
Partick Thistle	A	4/27/96	4-2	van Hooijdonk 2, Cadete, Mackay	14693
Raith Rovers	H	5/4/96	4-1	Cadete 2, Gray, Grant	37318
				Average home attendance	**34231**

Scottish League Cup

Ayr United	A	8/19/95	3-0	van Hooijdonk, Thom, Collins	9128
Raith Rovers	H	8/31/95	2-1 aet	van Hooijdonk, Donnelly	27546
Rangers	H	9/19/95	0-1		32803

Scottish Cup

Whitehill Welfare	Easter Road	1/28/96	3-0	van Hooijdonk 2, Donnelly	13313
Raith Rovers	H	2/17/96	2-0	Thom, Donnelly	30870
Dundee United	H	3/10/96	2-1	van Hooijdonk, McLaughlin	31403
Rangers	Hampden	4/7/96	1-2	van Hooijdonk	36333

European Cup Winners' Cup

Dynamo Batumi	A	9/14/95	3-2	Thom 2, Donnelly	18000
Dynamo Batumi	H	9/28/95	4-0	Thom 2, Donnelly, Walker	31969
Paris St.Germain	A	10/19/95	0-1		30010
Paris St.Germain	H	11/2/95	0-2		34822

Scottish League Premier Division   1996-97

Aberdeen	A	8/10/96	2-2	van Hooijdonk, Thom	18595
Raith Rovers	H	8/17/96	4-1	van Hooijdonk, Thom 2, Donnelly	46795
Kilmarnock	A	8/24/96	3-1	Di Canio, Thom, Cadete	15970
Hibernian	H	9/7/96	5-0	Cadete 2, O'Neil, van Hooijdonk, own goal	47148
Dundee United	A	9/14/96	2-1	van Hooijdonk, Mackay	12205
Dunfermline Athletic	H	9/21/96	5-1	Cadete, Di Canio 2, van Hooijdonk 2	49692
Rangers	A	9/28/96	0-2		50124
Motherwell	H	10/12/96	1-0	van Hooijdonk	49289
Hearts	A	10/20/96	2-2	van Hooijdonk 2	13352

Hibernian	A	10/26/96	4-0	Thom 2, van Hooijdonk, Donnelly	13930
Aberdeen	H	11/2/96	1-0	Di Canio	50124
Rangers	H	11/14/96	0-1		50009
Hearts	H	11/30/96	2-2	Di Canio, O'Neil	49804
Motherwell	A	12/7/96	1-2	Hay	11589
Dundee United	H	12/21/96	1-0	O'Donnell	46483
Aberdeen	A	12/26/96	2-1	Cadete, Di Canio	16748
Dunfermline Athletic	H	12/28/96	4-2	Cadete 2, van Hooijdonk, Donnelly	45751
Rangers	A	1/2/97	1-3	Di Canio	50019
Motherwell	H	1/4/97	5-0	Cadete 2, Di Canio, van Hooijdonk, Wieghorst	45259
Kilmarnock	H	1/8/97	6-0	Cadete 3, McNamara, Wieghorst, Hay	45535
Hearts	A	1/11/97	2-1	Cadete 2	15424
Raith Rovers	A	1/14/97	2-1	Cadete, Hay	8544
Hibernian	H	1/18/97	4-1	van Hooijdonk, McLaughlin, Cadete	48986
Dunfermline Athletic	A	1/29/97	2-0	McStay, Cadete	17919
Dundee United	A	2/1/97	0-1		12483
Raith Rovers	H	2/6/97	2-0	Cadete, Di Canio	44770
Motherwell	A	2/22/97	1-0	Cadete	12131
Hearts	H	3/1/97	2-0	Cadete, Di Canio	49578
Kilmarnock	A	3/11/97	0-2		15087
Rangers	H	3/16/97	0-1		49733
Dunfermline Athletic	A	3/22/97	2-2	O'Donnell, Donnelly	13092
Raith Rovers	A	4/5/97	1-1	Di Canio	7914
Aberdeen	H	4/20/97	3-0	Cadete 2, Thom	46989
Hibernian	A	5/4/97	3-1	Cadete 2, Di Canio	10546
Kilmarnock	H	5/7/97	0-0		42788
Dundee United	H	5/10/97	3-0	Cadete, Hay, Johnson	46742
				Average home attendance	**47528**

Scottish League Cup

Clyde	A	8/14/96	3-1	Cadete 2, Thom	7382
Alloa	Firhill	9/4/96	5-1	Cadete 3, Thom, van Hooijdonk	12582
Hearts	A	9/17/96	0-1 aet		14442

Scottish Cup

Clydebank	Firhill	1/26/97	5-0	Cadete 2, Mackay, van Hooijdonk, Di Canio	16285
Hibernian	A	2/17/97	1-1	O'Donnell	16000
Hibernian	H	2/26/97	2-0	O'Donnell, Di Canio	45880
Rangers	H	3/6/97	2-0	Mackay, Di Canio	49284
Falkirk	Ibrox	4/12/97	1-1	Johnson	45261
Falkirk	Ibrox	4/23/97	0-1		35879

UEFA Cup

Kosice	A	8/6/96	0-0		16000
Kosice	H	8/20/96	1-0	Cadete	44448
Hamburg	H	9/10/96	0-2		45412
Hamburg	A	9/24/96	0-2		29639

Scottish League Premier Division   1997-98

Hibernian	A	8/3/97	1-2	Mackay	13216
Dunfermline Athletic	H	8/16/97	1-2	Thom	45120
St.Johnstone	A	8/23/97	2-0	Larsson, Jackson	10266
Motherwell	A	9/13/97	3-2	Burley 2, Donnelly	11550
Aberdeen	H	9/20/97	2-0	Larsson 2	48843
Dundee United	A	9/27/97	2-1	Donnelly, O'Donnell	11668
Kilmarnock	H	10/4/97	4-0	Larsson 2, Donnelly, Wieghorst	47955
Hearts	A	10/18/97	2-1	Rieper, Larsson	16977
St.Johnstone	H	10/25/97	2-0	Larsson, Donnelly	48687
Dunfermline Athletic	A	11/1/97	2-0	Blinker, Larsson	12659
Rangers	A	11/8/97	0-1		50082
Motherwell	H	11/15/97	0-2		47464
Rangers	H	11/19/97	1-1	Stubbs	49427
Dundee United	H	11/22/97	4-0	Thom 2, Larsson 2	48200
Kilmarnock	A	12/6/97	0-0		15676
Aberdeen	A	12/9/97	2-0	Larsson, Jackson	16981
Hearts	H	12/13/97	1-0	Burley	49806
Hibernian	H	12/20/97	5-0	Burley 2, Wieghorst, McNamara, Larsson	48605
St.Johnstone	A	12/27/97	0-1		10485
Rangers	H	1/2/98	2-0	Burley, Lambert	49396
Motherwell	A	1/10/98	1-1	Lambert	12350
Dundee United	A	1/27/98	2-1	Donnelly, Burley	14004
Aberdeen	H	2/2/98	3-1	Wieghorst, Larsson, Jackson	45813
Hearts	A	2/8/98	1-1	McNamara	17657
Kilmarnock	H	2/21/98	4-0	Brattbakk 4	48477
Dunfermline Athletic	H	2/25/98	5-1	Brattbakk 2, Larsson, O'Donnell, Wieghorst	48576
Hibernian	A	2/28/98	1-0	Rieper	15137
Dundee United	H	3/15/98	1-1	Donnelly	48564
Aberdeen	A	3/21/98	1-0	Burley	18009
Hearts	H	3/28/98	0-0		49978
Kilmarnock	A	4/8/98	2-1	Larsson, Donnelly	18076
Rangers	A	4/12/98	0-2		50042
Motherwell	H	4/18/98	4-1	Burley 2, Donnelly 2	49351
Hibernian	H	4/25/98	0-0		49619
Dunfermline Athletic	A	5/3/98	1-1	Donnelly	12719
St.Johnstone	H	5/9/98	2-0	Larsson, Brattbakk	49701

Average home attendance   48532

Scottish League Cup

Berwick Rangers	Tynecastle	8/9/97	7-0	Donnelly 2, Jackson, Larsson, Thom, Blinker, Wieghorst	6267
St.Johnstone	A	8/19/97	1-0 aet	Donnelly	7488
Motherwell	H	9/10/97	1-0	Larsson	35582
Dunfermline Athletic	Ibrox	10/14/97	1-0	Burley	27796
Dundee United	Ibrox	11/30/97	3-0	Rieper, Larsson, Burley	49305

Scottish Cup

Greenock Morton	H	1/24/98	2-0	Brattbakk, Jackson	39933
Dunfermline Athletic	A	2/16/98	2-1	Mahe, Brattbakk	12322
Dundee United	A	3/8/98	3-2	Brattbakk, Wieghorst, own goal	12640
Rangers	Parkhead (neutral)	4/5/98	1-2	Burley	48000

UEFA Cup

Inter Cable-Tel	A	7/23/97	3-0	Thom, Johnson, Wieghorst	6980
Inter Cable-Tel	H	7/29/97	5-0	Thom, Johnson, Jackson, Hannah, Hay	41557
Tirol	A	8/12/97	1-2	Stubbs	6700
Tirol	H	8/26/97	6-3	Donnelly 2, Burley 2, Annoni, Thom	47017
Liverpool	H	9/16/97	2-2	McNamara, Donnelly	48526
Liverpool	A	9/30/97	0-0		38205

Scottish Premier League 1998-99

Dunfermline Athletic	H	8/1/98	5-0	Burley 3, Donnelly, Mackay	59377
Aberdeen	A	8/16/98	2-3	Larsson 2	16640
Dundee United	H	8/22/98	2-1	Burley, Burchill	59133
Dundee	A	8/29/98	1-1	Burley	9853
Kilmarnock	H	9/12/98	1-1	Blinker	58567
Rangers	A	9/20/98	0-0		50026
St.Johnstone	H	9/23/98	0-1		55745
Hearts	H	9/26/98	1-1	Donnelly	59283
Motherwell	A	10/3/98	2-1	Brattbakk, Lambert	12103
Dunfermline Athletic	A	10/17/98	2-2	Larsson, Brattbakk	10968
Aberdeen	H	10/24/98	2-0	Donnelly 2	59963
Kilmarnock	A	10/31/98	0-2		16695
Dundee	H	11/7/98	6-1	Larsson 3, Burchill 2, Donnelly	58974
St.Johnstone	A	11/14/98	1-2	Larsson	9762
Rangers	H	11/21/98	5-1	Moravcik 2, Larsson 2, Burchill	59783
Motherwell	H	11/28/98	2-0	Larsson, O'Donnell	59227
Hearts	A	12/6/98	1-2	O'Donnell	17334
Dundee United	A	12/12/98	1-1	Larsson	11612
Dunfermline Athletic	H	12/19/98	5-0	Larsson 2, Moravcik 2, Mjallby	59024
Dundee	A	12/27/98	3-0	Burchill, Riseth, Larsson	10043
Rangers	A	1/3/99	2-2	Stubbs, Larsson	50059

St.Johnstone	H	1/31/99	5-0	Brattbakk 3, Moravcik, Larsson	59746
Hearts	H	2/6/99	3-0	Larsson 3	59884
Kilmarnock	H	2/17/99	1-0	Riseth	59220
Motherwell	A	2/21/99	7-1	Larsson 4, Moravcik, Burley, Burchill	11963
Dundee United	H	2/27/99	2-1	Burley, Larsson	59902
Aberdeen	A	3/14/99	5-1	Viduka 2, Larsson 2, Burley	16825
Kilmarnock	A	3/21/99	0-0		14472
Dundee	H	4/3/99	5-0	Larsson 2, Burley, Viduka, Blinker	59269
Hearts	A	4/14/99	4-2	Viduka 2, Riseth, Blinker	16388
Motherwell	H	4/17/99	1-0	Larsson	59588
St.Johnstone	A	4/24/99	0-1		10393
Rangers	H	5/2/99	0-3		59918
Dunfermline Athletic	A	5/8/99	2-1	Johnson 2	8848
Aberdeen	H	5/15/99	3-2	Blinker, Johnson, Burchill	59138
Dundee United	A	5/23/99	2-1	Burchill 2	10062
				Average home attendance	**59208**

Scottish League Cup

Airdrieonians	A	8/19/98	0-1		8762

Scottish Cup

Airdrieonians	H	1/23/99	3-1	Larsson, O'Donnell, own goal	43609
Dunfermline Athletic	H	2/13/99	4-0	Larsson 3, Brattbakk	46887
Greenock Morton	A	3/8/99	3-0	Viduka 2, Larsson	12062
Dundee United	Ibrox	4/10/99	2-0	Blinker, Viduka	43491
Rangers	Hampden	5/29/99	0-1		51746

European Cup

St.Patrick's Athletic	H	7/22/98	0-0		56864
St.Patrick's Athletic	A	7/29/98	2-0	Brattbakk, Larsson	9500
Croatia Zagreb	H	8/12/98	1-0	Jackson	59397
Croatia Zagreb	A	8/26/98	0-3		27000

UEFA Cup

Guimares	A	9/15/98	2-1	Larsson, Donnelly	8000
Guimares	H	9/29/98	2-1	Stubbs, Larsson	38076
Zurich	H	10/20/98	1-1	Brattbakk	44121
Zurich	A	11/3/98	2-4	O'Donnell, Larsson	14500

Scottish Premier League   1999/2000

Aberdeen	A	8/1/99	5-0	Larsson 2, Viduka 2, Burchill	16080
St.Johnstone	H	8/7/99	3-0	Mjallby, Viduka, Wieghorst	60282
Dundee United	A	8/15/99	1-2	Berkovic	12375
Dundee	A	8/21/99	2-1	Mahe, Larsson	10531
Hearts	H	8/29/99	4-0	Berkovic 2, Viduka, Larsson	60107
Kilmarnock	A	9/12/99	1-0	Burchill	14318

Hibernian	A	9/25/99	2-0	Viduka 2	14747
Aberdeen	H	10/16/99	7-0	Larsson 3, Viduka 3, Berkovic	59931
St.Johnstone	A	10/24/99	2-1	Burchill, Wieghorst	9066
Motherwell	H	10/27/99	0-1		57898
Kilmarnock	H	10/30/99	5-1	Viduka 3, Wright, Burley	59791
Rangers	A	11/7/99	2-4	Berkovic 2	50026
Hearts	A	11/20/99	2-1	Wright, Moravcik	17184
Motherwell	A	11/28/99	2-3	Berkovic, Viduka	10730
Hibernian	H	12/4/99	4-0	Moravcik 2, Viduka, Wieghorst	60092
Aberdeen	A	12/11/99	6-0	Lambert, Mahe, Moravcik, Viduka, Blinker, Wright	16532
Dundee United	H	12/18/99	4-1	Blinker, Viduka, Moravcik, Burchill	58181
Rangers	H	12/27/99	1-1	Viduka	59619
Kilmarnock	A	1/23/00	1-1	Viduka	14126
Hearts	H	2/5/00	2-3	Moravcik, Viduka	59735
Dundee	A	2/12/00	3-0	Mjallby, Viduka, Healy	10044
Dundee	H	3/1/00	6-2	Johnson 3, Viduka 2, Petrov	55628
Hibernian	A	3/5/00	1-2	Viduka	12239
Rangers	H	3/8/00	0-1		59220
St.Johnstone	H	3/11/00	4-1	Burchill 2, Viduka 2	59331
Rangers	A	3/26/00	0-4		50039
Kilmarnock	H	4/2/00	4-2	Johnson, Blinker, Berkovic, Burchill	55194
Motherwell	H	4/5/00	4-0	Johnson 2, Blinker, Berkovic	55689
Hearts	A	4/8/00	0-1		16046
Dundee	H	4/15/00	2-2	Mahe, Burchill	56403
Hibernian	H	4/22/00	1-1	Mahe	56843
Motherwell	A	4/29/00	1-1	Burchill	7405
Dundee United	A	5/2/00	1-0	Burchill	7449
Aberdeen	H	5/6/00	5-1	Johnson 3, Moravcik 2	56235
St.Johnstone	A	5/13/00	0-0		6739
Dundee United	H	5/21/00	2-0	Lynch, Burchill	56749
				Average home attendance	**58162**

Scottish League Cup

Ayr United	A	10/13/99	4-0	Viduka, Blinker, Mjallby, Petta	8421
Dundee	H	12/1/99	1-0	Wieghorst	38922
Kilmarnock	Hampden	2/16/00	1-0	Moravcik	22926
Aberdeen	Hampden	3/19/00	2-0	Riseth, Johnson	50073

Scottish Cup

Inverness Caley Thistle	H	2/8/00	1-3	Burchill	34389

UEFA Cup

Cwymbran Town	Cardiff	8/12/99	6-0	Larsson 2, Berkovic, Tebily, Viduka, Brattbakk	8920
Cwymbran Town	H	8/26/99	4-0	Brattbakk, Mjallby, Smith, Johnson	46757

Hapoel Tel Aviv	H	9/16/99	2-0	Larsson 2	45171
Hapoel Tel Aviv	A	9/30/99	1-0	Larsson	6400
Lyon	A	10/21/99	0-1		37500
Lyon	H	11/4/99	0-1		54291

Scottish Premier League   2000-01

Dundee United	A	7/30/00	2-1	Larsson, Sutton	5896
Motherwell	H	8/5/00	1-0	Berkovic	59057
Kilmarnock	H	8/13/00	2-1	Larsson, Johnson	57258
Hearts	A	8/19/00	4-2	Sutton 2, Larsson, Moravcik	16744
Rangers	H	8/27/00	6-2	Sutton 2, Larsson 2, Petrov, Lambert	59476
Hibernian	H	9/9/00	3-0	Larsson 2, Burchill	60040
Dunfermline Athletic	A	9/18/00	2-1	Larsson 2	9493
Dundee	H	9/23/00	1-0	Petrov	59524
Aberdeen	A	10/1/00	1-1	Larsson	17580
St.Mirren	H	10/14/00	2-0	Sutton, Larsson	59788
St.Johnstone	A	10/17/00	2-0	Valgaeren, Larsson	8946
Dundee United	H	10/21/00	2-1	Larsson, Thompson	59323
Motherwell	A	10/29/00	3-3	Mjallby, Valgaeren, McNamara	12421
Kilmarnock	A	11/5/00	1-0	Thompson	13412
St.Johnstone	H	11/12/00	4-1	Larsson 2, Sutton, Moravcik	56952
Hearts	H	11/18/00	6-1	Larsson 2, Valgaeren, Moravcik, Mjallby, Petrov	59849
Rangers	A	11/26/00	1-5	Larsson	50083
Hibernian	A	11/29/00	0-0		14939
Dunfermline Athletic	H	12/2/00	3-1	Larsson, Moravcik, Johnson	59196
Dundee	A	12/10/00	2-1	Petrov, Agathe	10763
Aberdeen	H	12/16/00	6-0	Larsson 3, Vega 2, Smith	59677
St.Mirren	A	12/23/00	2-0	Agathe, Larsson	9487
Dundee United	A	12/26/00	4-0	Sutton 2, Larsson, Petrov	12306
Kilmarnock	H	1/2/01	6-0	Larsson 4, Sutton 2	59103
Hearts	A	2/4/01	3-0	Larsson 3	13077
Rangers	H	2/11/01	1-0	Thompson	59496
Motherwell	H	2/21/01	1-0	Moravcik	58736
Hibernian	H	2/25/01	1-1	Mjallby	59791
Dunfermline Athletic	A	3/4/01	3-0	Petrov, Larsson, Lennon	8779
St.Johnstone	A	3/14/01	2-1	Johnson, Larsson	8993
Aberdeen	A	4/1/01	1-0	Agathe	16064
Dundee	H	4/4/01	2-1	Johnson, Mjallby	59190
St.Mirren	H	4/7/01	1-0	Johnson	60102
Hearts	H	4/22/01	1-0	Moravcik	58708
Rangers	A	4/29/01	3-0	Larsson, Moravcik 2	50057
Hibernian	A	5/6/01	5-2	Thompson, McNamara, Larsson, Stubbs, Moravcik	8879
Dundee	H	5/13/01	0-2		58967
Kilmarnock	A	5/20/01	0-1		12578

Average Home Attendance   59170

Scottish League Cup

Raith Rovers	H	9/5/00	4-0	Johnson 2, Sutton, Thompson	30753
Hearts	A	11/1/00	5-2	Crainey, Smith, Healy, Moravcik, McNamara	13076
			aet		
Rangers	Hampden	2/7/01	3-1	Larsson 2, Sutton	50000
Kilmarnock	Hampden	3/18/01	3-0	Larsson 3	48830

Scottish Cup

Stranraer	A	1/28/01	4-1	Valgaeren, McNamara, Moravcik, own goal	5660
Dunfermline Athletic	A	2/17/01	2-2	Larsson 2	11222
Dunfermline Athletic	H	3/7/01	4-0	Vega 2, Larsson 2	33900
Hearts	H	3/11/01	1-0	Larsson	34529
Dundee United	Hampden	4/15/01	3-1	Larsson 2, McNamara	38699
Hibernian	Hampden	5/26/01	3-0	Larsson 2, McNamara	51284

UEFA Cup

Jeunesse Esch	A	8/10/00	4-0	Moravcik 2, Larsson, Petta	3587
Jeunesse Esch	H	8/24/00	7-0	Burchill 3, Berkovic 2, Riseth, Petrov	40282
HJK Helsinki	H	9/14/00	2-0	Larsson 2	40544
HJK Helsinki	A	9/28/00	1-2	Sutton	6530
			aet		
Bordeaux	A	10/26/00	1-1	Larsson	21318
Bordeaux	H	10/9/00	1-2	Moravcik	51242
			aet		

Scottish Premier League   2001-02

St.Johnstone	H	7/28/01	3-0	Lambert 2, Mjallby	57933
Kilmarnock	A	8/4/01	1-0	Larsson	13201
Hearts	H	8/11/01	2-0	Larsson 2	57715
Livingston	A	8/18/01	0-0		10024
Hibernian	A	8/25/01	4-1	Sutton 2, Moravcik, Larsson	14701
Dunfermline Athletic	H	9/8/01	3-1	Moravcik 2, Sutton	58004
Dundee	A	9/15/01	4-0	Larsson 2, Petrov, Maloney	9842
Aberdeen	H	9/22/01	2-0	Larsson, Petrov	59386
Rangers	A	9/30/01	2-0	Petrov, Thompson	50097
Motherwell	A	10/13/01	2-1	Moravcik, Larsson	9922
Dundee United	H	10/20/01	5-1	Hartson 3, Balde, Maloney	58873
Kilmarnock	H	10/27/01	1-0	Valgaeren	58845
St.Johnstone	A	11/3/01	2-1	Larsson, own goal	9041
Hearts	A	11/17/01	1-0	Larsson	15570
Rangers	H	11/25/01	2-1	Valgaeren, Larsson	59633
Hibernian	H	12/1/01	3-0	Hartson 2, Lennon	59220
Dunfermline Athletic	A	12/9/01	4-0	Hartson 2, Balde, Thompson	8207
Dundee	H	12/15/01	3-1	Sutton, Larsson, Hartson	57559
Aberdeen	A	12/22/01	0-2		18610
Livingston	H	12/26/01	3-2	Larsson 2, Moravcik	58407

Dundee United	A	12/29/01	4-0	Hartson, Petrov, Thompson, Larsson	12165
Motherwell	H	1/2/02	2-0	Larsson, Hartson	58105
Kilmarnock	A	1/12/02	2-0	Hartson, Lambert	11689
St.Johnstone	H	1/19/02	2-1	Larsson, Thompson	58516
Hearts	H	1/23/02	2-0	Larsson 2	57177
Livingston	A	1/30/02	3-1	Moravcik, Larsson, Hartson	8437
Hibernian	A	2/2/02	1-1	Hartson	12313
Dunfermline Athletic	H	2/9/02	5-0	Larsson 3, Hartson, Agathe	58987
Dundee	A	2/17/02	3-0	Larsson, Mjallby, Hartson	10642
Aberdeen	H	3/2/02	1-0	Thompson	59584
Rangers	A	3/10/02	1-1	Petrov	49765
Dundee United	H	3/16/02	1-0	Petrov	58392
Motherwell	A	3/19/02	4-0	Larsson 2, Lambert, Mjallby	10134
Livingston	H	4/6/02	5-1	Larsson 3, Hartson 2	59510
Dunfermline Athletic	H	4/13/02	5-0	Hartson 2, Lambert, Smith, Sylla	56715
Rangers	H	4/21/02	1-1	Thompson	59034
Hearts	A	4/28/02	4-1	Lynch 2, Maloney 2	13288
Aberdeen	A	5/12/02	1-0	Maloney	15332
				Average Home Attendance	**58508**

Scottish League Cup

Stirling Albion	H	11/6/01	8-0	Maloney 4, Hartson 2, Tebily, Healy	29933
Livingston	A	12/19/01	2-0	Balde, Hartson	8395
Rangers	Hampden	2/5/02	1-2	Balde	43457

Scottish Cup

Alloa Athletic	Brockville	1/8/02	5-0	Balde, Wieghorst,Maloney, Petta, Sylla	5763
Kilmarnock	A	1/26/02	2-0	Larsson, own goal	11249
Aberdeen	A	2/24/02	2-0	Hartson, Petrov	17082
Ayr United	Hampden	3/23/02	3-0	Thompson 2, Larsson	26774
Rangers	Hampden	5/4/02	2-3	Hartson, Balde	51138

European Cup-Champions League

Ajax	A	8/8/01	3-1	Petta, Agathe, Sutton	51859
Ajax	H	8/22/01	0-1		60000
Juventus	A	9/18/01	2-3	Petrov, Larsson	39945
Porto	H	9/25/01	1-0	Larsson	54664
Rosenborg	H	10/10/01	1-0	Thompson	54644
Porto	A	10/17/01	0-3		30303
Rosenborg	A	10/23/01	0-2		21500
Juventus	H	10/31/01	4-3	Sutton 2, Valgaeren, Larsson	57717

UEFA Cup

Valencia	A	11/22/01	0-1		38000
Valencia	H	12/6/01	1-0	Larsson	57299
			aet	Valencia won 5-4 on penalties	

Scottish Premier League   2002-2003

Dunfermline Athletic	H	8/3/02	2-1	Larsson 2	57415
Aberdeen	A	8/10/02	4-0	Sylla, Sutton, Lambert, Mjallby	17284
Dundee United	H	8/17/02	5-0	McNamara, Larsson, Sutton, Petrov, Hartson	56907
Partick Thistle	A	8/24/02	1-0	Larsson	8033
Livingston	H	9/1/02	2-0	Balde, Larsson	56988
Motherwell	A	9/10/02	1-2	Hartson	8448
Hibernian	H	9/14/02	1-0	Hartson	56703
Dundee	A	9/22/02	1-0	Larsson	9483
Kilmarnock	H	9/28/02	5-0	Larsson 3, Sutton 2	57469
Rangers	H	10/6/02	3-3	Larsson 2, Sutton	59027
Hearts	A	10/20/02	4-1	Larsson 2, Sutton, Petrov	13911
Dunfermline Athletic	A	10/27/02	4-1	Larsson, Thompson, Sutton, Petrov	9139
Aberdeen	H	11/3/02	7-0	Hartson 4, Balde, Larsson, Maloney	58526
Dundee United	A	11/10/02	2-0	Sutton, Hartson	10664
Partick Thistle	H	11/17/02	4-0	Petrov 2, Larsson, o.g	57839
Livingston	A	11/24/02	2-0	Larsson 2	10002
Motherwell	H	12/1/02	3-1	Larsson, Valgaeren, o.g	56733
Hibernian	A	12/4/02	1-0	Petrov	12024
Rangers	A	12/7/02	2-3	Sutton, Hartson	49874
Kilmarnock	A	12/15/02	1-1	Valgaeren	9225
Dundee	H	12/21/02	2-0	Larsson, Hartson	56162
Hearts	H	12/26/02	4-2	Hartson 3, Larsson	58450
Dunfermline Athletic	H	12/29/02	1-0	Larsson	58387
Aberdeen	A	1/2/03	1-1	Larsson	16331
Dundee United	H	1/29/03	2-0	Larsson, Hartson	55204
Partick Thistle	A	2/2/03	2-0	Sutton 2	7119
Livingston	H	2/9/03	2-1	Sylla, Sutton	57169
Hibernian	H	3/2/03	3-2	Hartson 2, Mjallby	57592
Rangers	H	3/8/03	1-0	Hartson	58787
Dundee	A	4/6/03	1-1	Thompson	9013
Kilmarnock	H	4/13/03	2-0	Larsson, Petrov	56966
Hearts	A	4/19/03	1-2	Larsson	15855
Rangers	A	4/27/03	2-1	Thompson, Hartson	49740
Dunfermline Athletic	A	5/3/03	4-1	Petrov 2, Larsson, Thompson	8923
Motherwell	A	5/7/03	4-0	Lambert 2, Petrov 2	12037
Hearts	H	5/10/03	1-0	Thompson	58175
Dundee	H	5/14/03	6-2	Thompson 2, Maloney 2, Larsson, Mjallby	57542
Kilmarnock	A	5/25/03	4-0	Sutton 2, Thompson, Petrov	16722

Average **Home Attendance** 57475

Scottish League Cup

Inverness Caley Thistle	H	10/23/02	4-2	Hartson 2, Thompson, Maloney	34592
Partick Thistle	H	11/6/02	1-1	Lambert	26333
			5-4	penalties	
Dundee United	Hampden	2/6/03	3-0	Balde 2, Larsson	18856
Rangers	Hampden	3/16/03	1-2	Larsson	52000

Scottish Cup

St.Mirren	H	1/25/03	3-0	Larsson 2, Sylla	29976
St.Johnstone	H	2/23/03	3-0	Hartson 2, Smith	26205
Inverness Caley Thistle	A	3/23/03	0-1		6050

European Cup - Champions League

FC Basel	H	8/14/02	3-1	Sylla, Larsson, Sutton	58520
FC Basel	A	8/28/02	0-2		30500

UEFA Cup

FK Suduva	H	9/19/02	8-1	Larsson 3, Valgaeren, Sutton, Hartson, Lambert, Petrov	36824
FK Suduva	A	10/3/02	2-0	Thompson, Fernandez	1200
Blackburn Rovers	H	10/31/02	1-0	Larsson	59553
Blackburn Rovers	A	11/14/02	2-0	Larsson, Sutton	29698
Celta Vigo	H	11/28/02	1-0	Larsson	53726
Celta Vigo	A	12/12/02	1-2	Hartson	26000
VFB Stuttgart	H	2/20/03	3-1	Lambert, Petrov, Maloney	59000
VFB Stuttgart	A	2/27/03	2-3	Thompson, Sutton	50600
Liverpool	H	3/13/03	1-1	Larsson	59759
Liverpool	A	3/20/03	2-0	Thompson, Hartson	44238
Boavista	H	4/10/03	1-1	Larsson	60000
Boavista	A	4/24/03	1-0	Larsson	11000
Porto	Seville	5/21/03	2-3 aet	Larsson 2	52972

Index